After Greenwashing

Businesses show their environmental awareness through green buildings, eco-labels, sustainability reports, industry pledges and clean technologies. When are these symbols wasteful corporate spin and when do they signal authentic environmental improvements? Based on twenty years of research, three rich case studies, a strong theoretical model and a range of practical applications, this book provides the first systematic analysis of the drivers and consequences of symbolic corporate environmentalism. It addresses the indirect cost of companies' symbolic actions and develops a new concept of the 'social energy penalty' – the cost to society when powerful corporate actors limit the social conversation on environmental problems and their solutions. This thoughtful book develops a set of tools for researchers, regulators and managers to separate useful environmental information from empty corporate spin, and it will appeal to researchers and students of corporate responsibility, corporate environmental strategy and sustainable business, as well as environmental practitioners.

FRANCES BOWEN is Professor of Innovation Studies at Queen Mary University of London. She is a leading authority on when and how companies innovate in response to current and future environmental regulation. She is the 2014 Chair of the Organizations and the Natural Environment (ONE) Division of the Academy of Management, and President-Elect of GRONEN, the Group for Research on Organizations and the Natural Environment.

T0380307

Organizations and the Natural Environment

Series editors

J. Alberto Aragon-Correa, *University of Surrey*
Jorge Rivera, *George Washington University*

Editorial board

The increasing attention given to environmental protection issues has resulted in a growing demand for high-quality, actionable research on sustainability and business environmental management. This new series, published in conjunction with the Group for Research on Organizations and the Natural Environment (GRONEN), presents students, academics, managers and policy-makers with the latest thinking on key topics influencing business practice today.

Forthcoming titles

Marcus   *Innovations in Sustainability*
Gouldson and Sullivan   *Governance and the Changing Climate for Business*

After Greenwashing

Symbolic Corporate Environmentalism
and Society

FRANCES BOWEN
Queen Mary University of London

CAMBRIDGE
UNIVERSITY PRESS

University Printing House, Cambridge CB2 8BS, United Kingdom

Cambridge University Press is part of the University of Cambridge.

It furthers the University's mission by disseminating knowledge in the pursuit of education, learning and research at the highest international levels of excellence.

www.cambridge.org
Information on this title: www.cambridge.org/9781107034822

© Frances Bowen 2014

First published 2014

A catalogue record for this publication is available from the British Library

Library of Congress Cataloguing in Publication data

ISBN 978-1-107-03482-2 Hardback

For Susan,
who helps separate my symbol from my substance.

Contents

List of figures   *page* viii

List of tables   ix

Acknowledgements   x

List of abbreviations   xiii

1   Introduction   1

2   After greenwashing   15

3   Perspectives on symbolic corporate environmentalism   39

4   Drivers and consequences of symbolic corporate
    environmentalism   76

5   Study 1: Symbolic gaps in environmental strategies   109

6   Study 2: Pollution control technology and the
    production of symbolic capital   140

7   Study 3: The evolution of measurement and
    performance standards   181

8   Measurement and methods   206

9   Implications and conclusions   226

Notes   251

References   260

Index   291

Figures

2.1 Number of articles mentioning greenwashing in academic
    and popular outlets, 1998–2012   *page* 18
4.1 Optimal firm investment in altruistic and coerced
    corporate environmentalism   80
4.2 Optimal firm investment in strategic corporate
    environmentalism   82
4.3 Delmas and Burbano's (2011) typology of firms based on
    environmental performance and communication   87
4.4 Brennan and Pettit's trade-off between investments in
    audience-seeking and performance-enhancing activity   89
4.5 Consumer utility from 'voluntary' green solutions   94
4.6 Social benefit S-curve   98
4.7 Social costs and benefits of symbolic corporate
    environmentalism   100
4.8 Social costs and benefits according to the two views of
    corporate environmentalism   107
5.1 Relationships between firm size and corporate
    environmentalism   115
5.2 Impact of monitoring within fields on the social energy
    penalty   138
6.1 Impact of power within fields on the social energy penalty   176
7.1 Impact of a standard's criteria on the social energy penalty 202
8.1 Allocational and distributional effects of monopoly power   214

Tables

2.1 Definitions of greenwashing   *page* 21
2.2 Greenwashing and symbolic corporate environmentalism   34
3.1 Comparing two perspectives on corporate
    environmentalism   49
3.2 Evaluating symbolic performance: Legitimacy, reputation
    and status   58
5.1 Studies included in the meta-analysis   124
5.2 Meta-analysis overall results   129
5.3 Meta-analytic weighted least squares analysis results   131
6.1 Carbon capture and storage demonstration projects   152
6.2 Types of cultural symbols   158
7.1 Three carbon accounting organisational fields   188
7.2 Discursive priorities of measurement criteria across three
    carbon accounting fields   193

Acknowledgements

I decided to write this book when I returned to the United Kingdom from Calgary, Alberta, in 2011. I had spent eight years living, researching and teaching in the oil and gas capital of Canada. While there, I witnessed up close the environmental challenges associated with providing our current production system with energy and other natural resources. Concerns about dirty oil, pipeline safety, water scarcity, climate change, carbon pricing, fracking, sustainable resource development, rapid urban growth and the health of First Nations communities dominated Calgary's public conversation. Through my executive teaching, research interviews and Stampede breakfasts, I saw generous and authentic efforts by inspirational sustainability leaders to address those challenges head on. I also saw the struggles of individuals and companies that simply did not know how to address the green problems to which their industry contributed or how to talk about them.

What I observed in my time in Calgary was, for the most part, not deliberate 'greenwashing' – that is, positive green communication by companies without positive environmental performance – but rather something more systemic. Dismissing corporate attempts to engage with environmental issues as greenwashing is too easy. We need better tools to understand a fuller range of symbolic corporate environmentalism and its consequences for society. I am deeply grateful to the Calgary-based managers, executives, consultants, activists, regulators, colleagues and students who gave me access to the inside of Canada's oilpatch when I was there. Although there are not many direct references to this context, I could not have written this book without the often candid and off-the-record conversations with individuals struggling with how to improve the environmental performance of Calgary companies.

Over the years, I tested the ideas in this book at many different fora, including meetings of the Organizations and the Natural Environment (ONE) Division of the Academy of Management and the Group for

Research on Organizations and the Natural Environment (GRONEN). Most recently, I received excellent feedback on the overarching frameworks presented in Chapter 4 at seminars hosted at Queen Mary University of London (QMUL), the University of Bath, and the University of Cambridge. Innumerable conversations with generous colleagues in seminars, vineyards and pubs encouraged me to sharpen and refine my ideas about symbolic corporate environmentalism. These colleagues may not realize how carefully I listened to them, but I can recall specific ways in which the book has benefitted from pivotal conversations with Tima Bansal, Stephanie Bertels, Kate Blackmon, Olivier Boiral, Steve Brammer, Magali Delmas, Minna Halme, Aoife Brophy Haney, Volker Hoffman, Kate Kearins, Julian Kölbel, James Meadowcroft, Andrew Millington, Jonathon Pinkse, Natalie Slawinski, Mike Toffel, Connie Van der Byl and Alain Verbeke. I know there were others, too, and I hope that they will forgive my forgetfulness and accept my thanks in the form of an appropriate beverage when I next see them.

I developed several of the chapters in collaboration with various co-authors and research assistants. I am therefore particularly indebted to Jessica Dillabough for contributing to the meta-analysis in Chapter 5, to Devin McDaniels for tracking down the carbon capture and storage (CCS) materials in Chapter 6, and to Bettina Wittneben and Chuks Okereke for initiating and shaping the carbon accounting project in Chapter 7. Lesley DiMarzo provided invaluable administrative support throughout my tenure as Director of the International Resource Industries and Sustainability Centre (IRIS) at the University of Calgary, including organising events that underpin this book and support in collating the references. Martha Prevezer, one of my new colleagues at Queen Mary, provided detailed and thoughtful comments on the entire first draft, significantly improving the manuscript and stimulating ideas for new research directions.

Various parts of the book were financially supported by the Haskayne School of Business and the Institute for Sustainable Energy, Environment and Economy (ISEEE) at the University of Calgary, where I worked from 2003 to 2011; the Smith School of Enterprise and the Environment at the University of Oxford, where I was on sabbatical in 2009; and the Social Sciences and Humanities Research Council of Canada (Grant Number 603-2007-0010).

It has been a pleasure to embark on the adventure of writing the first book in the Cambridge University Press and GRONEN series on

Acknowledgements
Organizations and the Natural Environment. I extend my kudos to Jorge Rivera and Alberto Aragon-Correa for initiating this enterprise and for their moral support and vital developmental comments. I am looking forward to seeing how the book series evolves and to the rich conversations it no doubt will stimulate. Paula Parish and Claire Poole at Cambridge gently cajoled me through the process and kept me on track. Constance Burt's expert copyediting significantly clarified the text.

I chose to dedicate this book to my partner, Susan Rudy, who suffered daily updates on what I had written with such grace and never let me get away with sloppy language. For giving me the idea that I could go to university in the first place, I thank my Mam and Dad, for whom this book is further proof that I may never grow up and stop being a student.

Abbreviations

BREEAM	Building Research Establishment Environmental Assessment Method
CCS	carbon capture and storage
CDP	Carbon Disclosure Project
CEO	Chief Executive Officer
CO	carbon monoxide
CO_2	carbon dioxide
CSR	corporate social responsibility
DECC	Department of Energy and Climate Change (UK)
DJI	Dow Jones Index
ENGO	environmental non-governmental organisation
EPA	Environmental Protection Agency (US)
EU ETS	European Union Emission Trading System
FSC	Forest Stewardship Council
G8	Group of eight of the world's largest national economies
GHG	greenhouse gas
GRI	Global Reporting Initiative
GRONEN	Group for Research on Organizations and the Natural Environment
IASB	International Accounting Standards Board
ICAP	International Carbon Action Partnership
IPCC	Intergovernmental Panel on Climate Change
ISO	International Organisation for Standardisation
ITC	International Trade Commission
LEED	Leadership in Energy and Environmental Design
MC	marginal costs
MR	marginal revenue
NCD	Natural Capital Declaration
NGO	non-governmental organisation
NO_2	nitrogen dioxide
NRBV	natural-resource–based view

NRDC	Natural Resources Defense Council
OED	Oxford English Dictionary
ONE	Organizations and the Natural Environment
PR	public relations
R&D	research and development
RBV	resource-based view
SFI	Sustainable Forestry Initiative
TV	technology value
UN	United Nations
USGBC	US Green Building Council
WBCSD	World Business Council for Sustainable Development
WRI	World Resources Institute
WTO	World Trade Organisation
WWF	World Wide Fund for Nature

1 | *Introduction*

Back in 2005, HSBC became the first large bank and the first of the one hundred largest companies listed on the London Stock Exchange to declare itself 'carbon neutral'. The bank committed to reducing to zero its net carbon dioxide (CO_2) emissions from more than ten thousand office buildings and from executive travel (Walck 2006). It planned to invest up to £4 million annually in planting trees, reducing energy use, buying green electricity and trading carbon credits to limit its CO_2 emissions (BBC 2004). Achieving carbon neutrality was intended to set a new benchmark in environmental performance for the financial services industry, a sector that had been slower to respond to calls for environmental improvement than more obviously dirty industries such as chemicals and oil. The bank was recognised as the '*Financial Times* Sustainable Bank of the Year' in 2006 (*Financial Times* 2006).

Yet, HSBC was persistently criticised for this strategic environmental decision. HSBC's own guidelines emphasised that it was reducing net rather than gross CO_2 emissions. The bank would continue to emit some CO_2 from dirty energy and staff travel and pay others to provide equivalent CO_2 reductions through carbon offsetting (HSBC 2011a). Greenpeace questioned whether planting trees is actually carbon neutral, asking 'What if there's a forest fire?' (BBC 2004).[1] Other critics pointed out that HSBC's commitments were related to emissions from its own banking operations, not the much larger indirect emissions arising from projects that the bank financed in carbon intensive industries (Gass 2011). Even HSBC's commitment to 'plant one virtual tree in our virtual forest' for every account switched to a paperless Green HSBC Plus Account in 2007 backfired. A journalist noticed the HSBC fine print – 'for every 20 virtual trees we promise to plant a real one' – as well as a backlog of 400,000 virtual trees from the first two years waiting to be planted (Pearce 2009).

Responding to this criticism, HSBC withdrew its carbon neutrality commitment in 2011. What began in 2005 as a pioneering attempt to lead the way in green banking had come to a messy end. HSBC was forced to explain its withdrawal from an environmental commitment made with such fanfare a few years earlier. Activists celebrated a victory over exposing a high-profile bank's flimsy environmental credentials. HSBC was highlighted along with other high-profile companies, from 'Apple to Coca-Cola, GE to McDonald's, and Starbucks to Walmart', as greenwashing their climate-friendly policies (Pearse 2012). Greenwashing misleads consumers about companies' environmental performance or the environmental benefits of a product or service, specifically by combining positive environmental communications with poor environmental performance (Delmas and Burbano 2011). Researchers and activists usually understand situations such as HSBC's carbon neutrality as greenwashing: the bank deliberately disclosed one element of its environmental performance (i.e., zero net CO_2 emissions) and withdrew from this commitment when activists exposed the mismatch between its proactive-sounding statements and much less favourable environmental impacts.

It is easy to dismiss firms' environmental activities as greenwashing that promises an advantage to the firm while imposing costs on society. However, HSBC's experiments with carbon neutrality highlight a tension in a company's role in mitigating society's environmental impacts. On the one hand, stakeholders demand environmental improvements and require evidence that firms are indeed taking seriously their environmental responsibilities. On the other hand, consumers and a broader range of stakeholders have developed a justifiable scepticism about the effectiveness of green solutions promoted by large corporations. Society is caught in a bind between needing better green information and a distrust of those who provide it. A shared language needs to be developed to describe corporate environmental changes; but, as the architects of change, firms can also influence the language used. New terms such as 'carbon neutral' can signify an abstract concept that was not needed before – that is, producing products or services with low or zero CO_2 emissions to combat climate change. The meaning of these new symbols evolves through conversations and interactions among many different actors in society. Sometimes firms can influence the symbols around corporate greening, sometimes they cannot. The new symbols may be socially useful or they may be a damaging distraction. Dismissing the symbolic aspects of corporate environmental actions as deliberate greenwashing tells only part of the story.

The past two decades have given rise to an enormous range of symbols of corporate environmentalism. Firms are labelled as carbon neutral, sustainable, eco- or green. Products can be organic, dolphin-safe, recycled, reclaimed, low-energy, renewable, efficient or environmentally friendly. There are increasingly more sophisticated-sounding technologies, programmes, management processes, industry associations and labelling schemes to reassure stakeholders that firms are environmentally sound. Some of these symbols are greenwashing – that is, deliberate attempts to communicate positive environmental information not matched by improved environmental impacts. However, some are more than merely symbolic and actually signify environmental improvements. All corporate environmental activities have a symbolic component. We must develop tools to identify which are socially wasteful distractions and which may be initial attempts to promote green solutions so desperately needed to mitigate society's impact on the natural world.

In this book, I show that expanding research beyond greenwashing to a broader symbolic corporate environmentalism generates new research questions and implications for environmental strategy and policy. 'Corporate environmentalism' is defined as changes made by managers inside organisations that they describe as primarily for environmental reasons. 'Symbolic corporate environmentalism' is defined as the shared meanings and representations surrounding these changes. All environmental activities have a symbolic component as managers and others learn to describe the new environmental solutions they are adopting. New language, symbols, terms, labels and shared meanings evolve to signify the abstract idea of making changes to solve environmental problems. Some symbolic corporate environmentalism is 'merely symbolic' in the sense that the proactive-sounding symbols do not match with substantive environmental improvements. As discussed in the next chapter, greenwashing is a specific subset of symbolic corporate environmentalism in which the changes are both 'merely symbolic' and deliberately so. In this book, I expand conventional corporate environmental strategy research to include a broader range of symbolic activities after greenwashing. Symbolic corporate environmentalism includes not only greenwashing but also unintended, merely symbolic activities and the symbolic components of environmental changes that actually have a positive, substantive impact on the natural environment.

Recasting HSBC's carbon neutrality through a symbolic corporate environmentalism lens provides a much richer explanation than dismissing it as greenwashing. HSBC chose to invest in a portfolio of green solutions, including adopting and maintaining the carbon neutral credential, launching green bank accounts, signing up to industry charters such as the Equator Principles, building the first Leadership in Energy and Environmental Design (LEED) Gold–certified buildings in Latin America and the Middle East to house its regional headquarters, keeping count of virtual trees and participating in an underdeveloped CO_2 offset market.[2] Despite these initiatives, the overall environmental footprint of HSBC's direct and indirect activities continued to rise. The bank placed a strategic bet that the carbon neutral label would be valued as a signal of environmental responsiveness as other firms and stakeholders better understood carbon management over time. HSBC may or may not have deliberately opened up a gap between the proactive-sounding carbon neutral label and its actual environmental performance. However, the net result was that carbon neutrality did not develop as a valuable asset as the firm had initially envisioned.

Condemning HSBC's actions as greenwashing implies that society would be better off now that the limitations of its version of the carbon neutrality label has been exposed. Taking a broader symbolic corporate environmentalism perspective suggests that the social impact may not be so simple: over time, HSBC's withdrawal might slow the development of proactive environmental management in the banking sector. Stakeholders may have lost the opportunity to challenge more banks to examine their carbon footprints by considering whether they could reduce carbon emissions like their sector leaders. Society needs experiments such as the carbon neutrality label to improve environmental performance. Yet, withdrawing from a public commitment can damage a firm's credibility and limit the learning gained from these experiments. The frameworks described in this book provide the analytical tools for evaluating why HSBC first opted in and then out of carbon neutrality, as well as the social consequences of those decisions.

As environmental issues have spread into the business mainstream, the symbolic component of corporate environmentalism has become increasingly pervasive. There are now more than four hundred active eco-labelling schemes worldwide, each claiming to give stakeholders useful information about the environmental performance of products ranging from cut flowers to cosmetics and from construction to carpets. More than one hundred environmental awards have been established to celebrate multiple dimensions of environmental performance, recognising the most innovative environmental technologies, the greenest car dealership in the United Kingdom or the 'Environment/Sustainability Manager of the Year'. There are at least 120 recognised voluntary standards listed by the International Trade Commission (ITC).[3]

These are only some of the more obvious symbols of corporate environmentalism. Firms also signal their environmental awareness by adopting a wide range of everyday practices that have become norms in contemporary business, including constructing green buildings, developing environmental visions, implementing environmental measurement and reporting systems, signing green industry pledges and supporting environmental technologies. Some of these symbols signify substantive improvements in a firm's environmental impact, such as emission reductions or improving air or water quality. Others are merely symbolic green solutions, disconnected from the underlying environmental impacts of corporate activities. Many other green solutions lie between these two extremes, where firms gain symbolic legitimacy for signalling environmental awareness, but the substantive impact is limited because they control the implementation of a new practice.

The symbolic aspect of corporate environmentalism was driven home for me when I visited Walmart's Canadian headquarters in 2006. Office buildings are powerful symbols of corporate cultures. I had visited the headquarters of several Canadian subsidiaries of foreign-owned multinationals during that same week. Most had reception areas in spacious, light-filled atriums in glitzy office buildings in prestigious downtown Toronto locations. In contrast, Walmart's Canadian headquarters was housed in one of its 'big-box' warehouse buildings in an out-of-town industrial area. I was struck by the no-nonsense building with a small reception area for visitors and suppliers, which signalled a low-cost corporate culture. What I did not expect was that the entire reception area had been recently painted a vibrant green, replacing Walmart's corporate blue and yellow colours. Walmart's literal greenwashing – covering the walls and chairs in the reception area with green paint – could be dismissed as a cynical ploy to show visitors the corporation's new green sheen. Alternatively, it could serve as a useful stimulus to visiting suppliers as well as employees to consider environmental costs. In recent years, the company has made impressive gains by improving environmental management. Since 2008, Walmart has saved $3.4 billion by reducing packaging waste. The company recently announced plans to expand its renewable-energy projects even more: it will build on its position in the United States as the leading user of onsite renewable power, which will eliminate the need for two more fossil-fuel power plants and thereby save the company $1 billion annually in energy costs by 2020 (Walmart 2013). The greening of the reception area may have helped with the symbolic support to enact behavioural changes in the company. It may also have helped spread environmental awareness through the supplier network and industry by reminding visitors of society's expectations for green performance. Or it may be merely a paint-thin veneer over low-cost business as usual. Current analytical tools simply cannot detect the difference.

Of course, some corporate environmentalism has been rightly dismissed as greenwashing. Shell was compelled by the Advertising Standards Authority in the United Kingdom to withdraw its print advertisements that featured flowers coming out of smokestacks. Lexus's UK print-advertising campaign, 'Put your carbon foot down', was similarly censured because the text stating 'a car that's better for the environment' did not provide any details of comparison cars or emission levels.[4] Attempts to launch environmental product ranges such as GE's Ecomagination campaign launched in 2005 (the same year as Walmart's sustainability programme) and IBM's Smarter Planet in 2008 often overstate material changes to firms' internal processes, programmes and policies.

Academic research is catching up with these deliberate initiatives and can now explain some drivers of overt greenwashing (Delmas and Burbano 2011; Lyon and Maxwell 2011). Far less is known about the more subtle but much more pervasive symbolic component of ordinary corporate environmental practices. Critics have long denounced corporate environmentalism as distracting 'spin' and a waste of societal resources. HSBC's commitment to plant 'virtual trees' is, at best, an inadequate disclosure of the firm's environmental performance, leading to less socially efficient decision making. At worst, it is a cynical attempt to cash in on consumers who may be willing to pay for a greener bank account without incurring the full cost of providing a greener service. Either way, the headline promise of a green bank account is not matched with adequate substantive tree planting or CO_2 absorption, yielding a social loss.

What about the longer-term effects of HSBC's symbolic corporate environmentalism? Offering green bank accounts, promoting a carbon neutrality vision and asking energy suppliers about the carbon intensity of their operations could lead to useful spillovers, thereby encouraging consumers, competitors, suppliers and regulators to incorporate green criteria into their own decisions. Even merely symbolic corporate environmentalism can lead to learning over time and a gradual rise in environmental performance expectations. We must pay closer attention to the effects of green solutions, in terms of both symbolic performance in the sense of positive social evaluations and substantive impact on the natural environment.

Substantial academic research in the past two decades aims to understand the effects of corporate environmentalism. Most of this research is in what I term the 'conventional view' of corporate environmentalism (see Chapter 3). The conventional perspective questions firm-level environmental strategy and performance: Does it pay to be green? When, why and how? In contrast, the 'critical view' interrogates the role of corporations as mediators and constructors of discourse surrounding environmental degradation and its consequences for which green solutions gain traction in society. The focus is more on asking what it means to be green and who has the power to decide that and how. Both views have something to offer in understanding symbolic corporate environmentalism. However, both views also have significant theoretical blind spots that limit our understanding of the symbolic components of greening. The conventional view tends to underplay the power of some social actors – particularly large firms and well-organised industry associations – to influence the rhetoric and resources around green solutions. Conversely, the critical view focuses so much on this corporate power and its potential abuses that companies' green solutions are routinely dismissed as merely symbolic, with little sense of the potential environmental and social benefits derived from developing shared meanings and learning about green solutions. Both views tend to neglect green solutions that are neither purely symbolic nor purely substantive but that might be symbolically useful in developing shared meanings and language around new environmental demands.

Despite the apparent explosion in research and practice-based talk on corporate environmentalism, industrial societies are pushing Earth's biosphere ever closer to and even beyond safe operating limits. Rockström et al. (2009) identified threshold limits of human impacts on nine natural systems – the carbon cycle, ocean acidification, stratospheric ozone, global phosphorus and nitrogen cycles, biodiversity loss, global freshwater use, land-system change, aerosol loading and chemical pollution – and showed how we are already operating beyond three of these natural limits. Critical researchers argue that twenty-five years of research in the conventional view has provided many symbols and some actions but not nearly enough substantive environmental renewal from industrial activity (see, e.g., Forbes and Jermier 2012 and Whiteman et al. 2012). They have a point: symbolic corporate environmentalism pervades our contemporary capitalist society.

However, we must not forget the analytical and empirical progress of twenty years of conventional corporate environmentalism research. In this book, my perspective is that problems in the natural environment are so urgent and important that we need to generate better short- to medium-term solutions within our current discursive, policy and strategy frames. Conventional corporate environmentalism has developed tools for understanding corporate environmental decision making. I intend to use and develop these tools from the conventional view to ask questions posed in the critical view: What are the drivers and consequences of symbolic corporate environmentalism and, most important, when might corporate environmentalism be bad for society?

The most obvious way in which corporate environmentalism is bad for society is when green solutions do not have any substantive impact on mitigating environmental damage. In this book, I present many studies that show firms adopting a particular green solution to gain positive social evaluations – whether an environmental policy, an eco-label, a pollution control technology or a new measurement and reporting system – but not improving substantive environmental impacts. I label these green solutions 'merely symbolic'. They are the most overt form of symbolic corporate environmentalism, the most misleading and, ultimately, the most wasteful. I also address green solutions that are not completely decoupled from substantive environmental improvements. There is a significant grey area in which green solutions promise some environmental benefit but apparently deliver more reputational and legitimacy benefits than are strictly warranted by the substantive improvement.

A good example is performance-based eco-labels such as the points-based LEED green building standard that HSBC adopted for all of its major buildings. Performance-based standards reduce the likelihood of merely symbolic corporate environmentalism, but they do not eliminate symbolic effects altogether. The conventional view tends to be pragmatic about performance-based symbols and broadly accepts that they represent underlying environmental improvements, as advertised. In the conventional view, the main areas of concern for these symbols are the strength of monitoring, sanctions and enforcement stringency around the symbol, and its proper implementation. The critical view, however, reminds us that someone somewhere decides how many points should be awarded to a specific building. The rules are written and the paperwork is evaluated by individuals, each with their own interests and biases. These evaluations are made within a relational context that gives some actors more status than others to award a recognised 'stamp of approval'.

Most green solutions suffer this type of problem. There may or may not be substantive environmental improvements, but there will always be a relational context within which shared meanings evolve and are influenced by those who may choose to exert their systemic power in society. I argue that this difficulty extends far beyond the typical symbols discussed in greenwashing – eco-labels, certificates, awards, schemes, marketing and other deliberate communicative practices – to the symbolic components of everyday corporate environmental practices. Instead of labelling corporate activities as 'symbolic' or 'substantive', I examine all of the symbolic or substantive effects of the initiatives. I argue that all green solutions have a symbolic component and that after greenwashing, we must be alert to the symbolic performance of all of a firm's greening activities, not only those that are deliberately communicative.

The gap between the rhetoric around firms' activities and the reality of environmental damage is a pressing social problem. Activists and academics have embraced the challenge to expose and analyse greenwashing. However, there are no easy solutions to the environmental challenges: governments are bound by public apathy, non-governmental organisations (NGOs) by the need to maintain legitimacy in a corporatist society, and firms by poor knowledge of environmental issues and inadequate incentives for action. Symbolic corporate environmentalism is here to stay, even after greenwashing. The challenge is to work out when the benefits of harnessing firms' creativity and resources to tackle environmental challenges might outweigh the costs of allowing them to drive the terms of the debate. My hope is that this book provides a 'call to arms' as well as analytical frameworks to understand symbolic corporate environmentalism and its social consequences.

Core ideas and contributions

This book is the first systematic examination of the drivers and social consequences of symbolic corporate environmentalism after green-washing. In it, I extend our theoretical and empirical understanding of the shared meanings and representations around firms' environmental activities. I contribute to debates about firms' environmental strategy and the social implications of widespread symbolic behaviour on green issues. By tapping into wider literatures in organisation theory, economics, sociology, anthropology and law, I build theoretical insights on the drivers and consequences of symbolic corporate environmentalism. This approach is novel in two main ways. First, I reinject notions of power and status back into analysing symbolic corporate environmentalism that have been lost in recent economic analyses of greenwashing. This provides a richer sense of how corporate engagement with a broader social greening conversation impacts the range of potential solutions to solve environmental challenges. Second, I bridge the typical firm level of analysis to the broader institutional field level and, ultimately, to the societal level. This highlights the social costs and benefits of symbolic corporate environmentalism that are often overlooked in the conventional literature, which tends to focus on firm-level environmental strategy.

Book structure

Chapter 2 begins the analysis by showing how the broader concept of symbolic corporate environmentalism is 'after greenwashing' in two significant ways. First, I show the rise and fall of greenwashing in the popular and academic literatures. New monitoring technologies such as smartphones and social media may limit the extent to which firms can continue to get away with deliberate greenwashing. After green-washing, however, we need to pay attention to a broader and more embedded phenomenon of symbolic corporate environmentalism. Second, symbolic corporate environmentalism is after greenwashing in the sense that it adopts the tradition of the earliest greenwashing literature. When the concept was first developed, greenwashing described a much broader range of activities than the deliberate, communicative activities of firms that it has come to represent today.

Chapter 3 builds on this by reviewing the current research literature on corporate environmentalism and how it has addressed gaps between firms' symbolic and substantive performance. I develop a detailed conception of symbolic corporate environmentalism and position it within two contrasting research traditions on corporate environmentalism: the conventional view and the critical view. Part of the research challenge in this area is to bridge the chasm in corporate environmentalism scholarship between conventional strategic approaches that focus on firm-level strategy and critical approaches that place firms as mediators and constructors of environmental discourse. The chapter outlines how this bridging could be accomplished and the novel research questions that such bridging would allow us to explore.

Chapter 4 presents a set of three conceptual frameworks for understanding the drivers and consequences of symbolic corporate environmentalism. It begins with a firm-level model of corporate environmental decisions and shows how relaxing some of the standard assumptions can lead to the overproduction of relatively more symbolic green solutions. The chapter then presents a static analysis of the welfare implications of investing in combinations of symbolic and substantive green solutions. This second framework demonstrates that when suppliers of green solutions have the power to limit the form of the solution, utility is lower compared with when there is full competition for green solutions. Finally, I put this social cost analysis into a more dynamic frame, showing how the social costs and benefits of a given green solution vary as the solution becomes entrenched as the dominant design. I argue that some of the disagreements between the two perspectives on corporate environmentalism are essentially reduced to differences in their assumptions about the shape of a social cost curve. The model offers instead a way to empirically identify contexts in which there is a particularly serious potential for social losses due to a firm's power to limit the supply of green solutions. This is a significant theoretical advance in the current tendency in the literature to simply assume that corporate power over green solutions leads to social welfare losses or that it does not.

Using three empirical studies, Chapters 5 through 7 explore various aspects of the model on the consequences of symbolic corporate environmentalism. I highlight three cultural manifestations of corporate environmentalism that lie beyond the typical greenwashing focus on deliberate communicative practices: environmental strategies, pollution control technologies and measurement systems. The overall approach in these three chapters is to use a range of empirical methods and research contexts to shed light on particular contingencies in the model. These chapters are full of research richness and empirical detail; readers who are less interested in the academic mechanics and more in the overall direction of the argument can safely skip the first few sections of each chapter and proceed to the 'Empirical Summary' section. Academics may appreciate each of the chapters as standalone contributions to specific research questions within the overall theme.

Chapter 5 begins with a meta-analysis of empirical studies of the drivers of corporate environmentalism from the past twenty years. I test hypotheses on environmental strategies of large firms to explain when gaps can emerge between what they say, what they do and, ultimately, their environmental impact. The strength of monitoring within a particular social field turns out to be a crucial driver of the social benefits of firms' environmental activities: there is more social benefit when fields are tightly monitored.

Chapter 6 delves more deeply into when and how social actors can exert discretionary power over the production of green solutions. In this chapter, the empirical context is a pollution control environmental technology: carbon capture and storage (CCS) demonstration projects. Through a discourse analysis of firms' and governments' symbols around these projects, I identify three different types of symbolic capital around environmental initiatives. I show that particular features of the field surrounding CCS demonstration projects suggest that the social costs of symbolic corporate environmentalism are likely to be higher in this field than for other types of environmental technologies.

Chapter 7 also examines the dynamics within fields but instead focuses on the discourses around carbon accounting. This is a good example of a field in which actors are coming together to define, develop and promote new environmental measurement and performance standards. I analyse the discursive priorities among different actors within the carbon accounting field and show how the distribution of actors and meaning systems around the new measurement system leads to an emphasis on symbolic rather than substantive green solutions. The analysis is a reminder to focus on the standalone technology value of a new green solution to maintain social benefit – a dimension that can become lost in negotiations about potentially costly and controversial green solutions.

The final two chapters conclude with ideas on where to focus research attention after greenwashing. Chapter 8 presents speculative sketches that describe how to estimate the social costs and benefits of symbolic corporate environmentalism. I use analogous measurement challenges from other theoretical traditions to suggest ways to expand the empirical treatment of greenwashing to include the full range of social costs and benefits of broader symbolic corporate environmentalism. Finally, Chapter 9 summarises implications of the frameworks and empirical studies presented in this book for research on corporate environmentalism and organisational theory more generally. The chapter includes a checklist of the social implications of symbolic corporate environmentalism that policy makers and activists may find useful in identifying priority areas for action.

Symbolic corporate environmentalism consists of shared meanings and representations around changes made by managers that they describe as primarily for environmental reasons. As consumers, voters and investors, we want these symbols to signal environmental quality and to provide reassurance that firms are serious about their societal responsibilities. However, some of these symbols are completely disconnected from the impacts that firms have on the natural environment, and many more have less substantive environmental impact than they symbolically promise. Despite apparently widespread corporate environmentalism, industrial activities are pushing society closer to and, in some cases, exceeding planetary boundaries. The gap between firms' symbolic activities and the reality of environmental damage endangers our natural surroundings and, ultimately, may threaten the stability of current economic and social systems.

We must develop sharper tools to distinguish damaging symbolic corporate environmentalism from that which has the potential to signal and coordinate authentic environmental improvements. This is particularly important when we realise that symbols tend to become entrenched over time. Some symbolic corporate environmentalism signals environmental information that would otherwise be unavailable to stakeholders, thereby assisting managers, consumers, investors and regulators in making more efficient decisions. However, this can also be a socially costly attempt to control the rhetoric and resources surrounding environmental issues. This book develops tools that can help to identify the difference.

2 | *After greenwashing*

Symbolic corporate environmentalism pervades all firms' attempts to address environmental issues but is not usually addressed explicitly in conventional corporate environmental strategy research. What we do have, however, is a growing body of research on the narrower concept of greenwashing. One aim of this book is to build theory on the drivers and consequences of symbolic corporate environmentalism in the tradition of research on greenwashing. As discussed in this chapter, the academic definition of the term 'greenwashing' has evolved in the past twenty years and has recently become more specific to deliberate, disclosure-based firm activities. In contrast, broader symbolic corporate environmentalism resonates after greenwashing in the sense that it builds on an earlier, more politicised and critical version of greenwashing from twenty years ago. This chapter demonstrates how symbolic corporate environmentalism is 'after greenwashing' in two significant ways. First, it is after greenwashing in time. I show the rise and fall of greenwashing in practice but caution against neglecting symbols around corporate greening in a post-greenwash era. Second, it is after greenwashing in tradition. I show how redirecting research attention from greenwashing to symbolic corporate environmentalism provides a richer understanding of corporate greening and also opens up new research challenges.

The rise and fall of greenwashing

In 1985, the US oil company Chevron started running its famous *People Do* advertisements in print media and on US television.[1] The ads show various scenes from nature – a grizzly bear settling down to hibernate; a turtle swimming free around a disused oil platform recast as a nature sanctuary; endangered birds basking under a Hawaiian sunrise – while a voiceover or text box asks rhetorical questions: 'Do people sometimes work through the winter so nature can have spring all to herself?' 'Do people help nature reach a new dawn?' The answer each time, beneath a corporate logo, is Chevron *People Do*. These grainy, low-resolution television adverts appear to be from a more naïve, pre-media-savvy era. But, in the late 1980s, Chevron recorded an improvement – compared with other oil companies – in its environmental-reputation rankings among consumers in areas where the ad campaign ran. In 1990, the campaign was recognised with an Effie Award from the American Marketing Association for effectiveness in marketing communications.

Fast-forward to 2007: Chevron launched a new global advertising campaign, this time based on *Human Energy*. The ads aimed to illustrate challenges related to the growing global demand for energy and what Chevron was doing to address them (Chevron 2007). Again, this campaign was praised for marketing effectiveness and awarded an Effie – by now the preeminent global award for advertising effectiveness – in the Corporate Reputation category in 2007. Chevron hoped to build on the success of the *Human Energy* campaign by launching a follow-up campaign, *We Agree*, on October 18, 2010. This time, the advertisements emphasised the 'common ground Chevron shares with people around the world on key energy issues' (*Chevron 2010*). The ads feature declarative statements in the passive voice, such as 'Protecting the planet is everyone's job' and 'It's time oil companies get behind the development of renewable energy'. The ads contain the signatures of a Chevron employee and a community partner and are stamped with 'We Agree' in red letters.

What might have been a business-as-usual attempt to put a green veneer on high environmental impact activities backfired on the very day Chevron launched the campaign. Unbeknownst to Chevron, details of the *We Agree* launch had been leaked to environmental activists at the Rainforest Action Network via an actor who received a casting call to appear in one of the television ads and by a street artist asked to help produce the print posters. The details found their way to 'The Yes Men', Andy Bichlbaum and Mike Bonanno, who are infamous for their credible but spoof impersonations of representatives from the world of big business, ranging from the World Trade Organisation (WTO) to Dow Chemical and Exxon.[2] A few hours before Chevron's official launch of the *We Agree* campaign, The Yes Men produced their own press release from a spoof Chevron domain announcing the launch and their own version of an accompanying website. The Yes Men's website featured 'improved' adverts that were almost indistinguishable from the Chevron originals other than the more direct, active voice messages: 'Oil companies should clean up their messes' and 'Oil companies should fix the problems they create' – each stamped 'We Agree' in red.

The hoax was revealed later that day and widely reported in the mainstream media, as well as being admired in environmental blogs and websites. For some commentators, this prank signalled that 'the era of greenwashing is over' (Werbach 2010). In our contemporary networked and digital social economy, it is becoming increasingly difficult for companies to maintain separation between positive environmental communications and not-so-positive actual environmental impacts. Chevron's experience demonstrates the rise – and, ultimately, the hubris – and fall of environmental marketing that does not quite match a firm's environmental performance.

As environmental marketing has matured, so have environmental non-governmental organisations (ENGOs) and consumer sophistication with environmental messaging. Although there will still be flagrant examples of greenwashed environmental communications, there also are well-informed, tech-savvy activists ready to expose them. The rise of greenwashing was driven by a combination of increasing environmental consciousness and poor environmental information through the 1980s and 1990s. Today, we may be witnessing the fall of greenwashing because the most egregious examples can be easily exposed by anyone with a copycat URL address, slick production values and the wit to help a spoof go viral. In our Web 2.0 era, websites such as greenwashingindex.com enable users even to view and rank examples of greenwashing posted by others.

The *Oxford English Dictionary* (OED) defines 'greenwash' as 'disinformation disseminated by an organisation so as to present an environmentally responsible public image' (Oxford Dictionary of English 2012). According to the OED, the term blends 'green', in the sense of environmental, with 'whitewash: a deliberate attempt to conceal unpleasant or incriminating facts about a person or organisation in order to protect their reputation'. Although the term likely originated in the 1980s, it entered the OED in 1999 and was identified by John Simpson, the then chief editor of the OED, as an emerging business buzzword for the new millennium (Simpson 2000).[3] Simpson's prediction proved accurate because the term began to appear more frequently

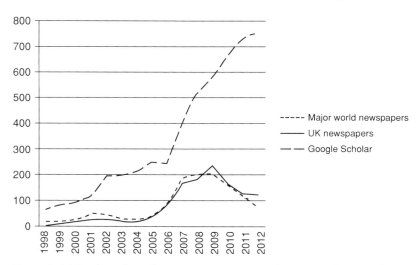

Figure 2.1 Number of articles mentioning greenwashing in academic and popular outlets, 1998–2012.
Sources: 'Google Scholar' series is number of unique hits per year on
scholar.google.co.uk. 'UK newspapers' is number of unique hits per year in the
content of all newspapers carried on LexisNexis that are published in the UK.
'Major world newspapers' includes articles in more than forty full-text newspapers within LexisNexis that are 'generally regarded by the reading public as
most comprehensive and reliable'.

in newspapers starting in 2005 (Figure 2.1). Greenwashing became a
common theme in the printed press, peaking in 2009 at more than two
hundred articles mentioning the term per year in the United Kingdom.
In 2008 seventy-three articles mentioned greenwashing in *The New
York Times* alone (with seventy-one in 2009).

The earliest widely cited works on greenwashing are Greer and
Bruno's (1996) *Greenwash: The Reality behind Corporate Environmentalism* and Tokar's (1997) *Earth for Sale*. Both of these books
are firmly rooted in the US environmental justice movement, focusing on the power and ideology related to corporate environmental
activities. The provenance of these early books explains a subtle difference in the definition of greenwashing between US and UK English.
The US-based *Merriam-Webster's Collegiate Dictionary* defines 'greenwashing' as 'expressions of environmentalist concerns especially *as a
cover for* products, policies, or activities' (emphasis added). In US
English, 'greenwashing' is derived from 'green' and 'brainwashing: a

forcible indoctrination to induce someone to give up basic political, social, or religious beliefs and attitudes and to accept contrasting regimented ideas' (*Merriam-Webster's Collegiate Dictionary* 2011). Thus, the early US use of the term 'greenwashing' is more ideologically loaded than the UK English 'whitewashing' of a reputation. Early US conceptions of greenwashing emphasised the importance of elite power and propaganda in successful greenwashing, and it is these resonances that ensure that Greer and Bruno (1996) and Toker (1997) are still widely cited in critiques of corporate environmentalism.

About the same time – and a full decade after the beginning of Chevron's *People Do* campaign – marketing scholars started to become more serious about examining environmental claims made in firms' advertising. For example, Polonsky et al. (1997) compared claims made about substantive changes in organisational environmental behaviour with claims designed to enhance a firm's environmental image in a sample of environmental advertising. They noticed cross-national differences in which firms in the United States made more environmental 'posturing' claims and less substantive claims than firms in Canada, Australia and the United Kingdom. They speculated about whether this was because at that time there was a higher cultural and regulatory tolerance in the US marketplace for efforts to position a firm as environmentally sensitive or perhaps because the other countries were farther along a path to greening.[4] These potential explanations highlight important aspects of greenwashing. First, greenwashing is a deliberate communication strategy by firms that, by definition, is disconnected from substantive greening. Second, the likelihood of greenwashing depends on the strength of monitoring in the institutional field surrounding a firm.

Similar to other new management phenomena (Abrahamson 1996), the increase in academic literature mentioning greenwashing lagged the increase in the popular press by a year or two. Unlike other management fashions (e.g., quality circles, lean production and total quality management), 'greening' was always a more difficult 'sell' than other management fashions with more obvious managerial benefits (Fineman 2001). Nevertheless, as academic interest in corporate environmentalism flourished, so did mentions of greenwashing in academic articles (see Figure 2.1). By 2012, Google Scholar listed more than two articles a day that mentioned the concepts of greenwash or greenwashing.[5] However, looking more closely at these articles reveals that, more often than not, greenwashing makes a guest appearance in most contemporary corporate environmentalism scholarship. Of the 752 Google Scholar hits in 2012, for example, fewer than a dozen were peer-reviewed academic journal articles that discuss greenwashing in more than a cursory way. These articles include two typical varieties of current academic research on greenwashing: (1) empirical studies on the incidence and consequences of deliberate environmental communication (see, e.g., Chen and Chang 2013 and Vidovic and Khanna 2012); and (2) evaluations of whether particular events or discourses are primarily about environmental image or substance (see, e.g., Allenby 2012 on the Rio+20 conference and Stephenson, Doukas, and Shaw 2012 on the discourse about shale gas). In a new development in the greenwashing literature, both Haack, Schoeneborn, and Wickert (2012) and Dauvergne and Lister (2012) echo the end of naïve greenwashing as exemplified by The Yes Men's *We Agree* hoax. They encourage us to go 'beyond simply greenwash' in the narrow sense of positive environmental communication coupled with poor environmental performance. The slowing growth in academic papers mentioning greenwashing – and early calls to place greenwashing within a broader organisational context – may signal the decline of narrow greenwashing in academic circles as well.

Academic conceptions and definitions of greenwashing have only recently become more refined (Table 2.1). Many have simply adopted variants of the original OED definition, such as Haack et al.'s (2012: 828) 'active dissemination of misleading information to present an environmentally responsible public image' (see also Laufer 2003; Ramus and Montiel 2005; and Vos 2009). Laufer's (2003) study of greenwashing in the socially responsible investment industry became a canonical early description of how 'corporations creatively manage their reputations with the public, financial community, and regulators, so as to hide deviance, deflect attributions of fault, obscure the nature of the problem of allegation, reattribute blame, ensure an entity's reputation and, finally, seem to appear in a leadership position' (Laufer 2003: 255). In this definition of greenwashing, firms deliberately propagate disinformation about their environmental activities through confusion, fronting and posturing (Beder 1997).

Definitions of greenwashing in marketing-oriented studies emphasise the nature of claims made by firms. Greenwashing is 'marketing hype to give a firm a green tinge' (Polonsky et al. 1997: 227) or

Table 2.1 *Definitions of greenwashing*

Source	Definition
Oxford English Dictionary (2012, first appeared 1999)	Disinformation disseminated by an organisation so as to present an environmentally responsible public image. *Origin: green + whitewashing*
Merriam-Webster's Collegiate Dictionary (2013, online)	Expressions of environmentalist concerns especially as a cover for products, policies or activities. *Origin: green + brainwashing*
Laufer (2003)	Disinformation from organisations seeking to repair public reputations and further shape public images.
Polonsky et al. (1997)	Marketing hype to give a firm a green tinge, without reducing the firm's detrimental environmental impact. Occurs when firms make fewer substantive claims and more posturing claims in environmental advertising.
Gillespie (2008)	Advertising or marketing that misleads the public by stressing the supposed environmental credentials of a person, company or product when these are unsubstantiated or irrelevant.
TerraChoice (2007)	The act of misleading consumers regarding the environmental practices of a company (firm-level greenwashing) or the environmental benefits of a product or service (product-level greenwashing).
Delmas and Burbano (2011)	The intersection of two firm behaviours: poor environmental performance and positive communication about environmental performance.
Walker and Wan (2012)	A strategy that companies adopt to engage in symbolic communication of environmental issues without substantially addressing them in actions. The difference between symbolic and substantive actions.
Forbes and Jermier (2012)	A superficial corporate environmentalism that is all style and no substance; a green ceremonial façade [that] focuses attention on one or a small number of highly visible green criteria and neglects all others.

(cont.)

Table 2.1 *(cont.)*

Source	Definition
Lyon and Maxwell (2011)	The selective disclosure of positive information about a company's environmental or social performance, without full disclosure of negative information on these dimensions, so as to create an overly positive corporate image.
Marquis and Toffel (2012)	A form of selective disclosure in which companies promote environmentally friendly programmes to deflect attention from an organisation's environmentally unfriendly or less savoury activities.

'supposed environmental credentials' that are 'unsubstantiated or irrelevant' (Gillespie 2008: 79). TerraChoice's (2007) definition separates claims about the environmental practices of a company (i.e., firm-level greenwashing) from claims about a product or service (i.e., product-level service). Its 'Six [later seven] Sins of Greenwashing' highlight claims that hide trade-offs, provide inadequate proof, are vague, are based on false labels, are irrelevant, are based on spurious comparisons or are simply false. Whereas marketing definitions imply a difference between a firm's claims and actions, this gap is more explicit in the most recent definitions of greenwashing. Both Delmas and Burbano (2011) and Walker and Wan (2012), for example, emphasise firms' simultaneous positive communication on environmental issues combined with poor substantive performance. From their symbolic organisational theory perspective, Forbes and Jermier (2012) also notice this symbol–substance gap, describing greenwashing as a firm's deliberate use of 'mere symbols' or 'a superficial corporate environmentalism that is all style and no substance' (2012: 561). Greenwashing focuses attention on highly visible green initiatives or criteria, thereby deflecting attention from a more comprehensive analysis.

Recent definitions of 'greenwashing' by strategy scholars and economists turn stakeholders' limited information and attention to a firm's advantage. They model greenwashing as a deliberate information management strategy in which firms can selectively disclose positive information about their environmental performance without full disclosure of less favourable activities (Lyon and Maxwell 2011; Marquis and Toffel 2012). The most careful, and narrowest, definition of all of these is Lyon and Maxwell's (2011: 9): 'selective disclosure of positive information about a company's environmental or social performance, without full disclosure of negative information on these dimensions, so as to create an overly positive corporate image'. This definition provides a foundation for Lyon and Maxwell's (2011) 'persuasion game' analysis of the drivers of greenwashing for firms with different levels of environmental performance. If we attempt to model greenwashing using economic game theory models such as this, then we certainly need more precise definitions of greenwashing. However, as with many economic models, the downside of idealised precision is that the definition of 'greenwashing' is much narrower than the politicised 'brainwashing' of the *Merriam-Webster Collegiate Dictionary* and the early writers in the US environmental justice movement.

A review of the definitions in Table 2.1 shows both the rise and the fall of the greenwashing concept. As greenwashing became more common in the popular press, academics followed with increasingly precise studies and definitions. Simply naming a phenomenon more carefully encourages others to examine it in more depth. As greenwashing becomes more delineated and easier for economists to study and model, the term begins to lose its broader ideological origins from the early literature. Most contemporary definitions of 'greenwashing' relate explicitly to a firm's choice about whether and what to disclose – not a choice about the form and substance of a firm's environmental actions in the first place. The earlier Merriam-Webster's definition focuses on broader 'expressions of environmentalist concerns'. Although these expressions might include selective disclosure through discretionary advertising or environmental reporting, 'expressions' also could take the form of actions that are understood symbolically in the field in which the firm operates. For example, Walmart's green reception area and IBM's Smarter Planet initiatives would not be captured within Lyon and Maxwell's (2011) 'selective disclosure' definition, but they surely would qualify as the more ideologically loaded 'expressions of environmentalist concerns especially as a cover for products, policies, or activities' (*Merriam-Webster's Collegiate Dictionary* 2011). Similarly, the OED definition includes the admittedly rather broad term 'disinformation', but this captures significantly more potential greenwash than the more specific 'positive information about a company's environmental or social performance' (Lyon and Maxwell 2011).

During the past thirty years or so, we have seen first the dramatic rise and then the beginnings of the fall of greenwashing. Newspaper articles mentioning greenwashing peaked in 2009, and early indications suggest that the number of academic articles may have reached a peak in 2012. There is no doubt about the wide variety of factors driving this trend, and answers to why greenwashing may have peaked in this way appear to be little more than speculation. However, it does seem sensible to suggest that the rise and fall in reporting about greenwashing in the popular press (at least) mirrors that of the attention given to environmental issues in newspapers more generally. Coverage increased as environmental awareness increased but then began to decline, along with media attention to environmental, energy and climate change since the financial crisis in 2008 and the failed United Nations (UN) climate talks in Copenhagen in 2009.

Looking past the decline in media coverage, Chevron's experience with the *We Agree* campaign and HSBC's 'virtual trees' suggest the potential for a real decline in the naïve greenwashing phenomenon. It is simply more difficult to maintain prima facie greenwash over time in an era of social media. Emerging research that theorises the impact of social media on greenwashing highlights the differences in corporate-stakeholder information flows between traditional and social media (Lyon and Montgomery 2013). Social media is nonhierarchical, lacks elite gatekeepers, is highly dynamic and public, and lacks formal controls within an environment of broad monitoring. Lyon and Montgomery (2013) further suggest that in a 'high information' social media context, there may be no greenwash at all – at least in the sense of simultaneous positive environmental information and poor environmental performance.

The decline of greenwashing seems likely to accelerate as new technologies enable anyone with a smartphone to directly monitor their environment and expose undisclosed, poor environmental performance. For example, HabitatMap – an ENGO based in New York that aims to raise awareness about the links between the environment and human health – launched AirCasting, 'a platform for recording, mapping, and sharing health and environmental data using your smartphone'.[6] Smartphone users can download the app and then use it to record, map and share sound levels recorded by the phone's microphone. Advanced users can connect this with AirCasting's air monitor (which records temperature, humidity, and carbon monoxide [CO] and nitrogen dioxide [NO_2] gas concentrations) and its custom-designed heart-rate monitor to record and share how users' heart rates respond to exposure to noise and air pollution. The commercial potential of this monitoring equipment has not gone unnoticed by major companies such as IBM, which launched a WaterWatchers app that enables mobile-phone users in South Africa to photograph and report water problems they observe (Simjee 2013). IBM's app is designed to centrally collect the water data and then distribute it to water planners, utilities and municipalities; however, it is not difficult to imagine a parallel, open-source water data collection platform operated by tech-savvy activists. Direct and diffused monitoring of environmental impacts is likely to further close the gap between naïve positive communication and poor performance on environmental issues. Social media, smartphones and smart monitoring will soon confine environmental advertising like Chevron's *People Do* campaign to the marketing history archives.

From greenwashing to symbolic corporate environmentalism

Outright greenwashing as it was in the 1980s, 1990s and early 2000s may soon take its place in history with other cultural phenomena of that era. But does this mean that companies have stopped trying to confuse, inflate, cover or creatively manage their reputations on environmental issues? Just because corporate environmentalism is maturing, can we now expect alignment between the symbolic and material components of firms' green activities? More important, can we expect firms to unquestioningly comply with societal environmental demands now that these are more clearly articulated and less uncertain? This does not seem likely. The stakes are high: for firms that require access to increasingly stressed ecosystem services, for NGOs and activists who want to protect natural systems, for consumers who demand a wide variety of goods and services at low prices, and for politicians who want to be reelected. It seems unlikely that a distributed force of informal monitors armed with smartphones and social media will stop 'big business' in its tracks. It is more likely that firms' tactics will change and that activists, academics and analysts will have to approach the contested terrain of who decides how to solve environmental problems in

a more sophisticated way. Throughout this book, I argue that we need
to expand our conception of the shared meanings and representations
around firms' environmental behaviour, from narrow greenwashing to
a much broader symbolic corporate environmentalism. It will always
be important for activists to expose examples of greenwashing and
for academics to develop increasingly robust and sophisticated analyses to understand this cultural phenomenon. However, greenwashing
is only part of a much broader and potentially more socially costly
contestation over how corporate greening is defined, described and
socially rewarded. Specifically, the academic literature on greenwashing is limited by four significant assumptions: it is focused on information disclosure decisions, it is assumed to be a deliberate strategy,
it is conceived primarily as a corporate phenomenon, and it is usually
assumed to be beneficial for firms and detrimental to society. Unpacking each of these assumptions provides a more realistic and powerful
analysis of symbolic corporate environmentalism after greenwashing.

Greenwashing is an information disclosure decision

Most of the definitions listed in Table 2.1 frame greenwashing as an
information disclosure decision. The focus is on a firm's communicative activities directed at particular stakeholder audiences. Greenwashing can be information that is directed at consumers through advertising (see, e.g., Gillespie 2008 and Polonsky et al. 1998); at investors
through environmental disclosure schemes such as the Carbon Disclosure Project (CDP) (see, e.g., Lyon and Maxwell 2011); or at a broader
public through corporate websites (see, e.g., Walker and Wan 2012).
Firms also signal environmental quality through disclosing awards or
certifications such as the International Organisation for Standardisation (ISO) 14001 standard. This focus on greenwashing as disclosure
is understandable. It is much easier for researchers to collect data on
large samples of firms based on visible metrics from publicly available data. Tracking memberships of industry clubs, the use of logos,
and responses to investor questionnaires has allowed researchers to
contrast positive environmental information with measurable environmental performance, such as toxic releases or carbon intensity of
operations.

Recent disclosure-based studies help in understanding the nature,
contingencies and dynamics of a particular type of greenwashing – but

focusing on disclosure does not tell the whole story. Lyon and Maxwell (2011: 9) recognised the limitations of defining greenwashing as selective disclosure and leaving 'for future research the important challenge of integrating a disclosure model with a model of corporate choice of environmental projects'. A fuller model should work backward from the decision to disclose environmental information to integrate it with the symbolic aspects of adopting a given green initiative in the first place. More important, focusing on disclosure draws attention to a firm's communicative practices such as reporting, public relations (PR) and marketing. However, Merriam-Webster's 'expressions of environmentalist concerns' can include a wide variety of firm practices, not only communicative practices. We must pay attention to the symbolic dimension of the ordinary activities of firms (Forbes and Jermier 2012). Moving beyond greenwashing as disclosure allows the broadening of greenwashing back to its ideological roots: that is, examining how powerful elites use the shared meanings surrounding a wide range of organisational artefacts and practices to redirect the environmental conversation. Firms may not actively disclose environmental information through their mission statements, organisational structures, environmental technology choices, human resource routines, cultural stories or workplace rituals, but these practices can be powerful symbolic manifestations of green activities (Forbes and Jermier 2012). We must relax the dominant assumption of greenwashing as being about disclosure choices to include the shared meanings around all of an organisation's green activities.[7]

Greenwashing is deliberate

A second assumption found in most of the definitions in Table 2.1 is that greenwashing is deliberate. It is 'a strategy that companies adopt' (Walker and Wan 2012), 'active dissemination' (Haack et al. 2012), or disclosure that is 'selective' (Lyon and Maxwell 2011; Marquis and Toffel 2012). All of these definitions imply that someone, somewhere in a firm decides to greenwash, whether it is the chief executive officer (CEO), marketing staff, PR department or whoever. This assumption about greenwashing makes sense among activists who are trying to expose particular firms or individuals for poor environmental performance. They need someone to blame for the lack of authentic action on environmental issues. It also makes sense among academics who study firms' decisions, including most economists, strategists, marketers and accountants. They need to ascribe agency to firms – or at least to managers within them – so as to contrast effective with ineffective firm actions. However, assuming that greenwashing is deliberate narrows the phenomenon and seriously limits how we conceptualise it.

Mintzberg and his colleagues famously pointed out that not all strategies are deliberate – some emerge from a pattern of actions rather than a pattern of decisions (Mintzberg and Waters 1985). A firm's words and actions on environmental issues can become disconnected because its intended strategies can be unrealised or because this disconnect emerges from a pattern of actions conducted in different parts of the firm. Contemporary decoupling literature builds on this disconnect to argue that it may not make sense to define 'decoupling' as separating stated intent from action; intentions may be generated simultaneously with actions or even after them (Bromley and Powell 2012).

Gaps between the symbolic and substantive effects of green activities might emerge as an unintended consequence of the process of corporate greening (Winn and Angell 2000). Gaps might arise for various reasons, including unexpected results from environmental programmes, poor project implementation, managers' cognitive biases, internal politics, middle managers' discretionary resource allocation and other external factors (Delmas and Burbano 2011). When HSBC announced in 2011 that it would no longer be carbon neutral, it stated that this was because the market for carbon offsets had not developed as expected when it made the commitment in 2005. According to HSBC's explanation, external factors led to an unintended mismatch between the firm's carbon neutral goals and its ability to meet them. Pointing out that symbolic gaps do not always need to be deliberate does not exonerate the cases of outright deception about firms' performance – these deliberate deceptions should always be exposed and corrected. Widening our understanding of how differences between green words and actions can occur to include unintended or emergent gaps will provide a richer and more realistic analysis of firms' environmental strategies.

Greenwashing is initiated by companies

The third assumption embedded in the academic definitions in Table 2.1 is that greenwashing is primarily a company-led activity. Delmas and Burbano (2011) define it as 'the intersection of two *firm* behaviours'; Marquis and Toffel (2012) note that it is *companies* that promote environmental programmes; and for Walker and Wan (2012), greenwashing is 'a strategy that *companies* adopt' (emphases added). Early and dictionary-based definitions do not have this embedded assumption about firms doing the greenwashing. Some definitions include no actor at all (e.g., *Merriam-Webster's Collegiate Dictionary*) or else a more general actor, such as 'organisations' (e.g., Laufer 2003 and *Oxford English Dictionary* 2012). In the transition to a more formalised approach in the management research literature, we somehow acquired the assumption that greenwashing is, by definition, a company-led activity. Many greenwashing examples are promulgated by companies, but other social actors can spread disinformation or deflect attention on green issues as well. Governments, public sector organisations, individual politicians and even NGOs have all been criticised for communicating false progress on environmental issues. Although recent greenwashing literature focuses on greenwashing in voluntary, industry-led regulation, we must understand a firm's environmental strategies in a context in which formal environmental regulation also may be primarily symbolic (Matten 2003; Newig 2007).

Of course, it may not always be obvious who is responsible for greenwashing. A crucial assumption in Lyon and Maxwell (2011) is that disclosures are verifiable by outside parties – that activists can audit and detect greenwash and act accordingly on this information. Active greenwash detection mechanisms using distributed monitoring via smartphones and social media may increase the likelihood that activists will be able to recognise outright communicative greenwashing. But what about more dispersed symbolic information embedded in the everyday activities of firms? It is notoriously difficult for participants in a social field to see past that field's shared symbolic meanings. Even a firm's own employees may be unable to see decoupling between a firm's words and actions (Boxenbaum and Jonsson 2008). Activist groups such as the Rainforest Action Network and the World Wide Fund for Nature (WWF) adopt corporate language, receive corporate donations, and enter into strategic partnerships with companies, thereby contributing to the generation of shared meanings about environmental responsibility. This has earned these groups criticism for participating in greenwash. These activists might counter that they need to strategically suspend disbelief around a company's environmental intentions to be able to engage in a productive dialogue; build relationships; and drive longer-term, deeper environmental change. The problem is that this also can drift easily into a collective self-deception that misrecognises reassuring symbols of environmental change from those in authority for real environmental improvement (Bourdieu and Thompson 1991; Newig 2007). It is not clear whether the merely symbolic greening begins with companies, with governments that generate stringent rhetoric without implementing green legislation, with well-intentioned ENGOs that want to participate in the green public debate, with a citizenry that is quite willing to accept false reassurances about environmental action, or with the interactions among all of these field participants. Assuming that greenwashing is a company-led activity absolves individuals as consumers, employees or voters from needing to change their own behaviour.

Greenwashing is beneficial to firms and costly to society

The fourth key assumption in current scholarship is that greenwashing is beneficial to firms and costly to society. On the one hand, firms can reap private reputational benefit from environmental disclosure that is ahead of true environmental performance by lowering regulatory costs, improving brand image and so on (Delmas and Burbano 2011). On the other hand, communicative activity that does not match a firm's underlying environmental performance imposes a negative externality on society that arises from the distortion of a company's image (Lyon and Maxwell 2011). So far, too little research has focused on the welfare implications of symbolic greening. Economists and strategists tend to assume that firms are deliberately greenwashing because they are responding rationally to incentives and payoffs to do so and that this gap is bad for society. However, we need to examine more closely the social and private costs and benefits of shared meanings about corporate greening. In considering costs, we must find a way to account for not only the direct costs of marketing and PR on firms but also the indirect cost of loss of productivity from diverting social energy into merely symbolic activities. We may be seriously underestimating the social costs of corporate control over the rhetoric surrounding environmental initiatives.

We also need a more sophisticated approach to the potential social benefits of environmental symbols. Even merely symbolic green initiatives may be beneficial to society in the long run. Labels, logos, programmes, policies and associations may help to integrate green issues into everyday business practice, communicate abstract scientific concepts, change employee attitudes and behaviour, and give managers tools to achieve apparent rationality in addressing nebulous environmental issues (see, e.g., Matten 2003 and Rhee and Lee 2003). Current research tends to define greenwashing as it relates to policy implementation depth – that is, the extent to which a disclosed policy is actually translated into improved firm-level environmental performance. This emphasises social costs because incorrect information about a firm's environmental quality creates distortions in firm valuation. However, analysing the breadth of the diffusion of symbols, rather than simply the depth, allows a more sophisticated understanding of how new greening ideas spread and become established in a particular organisational field. What may be dismissed as greenwash in the early stages of an institutionalisation process ultimately may lead to a broader social conversation and to a deeper environmental commitment (Haack et al. 2012). Gaps between a firm's words and actions may be costly to society in the short run but may help stabilise, legitimate and, ultimately, raise the quality of environmental solutions in the longer run.

From greenwashing to symbolic corporate environmentalism

Recent definitions of greenwashing are useful because they allow enough precision for greenwashing to be economically modelled and measured. However, deliberate, disclosure-based greenwashing initiated by companies is only part of the broader symbolic contestation over environmental issues. We need a wider perspective on how differences between the symbolic and substantive effects of green activities arise in an organisational field, as well as the social costs and benefits of these gaps in various contexts. In the tradition of the original wider scope of the 'greenwashing' term, I suggest that we consider a more general phenomenon: symbolic corporate environmentalism. This refers to the shared meanings and representations surrounding changes made by managers within firms that they describe as primarily for environmental reasons. Greenwashing is an important subset of activity within symbolic corporate environmentalism, but it is only a part of the broader shared meanings related to corporate greening. The broader concept of symbolic corporate environmentalism allows us to break out of the limitations imposed by the four assumptions about greenwashing in the recent literature to generate a richer explanation of the symbolic component of the environmental behaviour of firms. Although greenwashing may be on the decline, symbolic corporate environmentalism is unlikely to diminish in the near future. To provide a foundation to better understand this new concept, I next outline the differences between narrow greenwashing and symbolic corporate environmentalism.

The primary difference between greenwashing and symbolic corporate environmentalism is the way in which symbol and substance are connected. In conventional definitions of greenwashing, a firm's communications can be separated from actual environmental impacts. 'Greenwashing' is the label given when deliberate positive disclosure exists in parallel with poor substantive environmental performance. Thus, by definition, a firm's communications are disconnected from environmental impact. There is only a symbolic link between the signal – such as adopting an empty eco-label – and the abstract concept it is intended to signify (e.g., corporate environmental concern). In greenwashing, there is no necessary link between the symbol and materially improved environmental performance. Greenwashing is a special case within symbolic corporate environmentalism in which firms deliberately manipulate symbols so as to open up a gap between their symbolic and substantive performance.

Symbolic corporate environmentalism is both broader and more nuanced. This concept captures all of the shared meanings relative to changes that managers make for environmental reasons. All corporate environmental practices have both material and symbolic components (Forbes and Jermier 2012). For example, constructing a green headquarters building has the material components of high-efficiency lighting, a rainwater-utilisation system, a green roof or solar-power windows. It also has symbolic components such as showcasing environmental concern to internal and external stakeholders, signifying high status through association with a famous architect, and projecting an image of environmental responsibility through acquiring a green building certification (e.g., LEED Gold). Crucially, these components may or may not be linked with substantive environmental improvements. A green headquarters building has symbolic and material components regardless of whether it is actually beneficial for the environment. Indeed, even the most advanced green buildings may not match an absolute standard of building the greenest buildings (Pierre-Louis 2012). For example, the architect of HSBC's new North

American headquarters in Mettawa, outside Chicago, claimed that 'this is the most sophisticated environmentally sensitive building we've ever designed' (Hwa-Shu 2008), thereby vouching for the building's technologically advanced material components. But the Natural Resources Defense Council (NRDC) countered, 'What we really have here is yet another high-tech building calling itself "green" but that warrants the label only if you completely discount the sprawling, totally automobile-dependent location . . . [that] cause[s] far more carbon emissions from employees and visitors driving to and from than they save with energy-efficient building technology' (Benfield 2008). Obviously, it is not the building that calls itself green but rather the people commentating on and describing the building – in this case, *The New York Times*, HSBC and the LEED agency that awarded the Gold certification. The building's symbolic component evolves as shared meanings develop through interactions among actors within the field, and symbols like 'LEED Gold' and 'green building' come to represent the abstract concept of a building that does not damage the environment. The material and symbolic components of an environmental change may or may not be linked to reducing substantive environmental impact.

All environmental practices embody both material changes and powerful symbolic messages. Symbolic corporate environmentalism refers to the latter: the shared meanings and representations related to the environmental activities. Some symbolic corporate environmentalism has only a symbolic effect and is not linked to improved substantive performance. This type of symbolic corporate environmentalism is termed 'merely symbolic' (Short and Toffel 2010; Stevens et al. 2005). Greenwashing is a special case of 'merely symbolic' in which firms deliberately manipulate their communications and symbolic practices so as to build a ceremonial façade (Forbes and Jermier 2012).

However, there is another aspect of symbolic corporate environmentalism in which the symbolic and material components are indeed linked to substantive environmental improvement. It may be the case that the NRDC's criticism is too harsh: there may be substantive environmental improvements associated with HSBC's building. We could use a tool such as an environmental impact assessment or a life-cycle analysis of the building to assess this concern. Even if there is a substantive environmental impact improvement, it does not erase the symbolic function of social labels such as 'green buildings' and 'LEED

Table 2.2 *Greenwashing and symbolic corporate environmentalism*

	Greenwashing	Symbolic corporate environmentalism
Practices	Disclosure and communication practices only	All environmental practices
Examples of cultural manifestations	Environmental reports, advertising, eco-labels, corporate websites, certification schemes, public environmental policies...	... plus environmental technologies, job titles, strategic plans, internal environmental programmes, measurement and reporting systems, compliance registries, physical infrastructure, partnership agreements and so forth
Primary actors	Firms	Interactions among actors
Strategic focus	Deliberate strategy	Emergent strategy
Economic consequences	Beneficial to firms; costly to society	Costs and benefits for both firms and society
Link with environmental impact	Disconnected; symbolic effects only	May be connected or disconnected; symbolic and/or substantive effects

Gold'. The current corporate environmental strategy literature tends to underrate symbolic corporate environmentalism by looking only at merely symbolic activities, such as greenwashing, and not at the shared meanings around greening that might also have a substantive impact.

Table 2.2 illustrates how other features show that greenwashing differs from broader symbolic corporate environmentalism. First, symbolic corporate environmentalism is about more than environmental information disclosure. Contemporary greenwashing research has increasingly focused on easily visible environmental disclosures. Disclosure practices such as publishing sustainability reports, declaring support for green clubs, adopting labels and certification schemes such as ISO 14001 and EnergyStar, and participating in the CDP are all ways for firms to signal environmental quality. These environmental disclosures lend themselves to large-scale empirical studies in which firms can be easily categorised as disclosing support for a visible scheme or not. But we need to remember that the adoption of an internal environmental management system can signify environmental concerns as much as an ISO 14001 certificate. All changes to firm environmental practices are symbolically connected to the abstract idea of greening; all environmental practices embody a shared meaning that they represent an attempt to improve the natural environment. Therefore, symbolic corporate environmentalism includes not only disclosure and communication practices but also the symbolic aspects of the full range of environmental practices, including implementing an environmental technology, creating an environmental department, launching internal environmental programmes, instituting measurement and reporting systems and constructing physical buildings. We must expand our analysis beyond specific disclosure practices to include the symbolic components of all corporate environmental actions.

Second, symbolic corporate environmentalism may emerge as an unintended consequence of a firm's environmental decisions. Contemporary definitions of greenwashing tend to emphasise deliberate strategies. This view implies that firms make strategically interrelated deliberate decisions about disclosing environmental information and about levels of environmental performance. But a more realistic view recognises that the shared meanings about corporate greening emerge from a broader pattern of practices. Corporate environmentalism is a systematic pattern of voluntary practices across a firm (Aragon-Correa and Rubio-López 2007). Strategies often actually emerge as middle managers support their own pet projects and local managers respond to specific local environmental concerns or provide 'knee-jerk' reactions to a perceived environmental crisis. It is easy to see the potential for environmental practices within firms to become diffuse or contradictory. If a firm's practices are messy, then the symbolic aspects of those actions can also be messy. All environmental practices have symbolic meanings, whether or not those shared meanings are deliberately manipulated. The symbolic component of green practices may or may not accurately represent substantive environmental performance, regardless of whether a manager set out to deliberately mislead.

Third, symbolic corporate environmentalism is deeply embedded within an institutional field and may be constructed by a diverse range of actors or the interactions among them. Motivated activists are becoming better adept at recognising deliberate greenwash. However, they need to put aside their most critical voices to be able to maintain productive conversations with firms and governments. This can lead them to inadvertently support symbolic actions over no action at all. For an illustration of how this can work in practice, consider the WWF's response to the failed UN Rio+20 environmental summit in July 2012. The ENGO criticised the intergovernmental draft agreement, pointing out that it included the words 'encourage' fifty times and 'support' ninety-nine times but mentioned the words 'we will' and 'must' fewer than ten times in total (*The Economist* 2012). It criticised the negotiations as 'a process with no serious content' (WWF 2012). In the same press release, WWF praised the governments, banks, investors and large corporations – including Unilever, Puma and Dow Chemical – that collectively produced the 'Natural Capital Declaration' (NCD). Participants who signed the declaration 'wish to demonstrate our commitment to the eventual integration of natural capital considerations into private-sector reporting, accounting and decision making, with standardisation of measurement and disclosure of natural capital use by the private sector' (Natural Capital Declaration 2012a). The NCD lists benefits for firms in signing the declaration, such as showing leadership and commitment, risk management and reputational gains. It also reassures potential signatories that the NCD 'does not require from endorsers to report or disclose additional information' (Natural Capital Declaration 2012b). As discussed in Chapter 7, the more that high-status corporate actors are involved in designing a performance standard, the more likely that that standard is to be based on symbolic rather than substantive criteria. The WWF may be inadvertently promoting a new green initiative with little prospect for substantive change. Its support helps to construct and maintain cultural symbols related to corporate environmentalism – symbols that are misrecognised as legitimate by a disengaged public because of the high status of those promoting them. Giving more attention to how symbolic corporate environmentalism emerges within a field highlights the roles of power and status – dimensions that often are neglected in rational economic analyses of greenwashing.

Fourth, symbolic corporate environmentalism may have a range of private costs and benefits for firms as well as welfare costs and benefits at the societal level. At the firm level, individual companies might face both negative and positive consequences of merely symbolic greening. Private reputational benefits must be balanced against the potential private costs of loss of consumer confidence, lawsuits from false advertising, and other risks when consumers or NGOs question firms' claims (Delmas and Burbano 2011). We should also move the analysis from the firm to the social level and examine both the social benefits and the costs of symbolic corporate environmentalism. The Rio+20 environmental summit, for example, was rightly criticised for the excessive direct cost of convening thousands of participants from across the globe and the indirect cost of missing an opportunity for a step change in environmental cooperation. But it also gave rise to more than seven hundred voluntary commitments on various improvements towards sustainable development by individual companies, associations, governments and civil society groups.[8] Many of these commitments will turn out to lack substance or may have already been forgotten. But many, taken together, may plant the seeds of distributed incremental changes, each taken according to the self-interest of individual adopters, and which may raise the level of conversation and action on environmental improvement (Allenby 2012). A more dynamic view hints at the potential for social benefit as particular experiments for environmental improvement gain meaning, momentum and support. The main conceptual framework I introduce in this book provides a way to trade off the social costs and benefits of symbolic corporate environmentalism. A more contingent view of when symbolic corporate environmentalism may be most damaging is vital so that regulators and activists can focus their change efforts on the most socially harmful merely symbolic activities.

After greenwashing

This book is the first systematic analysis of the drivers and consequences of symbolic corporate environmentalism after greenwashing. I move beyond firm-centric greenwashing that is deliberate and disclosure based to include the symbolic component of a wider range of greening activities within institutional fields. Optimists argue that the 'bad days' of corporate greenwashing are behind us as academics and activists are becoming more adept at calling to account companies that commit greenwashing. Cynics dismiss corporate environmentalism as deflective manoeuvres by powerful social actors, and they emphasise the costs imposed on society by firms acting in their own self-interest.

Realists accept that stakeholders need corporate symbols to assess environmental quality but that these symbols are designed and promoted by actors that have a stake and a position to maintain in the field. Symbolic corporate environmentalism pervades contemporary organisational life. But when are these symbols particularly socially costly? Moreover, when might even merely symbolic changes be justified in the short run and outweighed by positive effects of information sharing, raising the quality of a public conversation or stimulating monitoring and surveillance? Providing guidance on these contemporary dilemmas is at the core of this book.

3 | *Perspectives on symbolic corporate environmentalism*

What is symbolic corporate environmentalism and how have aspects of it been theorised by others? Because symbolic corporate environmentalism is a new concept, there is no well-established and neatly defined body of research to analyse it. In this chapter, I expand the new concept of symbolic corporate environmentalism and draw on existing greenwashing research and broader theory to further describe it. I show how symbolic corporate environmentalism has been treated so far within two conflicting research perspectives: the conventional and the critical views. I define key ideas related to symbolic corporate environmentalism, including 'symbolic gaps' and 'symbolic performance'. I then place these ideas within broader organisational theory and strategy literatures related to firm symbolic performance, particularly on reputation, legitimacy and status. I use the theoretical foundations based on these two perspectives of symbolic corporate environmentalism to support the analysis in subsequent chapters.

'Corporate environmentalism' is defined as changes made by managers within firms that they describe as primarily for reasons connected with the natural environment. Researchers have variously focused on changes to firms' processes, practices and general modes of response to addressing environmental issues.[1] However, they usually have in common a focus on the selective adoption by firms of environmental changes that are beyond legal compliance (Prakash 2000) or 'environmentally friendly measures that are not required by law' (Lyon and Maxwell 2004: xi). Of course, the interpretations of 'environmentally friendly' and even 'what is required by law' are open to discussion. What matters here is how managers present the changes: corporate environmentalism entails changes that managers explain as voluntary responses to greening pressures in the natural, stakeholder or institutional environment that are not immediately required to meet current regulatory or legal obligations.

Corporate environmentalism is a general concept that captures a wide range of specific environmental practices. These practices can be product-oriented, such as when firms develop products that are somehow greener, or process-oriented, such as efforts to reduce waste or improve resource efficiency. Corporate environmentalism also includes investments in management systems – that is, internal infrastructural investments that affect the way production is managed (Klassen and Whybark 1999; Kolk 2000). Managers describe a variety of practices – from eco-labels to recycling schemes to buying carbon credits – as corporate environmentalism. It also includes firm involvement in a proliferation of environmental management standards, environmental reporting and accounting, partnerships, industry associations, employee training schemes, business consortia and conventions, which are all positioned as offering improvements in a firm's environmental performance.

In this book, I describe changes to environmental practices as 'green solutions' because they are responses by managers to solve problems in the natural, social, institutional and market surroundings arising from the natural environment. Some green solutions lead to improvements in substantive environmental problems, such as reducing water use, waste or carbon emissions. Other green solutions may address problems in the institutional environment, such as a threat of NGO activism or poor ratings in ethical investment rankings. Still other green solutions address a combination of both. The conventional view in corporate environmentalism research is that, properly implemented, green solutions should solve green problems. Yet, the discourse about the potential for corporate green solutions is far ahead of actual environmental improvements. Furthermore, as discussed in this chapter, a critical view of corporate environmentalism emphasises how recasting the conversation away from problems to solutions distracts social attention away from the environmental damage caused by industrial activity. According to the critical view, green solutions are designed and symbolically supported by those with the power to produce them.

Thus, simply because a manager (or, indeed, a researcher) describes a particular initiative, policy, strategy, investment or programme as a 'green solution', it does not mean that a 'problem' in the natural environment is necessarily 'solved'. Given this difficulty with the 'green-solutions' label, readers may wonder why I use it in this book.

One of the challenges in this controversial area is that there are no value-free labels. Most of the labels used to describe corporate environmentalism would suffer from this issue.[2] I choose to stay with the 'green solutions' label because it best reflects what managers, standard setters and designers of industry clubs claim that they are trying to do: that is, provide solutions to environmental problems, whether in the natural or institutional environment. However, given the controversy surrounding the solutions-based discourse, I use the label mindfully and certainly without any implication that a 'solution' will in fact 'solve' an environmental 'problem'.

In this chapter, I outline the contours of the academic literature that addresses the core concepts of corporate environmentalism, green solutions, symbolic performance and symbolic gaps. I begin by describing two widely held perspectives on corporate environmentalism – the critical and the conventional views – and how each view understands the shared meanings and representations related to everyday corporate activities. I show that proponents of each perspective have a quite different understanding of symbolic performance and symbolic gaps. I then position this difference within broader treatments of corporate symbolic gaps, borrowing ideas from organisational theory and strategy, sociology, psychology, anthropology, law and economics. The goals are to (1) provide key insights from the research to date on the important phenomenon of symbolic corporate environmentalism; and (2) generate themes, issues and questions that have not been fully addressed in the current literature.

Two perspectives on corporate environmentalism

Corporate environmentalism is the voluntary attempts of managers to adopt, implement and communicate solutions to environmental problems. Typically, corporate environmentalism is defined as environmental changes made by managers to firms' practices, processes or strategies beyond those required by law. This conventional approach questions the drivers and consequences of voluntary corporate greening. However, some critical theorists have been resisting this rather managerialist view of corporate environmentalism. They point out that expecting voluntary environmental leadership from firms and the rational 'eco-efficiency' rhetoric are actually quite recent, emerging only since the mid-1990s. Critical theorists term this conventional discourse the 'new corporate environmentalism' (Jermier et al. 2006) and instead propose a perspective anchored in the politics and rhetoric of environmentalism. A thorough analysis of corporate environmentalism should begin with understanding the key assumptions and concerns of both the critical and the conventional perspectives.

The conventional perspective

Corporate strategy is about matching a firm's internal resources with its external surroundings in order to secure advantage for the firm in the long term. In the late 1980s and early 1990s, managers began to adjust their strategies in response to changes to external environmental demands. Iconic events – including the Bhopal disaster in 1984, the Exxon Valdez oil spill in 1989, the Montreal Protocol that banned ozone-depleting substances in 1987, the original Rio UN Conference on Environment and Development in 1992, and, later, the Brent Spar controversy in 1995 – all heightened attention on environmental issues. Large, visible companies – particularly in the chemical, oil and natural resources sectors – faced questions from governments, NGOs, investors and the media on how their strategy could be affected by environmental concerns. At the same time, strategy scholars began to look inside firms to understand the foundations of competitive advantage, and they found an answer in the pattern of a firm's resources and capabilities (Barney 1991; Wernerfelt 1984). Corporate environmentalism research began to build on this theory to argue that investing in green solutions could enhance a firm's internal resources and, ultimately, its competitive position (Hart 1995; Sharma and Vredenburg 1998). Environmental concerns began to influence corporate strategy in both practice and theory.

The conventional perspective on corporate environmentalism focuses on how the natural environment affects firms' strategies and, ultimately, performance.[3] The approach is usually based on injecting environmental concerns into the resource-based view (RBV) of the firm. The RBV was built on an economic analysis of how firms invest and develop idiosyncratic resources to best position their activities to gain competitive advantage (Lockett and Thompson 2001; Penrose 1959). Hart (1995) famously adapted the framework to build a natural-resource–based view (NRBV) of the firm. His core insight was to turn potential limitations that firms might face due to resource scarcity and reliance on natural ecosystems into a basis for competitive advantage. Investing in specific strategic capabilities helps firms to build key resources and ultimately can secure competitive advantage. Hart's three green capabilities – pollution prevention, product stewardship and sustainable development – framed much of the subsequent conventional corporate environmentalism literature. Pollution prevention – or minimising emissions, effluents and wastes – can support a firm's continuous improvement and lead to lower costs than its competitors. Product stewardship develops a firm's abilities in stakeholder integration, preempting competitors' attempts to shape the stakeholder and regulatory environment. Furthermore, sustainable development – that is, minimising the environmental burden of firm growth and development – helps to develop a shared vision and a firm's future position.

Hart's NRBV formalised the prospect of win-win corporate environmentalism and offered mainstream strategy theory new insights about the foundations of competitive advantage (Berchicci and King 2008). By investing in green solutions, a firm could develop competitively valuable capabilities (Sharma and Vredenburg 1998), improve relationships with various stakeholders (Buysse and Verbeke 2003), and enhance its reputation (Russo and Fouts 1997). Developing a proactive corporate environmental strategy helps firms navigate contingencies in their external environment, thereby contributing to strategic success (Aragon-Correa and Sharma 2003). Numerous tests and extensions of the NRBV demonstrated the potential for investments in different types of green solutions to support a firm's competitive advantage (Sellers, Verbeke, and Bowen 2006).

A central research question in the conventional perspective of corporate environmentalism has been to test the relationship between environmental and financial performance: Does it pay to be green? In theory, firms can lower costs through eco-efficiency in their processes or products. Alternatively, they can differentiate through a reputation for beyond compliance leadership in their organisational processes or gain a price premium through eco-branding (Orsato 2006). However, the debate continues about how widespread these gains might be in practice, and recent reviews reveal mixed empirical evidence (see, e.g., Molina-Azorín et al. 2009 and Stefan and Paul 2008).

Because conventional corporate environmentalism research origi-
nates in economics and strategic management, there is an understandable focus on the private costs and benefits of green solutions for
firms. However, this perspective is rightly criticised for giving too little
attention to whether corporate environmentalism actually improves
the natural environment. Conventional research focuses on the more
easily visible and widely available indicators of environmental performance, such as adopting recognised labels, joining schemes and measures of single environmental issues (e.g., toxic emissions and climate
change) (Etzion 2007; Russo and Minto 2012; Whiteman et al. 2012).
Even studies based on the same green solution can give contradictory
results. For example, Pototski and Prakash (2005) found a positive
relationship between the adoption of the ISO 14001 environmental
management standard and substantive environmental improvements,
whereas Russo and Harrison (2005) found a negative relationship.

Conventional corporate environmentalism researchers sent insight-
ful 'postcards from the edge' of established strategy and economics
theory, shedding light on the origins of competitive advantage and on
industry self-regulation (Berchicci and King 2008). This 'second wave'
of corporate environmentalism placed green issues in the context of
a firm's overall strategic management (Hoffman and Bansal 2012).
Focused on showing the firm-level competitive benefits of green solutions, it also introduced a new language of corporate environmentalism
into contemporary business based on eco-efficiency, sustainability, and
environmental win-wins.

The critical perspective

There is no doubt that the conventional perspective helped to bring
concerns about the natural environment into conversations at corporate board meetings, business school conferences and academic journals. However, a set of alternative, critical perspectives argues that
'what business and the natural environment research has succeeded
in doing is to add the prefix "sustainable" to mainstream accounts
of organisational theory that continue to privilege growth, production
and consumption' (Banerjee 2012: 579). Advocates of a critical view
point out that the corporate environmentalism of the conventional
view should more accurately be thought of as a *new* corporate environmentalism because this particular version of corporate responses

to environmental pressures evolved only in the past fifteen years or so as a product of its sociohistorical moment. A more critical view points out that new corporate environmentalism functions as 'the *rhetoric* concerning the central role of business in achieving both economic growth and ecological rationality, and as a *guide* for management that emphasises voluntary, proactive control of environmental impacts that exceed or go beyond environmental laws and regulatory compliance' (Jermier et al. 2006: 618; emphasis in the original). The critical perspective looks past a firm-level analysis of corporate environmental strategy, positioning and competitively valuable resources and instead questions the structure and consequences of the rhetoric surrounding green solutions at the social-system level. The critical view asks: What does corporate engagement with a broader social conversation do to the potential solutions presented to pressing environmental challenges, and which solutions are ultimately preferred and implemented?[4]

A critical view highlights the fundamentally political nature of corporate environmentalism (Crane, Matten, and Moon 2008). Corporate involvement in inventing, selling, appropriating and deflecting green solutions is 'first and foremost about control': the critical questions are to ask who does and who should control the impact of industrial production on the environment (Jermier et al. 2006: 627). Critical researchers look beyond the conventional answer that managers and firms can and should self-regulate at the corporate, industry-sector or national level. Reducing complex, dynamic and interconnected environmental effects and portraying them as controllable oversimplifies the challenges ahead. A critical approach problematises the conventional received wisdom that business must have a key leadership role in a transition to a greener economy, whereas government's role is minimised. The discourse surrounding rational solutions to environmental challenges serves to maintain power structures and systems of influence that privilege corporate views.

The control problem boils down to two related corporate projects: controlling rhetoric and controlling access to resources. First, well-resourced and highly central firms have amassed considerable rhetorical and communicative skills that enable them to control the rhetoric surrounding corporate environmentalism. As Karliner (1997: 32) stated, transnational firms have 'appropriated the language and images of ecology and sustainability in an effort to ward off the threat that the environmental movement might convince the world's governments to force them to make much more far-reaching changes'. Large firms use extensive public relations and communications machinery to directly communicate about their corporate environmentalism and to indirectly limit the range of possible futures. The more visible 'war of ideas' (Beder 1997) related to corporate greening involves privately funded PR, front groups, think tanks, advertising and campaigns. More insidiously, environmentalism has been 'hijacked' as 'senior executives and their business clubs' reconstruct the environmental agenda (Welford 1997: x). Corporate executives and policy makers do not necessarily aim to eliminate debate or controversy because it is needed to maintain the (mis)perception of a functioning social debate. Rather, what is important is to maintain 'the power to limit the subject, scope and boundaries of the controversy' (Beder 1997: 282–283).

An important way in which powerful social actors reconstruct the environmental agenda is by reframing the environmental discussion from a source of problems to a source of solutions. As discussed previously, conventional perspectives promote win-win environmental initiatives, such as eco-efficiency, waste reduction and pollution prevention; managers simply need to find the profitable or socially acceptable ways to integrate green concerns to support their corporate strategy. Critical theorists resist redefining greening as an extension to 'business as usual'. They see the language of win-win solutions as a discursive device, removing environmental concerns from a conversation on moral responsibility and instead centring them in a technocratic, seemingly rational, and ultimately less threatening frame (Crane 2000). Further symptoms of the capture of solutions include the rise of the 'sustainable development industry' (Springett 2003) and, indeed, the rise of voluntary labels, codes, standards and everyday greening symbols that are at the core of this book. The critical view sees the solution-oriented discourse as a signal of corporate control over the rhetoric of greening.

The second dimension of the control problem involves controlling resources. The contestation over framing environmental issues is about maintaining current levels of access to the Earth's natural, physical and biophysical resources. The critical view is suspicious of tools common within the conventional perspective, such as the NRBV of the firm and valuing ecosystem resources because they simply subsume or co-opt natural resources into business as usual. Instead, critical theorists point out that these managerial devices are ways of diminishing the value of indigenous knowledge and ways of being – privileging Western frames over ecological sensemaking (see, e.g., Banerjee 2000 and Whiteman and Cooper 2011). Corporate control of natural resources is framed as another expression of neo-colonialism by large multinationals thirstily exploiting historical power relations to access natural resources wherever they can do so at lowest cost. This dynamic is all the more damaging because poor or marginalised groups are more likely to be the victims of disproportionate environmental damage (Shafik 1994). Thus, critical theorists are closely connected with the environmental justice movement, whether inequity is focused on the developing countries at the world scale or on marginal communities in richer countries.

Focusing on the political nature of corporate environmentalism invites questions about who is included and excluded in the environmental conversation. Critical organisational theorists ask who has the political skill and connections to exploit access to resources, as well as when and how they exert that control. Corporations have the means to engage in direct political influence through lobbying, think tanks and political action committees. At the global level, corporate diplomacy has become highly organised, with large companies participating in multilateral negotiations related to international environmental or trade rules either on their own behalf or through industry consortia. In her penetrating analysis of the global food supply, for example, Shiva (2000) traced how local food markets and policies were captured by large companies from North America and Europe and their influence on the international trade regime. Even environmental groups have been criticised for being elitist and imperialist. Race is the most important determinant of the location of risk-producing activities or, as economists might describe them, 'disamenities' (Shafik 1994). Yet, the role of race in reinforcing entrenched environmental inequalities too often is missing from analyses of the control of natural resources (Newell 2005). As Jermier et al. (2006) reminded us, even the multiplication of environmental social movements has not necessarily led to wider participation in environmental decision making because mainstream environmental groups need to gain access to power and resources to ensure their own survival.

A critical perspective on corporate environmentalism pays attention to underlying power structures, promotes ecological learning, broadens debate in the public sphere, emphasises citizenship capabilities and encourages inclusion. The most important contribution of critical corporate environmentalism is that theorists and managers should appreciate the fact that dominant discourses related to corporate environmentalism are constructed by the most powerful members of a social field. We should observe who decides what it means to be green. Critical theorists' emancipatory and deliberative instincts invite managers and researchers to resist the conventional view's reassuring integration of green issues into strategic concerns and to open conversation to a wider range of possible alternatives.

Comparing the corporate environmentalism perspectives

Table 3.1 summarises the previous discussion about the two main sets of perspectives on corporate environmentalism. The conventional perspective asks questions about firm-level environmental strategy and performance: Does it pay to be green? When, why and how? In contrast, the critical perspective interrogates the role of corporations as mediators and constructors of discourse surrounding environmental degradation and its implications. The focus is more on asking what it means to be green and who has the power to decide the answer and how. The two views evolved from entirely different families within the philosophy of science.[5] The conventional perspective is broadly based on variants of positivist thought, which assumes that there is a single reality 'out there' about which we can gather empirical evidence and use it to develop and test quite general social laws, similar to how we might for physical laws. However, the critical perspective is built on more constructivist foundations. This family of corporate environmentalism takes a critical stance with respect to taken-for-granted knowledge. It assumes that the concepts and categories we use to understand the world are historically and culturally specific, and it emphasises that our knowledge of the world is created and sustained by interpretations, particularly through language and symbols. It also assumes that behaviour and interpretation cannot be separated. Just as positivist views are 'dominant and traditional' in Western thought (Welford 1997: 45), perspectives on corporate environmentalism based on a positivist frame emerged as the conventional new

Table 3.1 *Comparing two perspectives on corporate environmentalism*

	Conventional perspective	Critical perspective
Corporate environmentalism		
Focal phenomenon	Corporate environmental strategy and performance	Corporations as mediators and constructors of environmental discourse
Key relationships	Economic relations	Power relations
Level of analysis	Firm	Field or system
Primary research questions	Does it pay to be green? (When, why, how . . .)	What does it mean to be green? (Who, why, how . . .)
Philosophical position	Positivist	Constructivist
Symbolic corporate environmentalism		
Environmental problem	Asymmetric information problem	Control problem
Analytical apparatus	Economics of signalling and reputation	Power relations within institutional fields
Motivation for symbolic behaviour*	Competitive gains from reputation	Controlling rhetoric and resources
	Managing legitimacy and social licence to operate	Maintaining status and authority

* For more detailed definitions of legitimacy, reputation and status, see Table 3.2.

corporate environmentalism in the past two decades. The conventional view's assumed objectivity makes it easier to bring the conventional corporate environmentalism's arguments, language and findings into corporate boardrooms and policy circles. But it also has the disadvantage in that the role of power in enabling some actors to control the rhetoric and resources surrounding environmental degradation is vastly underexplored in the conventional literature.

Thus, corporate environmentalism theory and practice is based on (at least) two fundamentally different perspectives. Conventional perspectives examine how natural environment issues are affecting business and how managerial decision making needs to change to manage them. Critical perspectives question how managers and organisations are defining and constructing the social conversation about environmental degradation in order to control access to the natural environment. There is an extensive and ongoing discussion within organisational theory – and the philosophy of science more broadly – on whether these two worldviews are intrinsically incompatible. Without discussing the details of those debates, it is sufficient to note that these views have fundamentally different implications for the theory and practice of corporate environmentalism. The corporate environmentalism research conversation is active within both perspectives; however, the premier business academic journals tend to publish more papers from the conventional view rather than the critical view. Both perspectives also are in evidence in management training and even management practice, in which we can contrast the conventional focus on management strategies, systems and processes with approaches that emphasise critical reflection, mindful leadership and deliberative processes.

To attempt to fully integrate or reconcile these two different worldviews would be a monumentally ambitious and possibly foolhardy enterprise. Nevertheless, given the urgency of environmental problems and the increasing legitimacy of conventional environmental research and practice, it seems vital to use aspects of the critical view to deepen conventional insights. Philosophical differences too easily can become an excuse for the critical and conventional camps to talk past one another. In this book, I hope to contribute to the more modest task of seriously interrogating each perspective's assumptions about symbolic corporate environmentalism and to use this to generate deeper insights into when green solutions are in the best interest of society and when they are not.

Symbolic corporate environmentalism

Contemporary research in the conventional perspective is beginning to find empirical evidence for a gap between stated corporate environmental commitments, the adoption of green solutions and environmental impacts. Evidence from contexts such as the adoption of sustainability certifications (Blackman and Rivera 2011), environmental management systems (Boiral 2007; Russo and Harrison 2005), voluntary disclosure programmes (Kim and Lyon 2011; Short and Toffel 2010) and industry voluntary agreements (Darnall and Sides 2008; Delmas and Montes-Sancho 2010) all show that firms that commit to proactive green solutions are no more likely – and, in some cases, are even less likely – to improve their substantive environmental performance. This line of thinking fits with the literature on greenwashing outlined in Chapter 2. However, there is more to the symbolic aspect of corporate environmentalism than deliberate, overt communicative efforts by companies to embellish their 'true' environmental performance. Symbolic corporate environmentalism is broader and refers to the shared meanings and representations related to all of the changes made by managers within firms that they describe as primarily for environmental reasons.

Both the conventional and critical perspectives acknowledge the existence of symbolic corporate environmentalism. However, there are fundamental differences in the functions that symbols are assumed to fulfil and how symbolic corporate environmentalism should best be understood and analysed (see Table 3.1). Within the conventional view, symbolic corporate environmentalism arises from information asymmetries and firms' attempts to signal their reputation and social legitimacy on environmental issues. Within the critical view, symbolic corporate environmentalism is a potential answer to a control problem, in which influencing symbols can allow firms to appear to be responding to environmental demands while maintaining control over rhetoric and resources. Thus, examining symbolic corporate environmentalism has become a contemporary research concern for researchers from each perspective but with quite different explanations for why managers and firms shape and influence the symbols around green solutions.

Forbes and Jermier (2012) recently revisited the new corporate environmentalism literature, this time casting it through the lens of symbolic organisation theory. This perspective, with its roots in symbolic anthropology, focuses theorists' attention on the public impressions of a phenomenon, organisation or action compared with 'behind-the-scenes' operations. All green solutions have a symbolic meaning that is shared, interpreted and deciphered by individuals both inside and outside of the organisation. However, Forbes and Jermier (2012: 360) remind us that 'some are "mere symbols", a concept we use to refer to the material and other tangible phenomena that distract or mislead by intentionally presenting an image that does not accurately represent environmental costs and benefits'. Making environmental changes to a firm's mission statement, organisational structure, disclosure practices, physical buildings, products or technologies may be substantive

green solutions if they reduce the firm's environmental impacts. If they
do not, then they are 'mere symbols' or what I call 'symbolic green
solutions'.

The main conventional explanation for why managers adopt symbolic green solutions is to signal a firm's environmental responsiveness
to stakeholders who otherwise might be unable to observe it. Stakeholders involved in a firm have poor information about the quality
of its environmental actions, but managers would like to be able to
demonstrate acceptable indicators of their firm's environmental quality. The symbolic component of green solutions can be an answer to
this information asymmetry, as managers adopt practices recognised
by stakeholders as signs of commitment to managing environmental
issues, effectively joining a 'green club' (Prakash and Potoski 2006).
Adopting a green solution with a well-established shared meaning low-
ers monitoring costs for individual stakeholders and eliminates the
need for a proliferation of many different schemes and labels, ultimately lowering the cost of achieving the same level of information
(Christmann and Taylor 2006). For example, research in the conventional perspective has shown that firms use the ISO 14001 certification scheme symbolically to communicate environmental credentials
when their supply chain exchange partners lack information (King,
Lenox and Terlaak 2005) and to signal to regulators when regulations are stringent but flexible (Potoski and Prakash 2005). The fear
of falling behind apparently greener competitors may lead firms to
state proactive environmental intentions or join green schemes that
are largely symbolic without incurring the additional costs of actually
making substantive environmental improvements. According to this
view, adopting a green solution is more likely to be symbolic when
there is poor transparency, low penalties for lack of substantive adoption and weak monitoring (Delmas and Montes-Sancho 2010; Lyon
and Maxwell 2011).

As noted previously, the conventional view generates a rich research
literature on the drivers of substantive green solutions but has given
far less attention to predictors of symbolic green solutions. In a recent
review of the drivers of greenwashing,[6] Delmas and Burbano (2011)
identified potential antecedents of symbolic corporate environmentalism at the institutional, organisational and individual levels. According to their review, firms are more likely to drive a wedge between

their symbolic and substantive performance based on pressures from market actors (i.e., consumers, investors and competitors) and non-market actors (i.e., regulators and NGOs); organisational structure, climate and communication; and cognitive biases of individual managers. Others emphasise characteristics of the proposed green solution itself, noting that symbolic corporate environmentalism is easier when these voluntary initiatives are self-monitored rather than externally certified (Darnall and Sides 2008); when auditing, monitoring and sanctioning processes are weak (Christmann and Taylor 2006); and when it includes either strong or weak environmental performers (Terlaak 2007).

The primary motivations for merely symbolic greening within the conventional view are to gain a licence to operate or to signal favourable environmental quality. However, the empirical evidence on whether green solutions actually lead to positive firm-level outcomes is mixed. Walker and Wan (2012) found a negative relationship between merely symbolic corporate environmentalism and financial performance, whereas Berrone, Gelabert, and Fosfuri (2009) found a positive relationship between some symbolic green solutions and gaining environmental legitimacy. Notably, these studies have in common a feature of much of the conventional perspective: the motivations for and outcomes of symbolic corporate environmentalism are focused at the firm level.

In contrast, the critical perspective raises the level of analysis to the field or system level and explains symbolic corporate environmentalism as a solution to a control problem. Greenwashing, in the language of symbolic organisational theory, is a 'green ceremonial façade', which "greens" the organisation in its surface appearance, but it likely has little to do with actual environmental performance' (Forbes and Jermier 2012: 561). Indeed, a central idea in the critical perspective is that the new corporate environmentalism strongly emphasises voluntary corporate environmental leadership and new business norms at the level of rhetoric but only incremental changes (at best) at the level of practice. Symbolic corporate environmentalism helps maintain current power relations within institutional fields by developing rhetoric and symbols that signal reassurance about the established orthodoxy as well as controllability of environmental issues while providing stakeholders with a sense that companies are taking action. This is achieved not only through deliberate greenwashing by managers but also can emerge as a rational response to the myths and discourses surrounding the effectiveness of green solutions (Boiral 2007).

Whereas conventional views emphasise the firm-level strategic benefits of joining green clubs (e.g., ISO 14001) (Prakash and Potoski 2006), critical views claim that environmentalism was 'hijacked' as 'senior executives and their business clubs' reconstructed the environmental agenda (Welford 1997: x). Adopting the legitimising symbolic green solutions leads to standardisation and uniformity in symbols rather than to environmental innovation and leadership, and adopting green symbols often is disconnected from what is actually occurring inside a firm (Jiang and Bansal 2003). The critical view sees the primary function of voluntary green solutions as evading public demands for stronger government regulation and control. For example, Karliner (1997: 185) accepted that green solutions such as ISO may help implement strong, uniform, voluntary standards in places where they are not required by law but also pointed out that ISO is 'a private-public organisation dominated by large transnational corporations'. Within the scheme, firms contract and pay their own choice of external auditors, and the relatively short audits are based mostly on documentary evidence provided by a firm (Boiral and Gendron 2011). This facilitates 'decoupling between the image of rigour of ISO certification and the backstage of internal practices' (p. 388). Firms may appear to be making investments in green solutions; however, even among leading firms that experience high institutional pressure, implementing formal green solutions such as ISO 14001 can be 'ritualistic and documentary' (Boiral 2007: 139). The adoption of symbolic green solutions functions as an organised exhibition of authority by high-status actors to develop acceptable signals of environmental responsiveness.

Both the conventional and critical perspectives concede that it may be difficult to differentiate between symbolic and substantive corporate environmentalism. For conventional researchers, this is a practical, empirical problem. For example, Berrone et al. (2009) considered environmental trademarks to be symbolic but environmental patents to be substantive green solutions, without really explaining why. Similarly, Walker and Wan (2012) operationalised both symbolic and substantive green solutions by evaluating company websites. For them, backward-looking statements on past accomplishments were labelled 'substantive' whereas forward-looking statements on company plans and commitments were labelled 'symbolic'. Neither of these operationalisations would be acceptable to critical theorists who emphasise that all green solutions have a symbolic dimension. What is important here, however, is to separate out green solutions that are 'merely symbolic' in the sense that they do not lead to any improvements in environmental impact. Does a given green solution lead to improvements in any of the nine ecological system boundaries identified by Rockström et al. (2009) and Whiteman et al. (2012)? In the short term, substantive green solutions do but symbolic green solutions do not.

In summary, the now substantial literature on corporate environmentalism can be categorised broadly into research and practice based on either (1) a conventional analysis of firm-level corporate environmental strategy and performance, or (2) a critical analysis of corporations as mediators and constructors of environmental discourse. Both perspectives recognise that green solutions can be symbolic and/or substantive but that their emphasis differs. Conventional approaches tend to assume that corporate environmentalism is a deliberate choice at the firm level and can affect both firm and substantive environmental performance. Critical approaches tend to theorise the discourse and rhetoric of symbolic green solutions first and only later consider whether there is potential for substantive environmental change. The conventional perspective is beginning to take seriously the empirical evidence that merely symbolic corporate environmentalism is widespread. Critical theorists take this for granted and highlight the system-level cost of symbolic activity without necessarily suggesting practical alternatives. The current research challenge is to bridge the chasm in corporate environmentalism scholarship between positivist strategic approaches that focus on firm-level strategy and interpretive approaches that place firms as mediators and constructors of environmental discourse. One of the goals of this book is to uncover mechanisms underlying the drivers and consequences of symbolic corporate environmentalism.

Symbolic performance and symbolic gaps

The obvious problem with operating at the symbolic level on environmental issues is that it can lead to dangerous substantive harm on the natural environment. We must pay closer attention to whether a green solution has a positive impact on the natural environment in terms of minimising biophysical harm (i.e., substantive performance) or whether it leads to only positive social evaluations (i.e., symbolic performance). It is possible that a green solution does not lead to either symbolic or substantive performance or to some of both. Others classify types of strategies based on managers' intentional green solution investments: that is, the extent to which they invest in communicative practices around environmental issues compared with practices that actually alter a firm's environmental impacts (see, e.g., Delmas and Burbano 2011). Greenwashing is focusing more on the former practices than the latter. Thinking of symbolic corporate environmentalism more broadly requires us to not only consider deliberate, communicative practices by firms but also how symbolic activities are understood and rewarded (or not) by interested stakeholders. Firms make investments in green solutions, but it is the stakeholders who award improved symbolic performance. Moving beyond greenwashing requires giving more attention to separating the extent to which particular green solutions lead to symbolic or substantive performance.

A core concern of this book entails the social consequences of symbolic corporate environmentalism. Before we can analyse the consequences, however, we need to understand the drivers. Seeking symbolic performance and maintaining distance between merely symbolic and substantive practices is not unique to environmental decision making. There is a well-established research literature on mismatches between firms' symbolic and substantive adoption of new practices (see, e.g., Endelman 1992; Meyer and Rowan 1977 and Westphal and Zajac 1994). A central tension in this literature is that although firms may gain social legitimacy through symbolic strategies, they may lose it if the difference between symbol and substance is exposed (Ashforth and Gibbs 1990; Fiss and Zajac 2006). Firms face pressures to maintain symbolic performance on environmental issues, yet corporate environmentalism often is dismissed as a green ceremonial façade. Borrowing ideas on symbolic performance from broader organisational theory and strategy, sociology, anthropology, psychology, law and economics can help us to theorise symbolic corporate environmentalism beyond the deliberate communicative practices of corporate greenwashing.

Symbolic performance

Symbolic performance is the extent to which an action – in this case, investing in green solutions – generates positive social evaluations (Heugens and Lander 2009). Managers implementing green solutions may be trying to improve their firm's impacts on the natural environment – that is, improving substantive performance – but they are also at least partly trying to improve their firm's symbolic performance as evaluated by stakeholders. According to the conventional view, managers are attempting to signal their firm's quality or social appropriateness through corporate environmentalism. The critical view emphasises how new corporate environmentalism helps a firm maintain the established social order. Organisational theorists and economists usually operationalise symbolic performance as a firm's reputation, legitimacy or status. Conventional approaches emphasise the reputation and legitimacy dimensions of symbolic performance, whereas critical perspectives highlight the role of status (see Table 3.1). Recently, organisational theorists have given more attention to the similarities and differences among each of these dimensions of symbolic performance and their implications for symbolic behaviour.[7] All three dimensions can be indicators of symbolic performance, but reputation, legitimacy and status are quite distinct concepts, each of which is relevant to understanding symbolic corporate environmentalism (Table 3.2 is a summary). There is insufficient research on how reputation, legitimacy and status interrelate to underpin symbolic corporate environmentalism.

Reputation is 'a set of attributes ascribed to a firm, inferred from the firm's past actions' (Weigelt and Camerer 1988: 443) or an indicator of the 'firm's relative success in fulfilling the expectations of multiple stakeholders' (Fombrun and Shanley 1990: 235). Most useful here is the dimension of reputation that Lange, Lee, and Dai (2011: 155) identify as 'being known for something' or the 'perceived predictability of organisational outcomes and behaviour relevant to specific audience interests'. A good reputation is a signal of firm quality and behaviour, which can differentiate it from its competitors. Reputations are intangible and socially complex, making them difficult to imitate and a potential source of sustainable competitive advantage (Barney 1991; Roberts and Dowling 2002). Because of this potential to gain advantage from reputation, strategy scholars and information economists devote considerable theoretical attention to the economics

Table 3.2 *Evaluating symbolic performance: Legitimacy, reputation and status*

	Legitimacy	Reputation	Status
Definition	Perceptions of appropriateness	Signal of quality and behaviour	Agreed-upon social rank
Judgment question	• Does the organisation belong to a familiar class or category? • Does the organisation conform to societal norms?	• How will the organisation perform or behave in the future relative to other organisations in the set?	• Where does the organisation fit in the ranked order of similar organisations?
Key criteria	• Taken-for-grantedness • Congruence with norms • Social licence to operate • Appropriateness	• Prominence • Past quality performance and relative success • Reputation for something	• Prestige due to hierarchical position • Privilege • Hierarchical position
Logic	Sociopolitical	Economic	Sociopolitical
Indicators	Symbols	Signals	Symbolic capital
Measurement scale	Dichotomous	Interval	Ordinal
Mechanism	Homogenising	Differentiating	Segregating/discriminating
What is valued	Similarity/conformance	Advantage	Distinction

Sources: Adapted and expanded from Bitektine (2011); Deephouse and Carter (2005); Deephouse and Suchman (2008); Devers et al. (2009); Lange, Lee, and Dai (2011); Rao (1994); and Washington and Zajac (2005).

of signalling and reputation (see, e.g., Axelrod 1984, Camerer 2003, and Connelly et al. 2011).

Conventional research has found that corporate environmentalism influences reputation at the industry, firm and product levels. For example, King, Lenox, and Barnett (2002) analysed a 'reputation commons problem', wherein firms in the same industry can be 'tarred with the same brush'. Firms strategically adopt various types of green solutions in order to navigate their industry's reputation. At the firm level, corporate environmentalism is more likely to lead to reputational benefits when environmental issues are highly salient (Brammer and Pavelin 2006). Philippe and Durand (2011) agree that signalling compliance with social norms has a positive impact on reputation and that this positive effect is stronger when signals about environmental goals are supported by signals of procedural commitment. This highlights a key problem with green reputation: to gain from a positive reputation, firms must overcome the problem of establishing the credibility of information about environmental quality (Jahn, Schramm, and Spiller 2005; Reinhardt 1998).

Whereas reputation emphasises the economic advantages to firms of being different, legitimacy captures the sociopolitical benefits of conforming to social norms. A central tenet of institutional theory is that when managers face uncertainty about an organisational practice, they may adopt it to be perceived as socially acceptable and appropriate rather than basing their decision on rational efficiency criteria (Lawrence 1999; Meyer and Rowan 1977). As firms adapt to institutional pressures, stakeholders such as shareholders, government, NGOs and other firms determine whether the firm fits with social norms (Dacin, Oliver, and Roy 2007). Evaluating symbolic performance through legitimacy is rooted in neo-institutional social theory, in which organisations are understood to be subject to isomorphic pressures that make them more alike over time, gradually defining which behaviours and practices are acceptable within a particular social field (see Deephouse and Suchman 2008 and Bitektine 2011 for detailed reviews). The legitimacy concept also has branched out from sociology and is commonly used within legal scholarship that examines the connections among legal frameworks, social norms and decision making (see, e.g., Edelman and Suchman 1997 and Posner 2002), as well as increasingly within psychological studies of why individuals adhere to social norms (see Tyler 2006 for a review). Across all of these literatures, evaluating symbolic performance as legitimacy involves asking whether a particular organisation or its activities are acceptable, appropriate, expected or endorsed or if it fits with norms. Thus, legitimacy is a dichotomous variable in the sense that an organisation either does or does not have legitimacy in a particular decision domain.

Because legitimacy reflects the extent to which firms are meeting societal expectations, it is a popular concept within both the conventional and critical corporate environmental literatures. The conventional approach tends to emphasise the extent to which the approval of various stakeholder groups influences environmental strategy (see, e.g., Darnall, Henriques, and Sadorsky 2010 and Kassinis and Vafeas 2006). In contrast, the critical approach delves more deeply into the processes by which firms seek and earn legitimacy through their environmental discourses and actions (see, e.g., Crane 2000 and Fineman and Clarke 1996). Although strategic management scholars typically are more interested in what makes firms different from rather than similar to one another, the environmental context has proven useful for unpacking the more nuanced aspects of corporate legitimacy management. For example, Delmas and Toffel (2008) demonstrated how firms emphasise green solutions in domains that are crucial for maintaining legitimacy. Active legitimacy and impression management on green issues has been shown to decrease company-specific stock market risk (Bansal and Clelland 2004).

It is popular in the conventional view to contrast economically based reputation motives with more sociopolitically based legitimacy motivations for symbolic corporate environmentalism. However, there has been far less focus on the role of status in driving environmental decision making. Washington and Zajac (2005: 284) defined status as the 'socially constructed, inter-subjectively agreed-upon and accepted ordering or ranking of individuals, groups, organisations or activities in a social system'. Status is fundamentally different from legitimacy and reputation in that it is explicitly hierarchical and distinguishes particular individuals or organisations as worthy of privilege or prestige. An organisation's status, as reflected by its positional ties within a network or market, influences how other social actors evaluate it under uncertainty (Podolny 1994, 2001). High-status actors are awarded higher symbolic performance than lower-status actors even if their output is the same. This so-called Matthew effect (Merton 1968), which is found in a diverse range of organisational contexts, emphasises how symbolic performance evaluations are shaped by social positions. Sociologists typically assume that such positional status is unearned and often is misrecognised by those who grant it because they do not see the arbitrary power structures that underpin these distinctions (Bourdieu and Nice 1984). In contrast, psychology has a long tradition of analysing individuals' status-seeking behaviours (see, e.g., Hyman 1942 for a classic review and Huberman, Loch, and Önçüler 2004 for a contemporary review). Recent work has begun to explore the potential of greening to generate symbolic performance in the sense of social status (see, e.g., Dastrup et al. 2012), but this is still a largely unexplored area.

An advantage of evaluating symbolic performance through status is that this hierarchical approach brings power and relational positions explicitly into the analysis. Privileged individuals and organisations are granted more authority to define appropriate responses to social demands than those with less power. In the environmental context, high status and authority can lead directly to authorship of key green standards and codes. Popular and well-established standards such as the LEED building standards in the United States and the ISO 14001 certification series may appear, at first glance, to be impartial endorsements of firms' green performance. But a closer look reveals that key industry players were heavily involved in the authorship of both schemes, which have largely displaced the more rigorous standards that were originally proposed.[8] Scholars bridging organisational theory and political science have asked how authority is granted to particular green symbols, calling for more attention to be given to which social actors dominate policy networks related to particular environmental issues (see, e.g., Cashore 2003 and Cashore and Vertinski 2000). The lesson for conventional corporate environmentalism researchers is to be more observant of the role of status in framing evaluations of legitimacy and reputation in the greening context. Symbolic performance evaluations are reflections of not only firms' relative quality or social acceptability but also of their social rank.

Symbolic performance, then, can be an evaluation of a firm's reputation, legitimacy or status. It is evaluated by stakeholders who observe firms' green solutions as signals, symbols and symbolic capital. The differences among signals in the sense used by information economists – and the broader symbols indicating conformance with social norms – have been long established within organisational theory (see, e.g., Feldman and March 1981). Signals typically are deliberate communications of positive information about an unobservable characteristic in an effort to convey positive organisational attributes (Connelly et al. 2011), whereas symbols are 'an image that refers to a system of beliefs that are generally known, if not necessarily shared, by the person who observes the symbol' (Posner 2002: 112). The emerging literature on greenwashing is largely interested in deliberate communication or disclosure of signals; however, there is a much broader symbolic domain surrounding corporate environmentalism. Furthermore, that symbolic domain also includes cultural symbols that are granted higher symbolic performance because of the status of those associating with them. Moving beyond conventional corporate environmentalism's concerns about reputation and legitimacy to include status also requires moving beyond signals and symbols to consider 'symbolic capital'. An individual or organisation can gain symbolic capital when it possesses cultural symbols that are associated with high prestige, whether or not that prestige is warranted.[9] To date, there has been little or no analysis of symbolic performance as it relates to the production and maintenance of symbolic capital in the greening context.

Throughout this book, I explore how reputation, legitimacy and status are interrelated in underpinning symbolic corporate environmentalism. Although corporate environmentalism research has separately relied on each of these symbolic performance dimensions, it is rare to integrate across all three dimensions to argue when each might be particularly important. Specifically, conventional corporate environmentalism research gives too little attention to the role of status and symbolic power in legitimacy seeking.

Symbolic gaps

A 'symbolic gap' is the difference between a firm's symbolic performance – in the sense of positive social evaluations – and substantive environmental improvements. A key empirical finding within corporate environmentalism in recent years is that there seem to be persistent symbolic gaps around firms' environmental performance. This presents a compelling puzzle: If much corporate environmentalism is understood to be symbolic, why are symbolic gaps not exposed and symbolic performance evaluations adjusted to match substantive environmental performance? An answer based on greenwashing would suggest that firms' communication strategies are somehow so sophisticated and so poorly monitored that their deliberate attempts to exaggerate, deflect or otherwise disconnect their symbolic from substantive environmental actions are not noticed by stakeholders. Alternatively, even if greenwashing is noticed, stakeholders are powerless to do anything about it. But we should remember an important difference between greenwashing and broader symbolic corporate environmentalism: whereas greenwashing is based on a firm's deliberate communicative efforts, symbolic gaps are based on social evaluations assigned to firms by interested stakeholders, which managers may be able to control to only a limited extent. Greenwashing is assumed to be deliberate in the sense that a company produces the greening communications. However, symbolic gaps can be the deliberate or unintended consequence of corporate environmentalism because symbolic performance is a social evaluation that is only partly determined by a firm's own actions.

There is a significant amount of research literature on the gap between what firms say and do in the broader organisational theory and strategy literatures. Often framed as contrasting 'talks and actions' or 'rhetoric and reality',[10] organisational theory studies emphasise decoupling; that is, organisations only ceremonially adopting new practices to meet social demands without necessarily fully implementing them (Meyer and Rowan 1977). Alternatively, strategy scholars often present symbolic gaps as a strategy implementation process problem, in which top managers' stated intentions and visions run ahead of implementation actions deep inside the firm (Andrews 1971). Marquis and Toffel (2012) recently added a more deliberate 'attention-deflection' strategy, in which managers deliberately adopt alternative but acceptable practices to avoid being coerced into potentially more costly alternatives.

So far, corporate environmentalism researchers have relied most heavily on decoupling explanations for symbolic gaps. Recent organisational theory research on decoupling addresses how symbolic gaps evolve over time (Tilcsik 2010), simultaneous causes and consequences (Weber, Davis, and Lounsbury 2009), and effects on organisational insiders (MacLean and Behnam 2010). Bromley and Powell (2012) argue powerfully that in our contemporary, more highly monitored and audited society, decoupling may be shifting from a gap between policy and practice to a gap between means and ends. Other researchers recently revisited Tolbert and Zucker's (1983) classic insight that late adopters of a new practice are more likely to only symbolically adopt a practice to gain social legitimacy (see, e.g., Delmas and Montes-Sancho 2010; Kennedy and Fiss 2009). However, these contributions downplay an important corollary to decoupling: because institutional pressures lead to decoupling, organisations will do their best to avoid scrutiny – or at least attempt to control the process of scrutiny (Boxenbaum and Jonsson 2008: 81). This raises questions about how the strength of monitoring and the relative power between firms and those that monitor them influences the potential for persistent symbolic gaps.

Evidence suggests that firms are likely to decouple when there is strong pressure from market stakeholders including suppliers, customers and shareholders (Oliver 1991; Stevens et al. 2005) but also that adoption is more likely to be substantive when it is monitored (Christmann and Taylor 2006). Similarly, although managers may become more aware of the potential for decoupling through their social networks (Westphal and Zajac 2001), social networks can be a source of support for monitoring whether or not adoption is substantive (Lounsbury 2001). Thus, although late adopters may be tempted to adopt symbolically for social legitimacy reasons (Tolbert and Zucker 1983), these same adopters may find themselves in a stronger normative context in which both the practice and the monitoring stakeholders are more mature (Phillipe and Durand 2011).

The primary fault line in the literature on symbolic corporate environmentalism is whether symbolic gaps are deliberate or an unintended consequence of the incentives and social structures within which managers operate. The greenwashing literature tends to portray symbolic gaps as deliberate, almost by definition. Recall some of the definitions of greenwashing in Chapter 2: '*the act of misleading* consumers regarding the environmental practices of a company' (Delmas and Burbaro 2011: 66; emphasis added); '*a strategy that companies adopt* to engage in symbolic communications of environmental issues without substantially addressing them in actions' (Walker and Wan 2012: 227; emphasis added); and firms 'creatively manag[ing] their reputations' (Laufer 2003: 255). These definitions imply some agency for firms – or at least managers within them – in deliberately opening up a gap between symbol and substance.

A strategic approach to corporate environmentalism tends to support this deliberate view of symbolic gaps. Economists commonly model corporate environmentalism as a strategic game in which firms can choose levels of substantive and symbolic environmental performance and in which activist stakeholders monitor, audit and sanction noncomplying firms depending on the information available to them (see, e.g., Lyon and Maxwell 2011). Marquis and Toffel (2012) identify three deliberate symbolic compliance strategies in addition to decoupling. 'Social image bolstering' is when firms adopt green solutions to enhance their reputation and deflect attention from less admirable activities, such as when they selectively and strategically adopt symbols, eco-labels and certification schemes (Corbett and Muthulingam 2007; Darnall and Kim 2012). 'Substitution' is when organisations create a less rigorous practice as a substitute to practices demanded by stakeholders. Examples include the commitment to use only Sustainable Forestry Initiative (SFI)–accredited wood products rather than the more stringent Forest Stewardship Council (FSC)–certified products (Cashore 2003) and the active promotion of carbon markets and earning carbon neutrality labels by offsetting rather than direct emissions reduction (Meckling 2011). The third strategy, 'selective disclosure', is the strategy most similar to greenwashing, in which firms disproportionately disclose positive information to create an impression of environmental proactivity and social conformance. There is a long history of scholarship in accounting that shows how firms selectively reveal information about their environmental performance in an attempt to gain social legitimacy.[11]

The critical view also often argues that firms deliberately open up symbolic gaps. A core assumption about symbolic behaviour is that 'through symbols, humans have the capacity to stimulate others in ways other than those in which they themselves are stimulated' (Welford 1997). By publishing an environmental report or painting a reception area green, for example, firms hope to favourably influence stakeholders, even if they themselves are polluting. Karliner (1997) argued that the symbols, language and messages of corporate environmentalism are deliberately designed to deflect environmental demands. Firms cope with institutional pressures by setting up symbolic diversions. In this 'war of ideas', symbolic diversions such as corporate front groups, weak self-regulatory mechanisms and green window-dressing are all the more dangerous because they are designed to go unnoticed (Beder 1997).

However, there is another way of looking at the emergence of symbolic gaps that does not rely on deliberate, malicious or devious corporate activities. Symbolic gaps can arise as an unintended consequence of other corporate or social processes for at least four reasons. First, symbolic gaps can be an unintended consequence of profit-maximising investments in green solutions. As discussed in more detail in Chapter 4, firms choose to invest in particular green solutions for strategic, profit-maximising reasons. But we need to understand corporate environmentalism as a strategic process that is as fallible as any other change process within an organisation. Winn and Angell (2000: 1131) admitted that 'unrealised greening' can be a consequence of deliberate greenwashing, but it also can be seen as 'an intermediary stage for firms in the process of ramping up to implementation'. Symbolic gaps also can arise through a simple disconnect between upper and middle management: some strategies simply do not become realised despite the best intentions of top managers (Mintzberg and Waters 1985). Announcing investments or committing resources to adopt a particular green solution does not necessarily guarantee that it will be fully implemented within the organisation. This opens up the possibility that firms may be rewarded through positive symbolic performance evaluations for adopting the green solution – even if it does not result in substantive improvements.

Second, symbolic gaps can arise from inertia. Internal inertia arises from existing firm structures and incentives, which explain a natural lag between senior management's declaration of commitment and the adaptions needed in the rest of the company to realise that intention (Delmas and Burbano 2011). Highly specific knowledge, organisational structures and poor communication can lead to knowledge-transfer difficulties among the marketing, product development, operations, legal, communications and other functions that need to collaborate on environmental issues. Outside of the firm, there can be a broader social inertia that tends to favour early, satisficing solutions to environmental problems. Moreover, any given green solution tends to gradually 'thicken in apparent objectivity' over time (Welford 1997). Because it can be difficult to break out of current language, symbols and acceptable solutions, it often is easier to repurpose or adopt existing words, solutions or symbols, which further feeds inertia. The result is that green solutions can become unchangeable social facts that are passed on to new field members – even if the solution does not positively impact the environment.

Third, symbolic gaps can arise as an unintended consequence of managerial cognitive biases. Managers may suffer narrow decision framing, hyperbolic inter-temporal discounting or optimism biases that lead them to overstate what might be possible in terms of green solutions or to underperform in implementation (Delmas and Burbano 2011). The broader strategic management literature is beginning to more seriously integrate cognitive and social psychology with standard strategic management theory.[12] Symbolic corporate environmentalism could be a fruitful context within which to deepen and empirically test explanations for persistent symbolic gaps arising from cognitive biases. For example, Walker and Wan (2012) point out that substantive performance evaluations are based on what firms have done in the past, whereas symbolic performance often is based on statements about what firms plan to do in the future. Optimism bias can lead managers to overstate the potential of future-oriented green solutions. If the desired substantive changes subsequently do not occur, this could lead to a symbolic gap. Alternatively, given the uncertainty surrounding green solutions, managers' decision framing often is based on analogical situations and how to cope with similar decision situations. Yet, unthinking analogical strategic decision making can lead decision makers astray (Gavetti, Levinthal, and Rivkin 2005). Over-reliance on proactive metaphors and discourse can entrench persistent gaps between the rhetoric and the reality of corporate greening (Milne, Kearins, and Walton 2006). Even well-intentioned attempts to frame unfamiliar greening choices as similar to other management innovations such as the introduction of total quality management or adapting to new trade regulations can open up a gap between proactive-sounding symbolic components and less-impactful material components of green solutions.

Finally, a more critical approach emphasises that symbolic gaps arise because of broader sociopolitical processes within the political economy of late capitalism (Bromley and Powell 2012; Fleming and Jones 2013). Consumers and producers are trapped within a 'culture of consumption, materialism and greed which now dominates human behaviour in the West' (Welford 1997: ix). It is difficult to break through the entrenched interests of incumbent firms within the status quo. New ideas – particularly those that might challenge current production and political processes – do not have legitimacy, especially if they emerge from the fringes of the field, as with environmentalism. Threatened incumbents experience safety in numbers from stakeholder scrutiny, so there is a tendency to adopt whatever labels and language are available rather than question whether they actually are fit for purpose. We should remember that the myths surrounding ceremonial behaviour and decoupling are apparently 'rational' in the sense that both producers and consumers of green solutions value reassurance that something is being done on environmental issues – even if that 'something' is not particularly effective (Boiral 2007). Yet, symbolic performance is not necessarily based on earned improvements in practices. Symbolic performance can be misrecognised as stakeholders award firms positive social evaluations but do not notice that their esteem is based on status rather than environmental improvements. This power dynamic serves to reinforce the social structures within the economy (Bourdieu 2005).

Some symbolic corporate environmentalism, and the symbolic gaps that arise from it, is deliberate. But if we are interested in understanding corporate environmentalism within a mature issue domain, then we also need to account for emergent strategies and their sometimes unintended consequences. Analysing broader symbolic gaps rather than more specific greenwashing is useful because it goes beyond deliberate communicative practices, which fuels a sensible suspicion of voluntary environmentalism. We do need symbols of corporate environmentalism to help with an information asymmetry problem. We also need to be aware of persistent symbolic gaps, ideally without fully adopting the pessimism and scepticism of the critical perspective. A core question in this book is about when symbolic gaps are likely to emerge and when they will continue to be persistent. In answering this question, I join efforts to explore the boundary conditions around conventional corporate environmentalism by injecting useful ideas from the critical view on power, status and dominant discourse (Banerjee 2012). Moving beyond greenwashing to symbolic gaps builds more realistic foundations and better normative implications for conventional corporate environmentalism research.

Consequences of symbolic corporate environmentalism

One of the ways in which Banerjee (2012) encourages us to explore the limits of corporate environmentalism and green solutions is by moving the level of analysis. Conventional research focuses on firm-level, private costs and benefits of corporate environmentalism. This is useful to analyse corporate decision making but less useful for evaluating whether there is a net social benefit from corporate environmentalism. Raising the level of analysis allows us to evaluate the social costs and benefits of corporate environmentalism. As Banerjee (2012: 585) stated: '[I]f corporations are to carry out activities once the purview of governments, then there is a need to examine the processes and outcomes of corporate involvement in political and social domains'. The conventional literature is beginning to make progress on understanding greening processes and private, firm-level outcomes; so far, however, there has been insufficient examination of social outcomes.

Critical theorists regularly remind us of the consequences of symbolic corporate environmentalism: 'It camouflages what is actually going on in a field of action, obscuring the negatives while trumpeting the positives' (Forbes and Jermier 2012: 560). Institutional organisational theorists have called for more research on the 'dark side' of symbolic behaviour because powerful actors use symbols to privilege some societal interests while relegating others. In the introduction to their *Handbook on Organisational Institutionalism*, the editors remind us that 'we too often neglect to assess the societal consequences of institutionalised corporate behaviour' (Greenwood, et al. 2008: 25). Even well-established and highly regarded standards such as ISO 14001 can have undesirable consequences at the economy or society level. For example, as ISO rules become established as the dominant symbols, international organisations such as the WTO may be able to use them to strike down other, stricter environmental controls as trade barriers. In another example, the existence of ISO standards as a potential green solution can serve as a diversion from the creation of international, binding standards (Karliner 1997). Both examples can impose externalised costs on society in the longer run because of the way that the green solutions are designed and promoted in the first place.

These indirect social costs are in addition to the private firm-level direct cost of funding PR teams, reporting about sustainability, adopting eco-labels, participating in industry associations and so forth. There may be a deadweight loss to society because high-status social actors exert monopoly power over acceptable symbols of corporate environmentalism in the public discourse. This limits the supply of green solutions to those that central social actors are willing to tolerate. Conventional wisdom is that a firm's strategic adoption of green solutions can be welfare-enhancing compared with coerced solutions (see, e.g., Husted and Salazar 2006 and Maxwell, Lyon, and Hackett 2000). However, these analyses neglect the importance of firms exerting control over the range of solutions available. If managers were truly indifferent about the form taken by their voluntary corporate environmentalism, then the best option from a welfare perspective would be for them to donate cash to a neutral body that then could allocate these resources to the best societal use.[13] Yet, part of the strategic advantage of voluntary corporate environmentalism is that firms do not give up this control over resource allocation and supporting particular solutions. Non-monetary donations are always inefficient but they facilitate signalling (Ellingsen and Johannesson 2011). As an illustration, to signal generosity, a person is more likely to volunteer to help a friend to move house than to offer to pay for a professional – even if doing so would be more efficient for all involved. In the same way, voluntarily allocating staff time to participate in community environmental projects appears generous, but it is actually less efficient than donating the equivalent cash to contract professionals to complete the work. Thus, to the extent that the donor of a particular green solution controls the exact form that the solution takes, there is a social welfare loss as more allocatively efficient alternatives are forgone.[14]

This insight puts us in the somewhat depressing position of being sceptical about not only the motivations of firms but also the social consequences of corporate environmentalism – even for apparently well-intentioned green solutions. Environmental managers within firms fight hard to be able to join green certification schemes, produce robust environmental reports, and find time to attend green industry association events. Yet, all of these initiatives usually impose a social cost precisely because firms control their design.

Fortunately, simply because there is a social cost, it does not mean that we should avoid all corporate environmentalism. There may be potential longer-term benefits from environmental rhetoric. Even Forbes and Jermier (2012: 566) acknowledge the benefits of some symbolic management on environmental issues:

We do not think that all contemporary approaches to organisational green-ing should be completely dismissed as mere empty symbols – epiphenom-ena that mislead and distract from shameful practices. Some organisational greening initiatives that begin with seemingly superficial symbols, such as the plans and policy statements of ISO 14001 or the LEED-certified corporate HQ buildings, might lead to further steps along the pathway to eco-centric organising.

Even largely symbolic green solutions can eventually generate social benefit by changing employee attitudes and behaviour (Field and Ford 1995), by giving managers tools to be able to sell an environmentally sound business case (Cornelissen and Lock 2000), by changing the mindset of employees as rhetoric leaves behind useful ideas and tech-niques (Rhee and Lee 2003), and by opening up organisational spaces to gather environmental information that is eventually put to substan-tive uses (Feldman and March 1981). As Feldman and March (1981: 180) stated: 'It is not easy to be a stable hypocrite'. A static analysis may suggest that symbolic corporate environmentalism entails social costs, but a more dynamic analysis highlights the possibility of social benefits. In the next chapter, I model this difference as a trade-off between utility losses due to corporate control and the social benefits of diffusion.

New directions and framing questions

During the past twenty years, tenacious scholars and practitioners succeeded in bringing corporate environmentalism 'in from the cold'. Corporate environmental researchers are no longer sending 'post-cards from the edge' of strategy and organisational theory. They have inspired, educated and learned from a growing cohort of environmen-tal management professionals. But, in this process, nature has been transformed from a biophysical context within which social activities are organised into an environmental issue to be managed. Critical man-agement researchers offer a sound argument about the conventional view's tendency to downplay power structures and the arbitrariness of social evaluations. There are distortions arising from the social com-petition to control resources and rhetoric that are largely ignored in a conventional corporate environmentalism analysis. We need to give more attention to the performativity of corporate environmentalism and the power structures that underpin it.

Seeking win-win solutions through building a firm's reputation or managing legitimacy can have a negative side effect on society. There simply is not enough research that considers the social consequences of symbolic corporate environmentalism. If we integrate the most realistic assumptions within the conventional and critical views, then we can develop a more sophisticated understanding of the relationships between symbolic corporate environmentalism and society. Symbolic corporate environmentalism often is associated with decoupling and can serve as a distraction, but it also can help the diffusion of more environmentally sound industrial activities. Conventional researchers focus on the positive firm-level performance benefits of implementing green solutions; critical researchers focus on the negative social side effects of green solutions being controlled by the powerful elite in society. A more comprehensive model would consider both approaches to assess the social costs and benefits of symbolic corporate environmentalism. The question then becomes: When might social costs outweigh the social benefits, leading to a social energy penalty? Conversely, when might the social benefits be larger than the social costs, potentially leading to a social energy premium?

Of course, integrating incommensurate perspectives is too ambitious to unravel in one book – generations of researchers so far have not managed to do so. We should also remember that the conventional and critical views are based on fundamentally different philosophical foundations (see Table 3.1). Nevertheless, it is a worthwhile ambition to expose and juxtapose the key assumptions within each perspective. In this book, the critical concerns of interests, power and control are taken seriously. However, problems in the natural environment are so urgent and important that we must generate short- to medium-term solutions within our current discursive, policy and strategy frames. A truly critical approach, perhaps rightly, calls for radical, deliberative and reflexive change; or, failing that, a philosophical shrug of the shoulders. My more pragmatic goal is to confront the conventional view with vital insights from the critical view and to advance our thinking on the consequences of corporate environmentalism. I use some of the apparatus and implications of the conventional perspective to persuade conventional researchers to take the critical view more seriously. Simultaneously, I aim to help the critical view to transcend its theoretical 'comfort zone' by analysing empirical studies that explore the contingencies and boundaries of the critical approach.

In this book, I incorporate four elements of the critical view to enrich conventional perspectives on symbolic corporate environmentalism. First, my approach aims for a critical evaluation of the limits and boundary conditions of voluntary corporate environmentalism. Despite a recent rise in conventional research that takes more seriously the symbolic adoption of green solutions, most conventional researchers downplay differences among proactive green stated intentions, the implementation of green solutions and their eventual environmental impact. However, many of the green solutions that companies designed, joined or adopted have now been around for two or three decades. The chemical industry's Responsible Care programme was initiated in 1985, the ISO 14001 series in 1996, and FSC certification in 1993. Also, numerous empirical studies have been conducted since the rise of the new corporate environmentalism in the 1990s. Corporate environmentalism is becoming a mature issue domain, in both research and practice. This longer experience and extensive evidence base now allows us to use empirical data on firms' adoption, implementation and consequences of green solutions to explore the boundaries of conventional corporate environmentalism. To what extent do green solutions actually translate into the mitigation of environmental damage? When are symbolic gaps most likely to emerge and persist? I address this theme most clearly in Chapter 5 in which I present a meta-analysis of the many quantitative, conventional studies of corporate environmentalism.

Second, I give particular attention to the importance of power – in the sense of controlling both rhetoric and access to resources. The material, discursive and positional power of those who write the rules is central to the analysis. So far, conventional researchers have under-explored when and how actors can exert discretionary power over the production of green solutions. The meta-analysis in Chapter 5 addresses this theme by showing how the strength of monitoring and the relational power imbalance among firms and those who monitor them influences the potential for symbolic gaps. I delve more deeply into this theme in Chapter 6 by analysing the political and rhetorical competition concerning CCS demonstration projects and how this links to the competitive strategies of firms that adopt the technology. Incumbent firms attempt to control resources by gaining subsidies and influencing political channels. They also attempt to control the rhetoric surrounding CCS by presenting it as a low-carbon solution, an engine of green growth and supporting energy security. Due to the highly politicised nature and concentrated structure of the traditional energy industry, power is vital to understanding the carbon strategies of firms in this industry but is often neglected in conventional win-win analyses. We need to further investigate how power is used to limit the subject, scope and boundaries of environmental controversies.

Third, I expand the conventional view by explicitly including status in understanding symbolic performance. The conventional view tends to treat symbolic performance as reputation or legitimacy, but corporate environmentalism is just as likely to be influenced by status as a reflection of a firm's or an association's hierarchical privilege. This link between status and the control of rhetoric or resources typically is underplayed in the conventional view. For example, the LEED building standards are acknowledged as the leading green building standards in the United States. To support their reputation for environmental quality or to maintain their social licence to operate, firms proudly announce that their headquarters or other facilities are LEED-certified. The standards are developed by the US Green Building Council (USGBC), which lends credibility to the standard. However, the USGBC often is mistaken as a government agency (it is not), and this misinterpretation of the independence and prestige of the standard is enhanced by the high status of the USGBC and the companies that adopt LEED. We must look for signs of dominance over greening solutions and the cultural symbols that reproduce it. Is there evidence that high-status firms use their power to shape legitimacy within fields? How and when? These themes are discussed in the empirical studies on CCS (see Chapter 6) and carbon accounting (see Chapter 7). Status can create distortions in symbolic performance evaluations that are underplayed in the conventional view. This is a problem especially during the process of developing measuring and reporting systems over time, as in the case of carbon accounting.

Finally, I raise the level of analysis from the firm to the broader institutional field or system level. Management researchers within the conventional perspective are familiar with the idea that demands for environmental improvement come from the broader stakeholder or institutional environment, but they usually limit the consequences of responding to those demands to evaluations of substantive or symbolic performance at the firm level. Investing in reputation or maintaining legitimacy focuses on the private benefits of symbolic corporate environmentalism, but we often overlook the potential social cost. Some scholars in the conventional tradition explored whose interests are served through voluntary environmental programmes and asked whether they are in the common interest (Steelman and Rivera 2006). I bridge the gap between these and more critical views that focus on the social welfare implications of corporate environmentalism. When are firm-sponsored green solutions in the best interests of society – even if they are symbolic – and when are they not? More specifically, when might the social costs of corporate environmentalism outweigh the social benefits, leading to a social energy penalty? When is the social energy penalty larger? How does it develop? What are possible ways to overcome it?

In the next chapter, I develop a model of the social costs and benefits of corporate environmentalism at the field level. Evaluating allocative efficiency or the welfare implications of firm-level decisions is typically the domain of economists and legal scholars, but these decisions have important implications for firm-level strategy and the policy designed to frame it. Managers and firms are part of a broader social conversation on greening. Management scholars are increasingly realising that we may have overly neglected the influence of management theory on social welfare. By examining the interactions between the firm and system levels of analysis, I hope to contribute to an ongoing discussion about the social implications of voluntary regulatory approaches. I also hope to provide inspiration to curious economists who may be able to more formally model and test some of these initial insights. The model is intended to bridge the critical and conventional perspectives and to help understand the costs and benefits of symbolic corporate environmentalism in society.

4 | *Drivers and consequences of symbolic corporate environmentalism*

After greenwashing, we need to investigate the broader concept of symbolic corporate environmentalism. Two specific extensions to current research are required to move beyond our current understanding of greenwashing. First, we need to move backwards from a strategic disclosure decision to integrate a richer analysis of firms' investments in green solutions in the first place. We need to broaden the analysis from managers' decisions regarding how to communicate about a firm's environmental choices to include how firms can gain positive social evaluations by investing in a portfolio of green solutions. Second, we need to analyse more closely the welfare implications of symbolic corporate environmentalism. The critical perspective has usefully identified social costs of symbolic activities, but focusing on the dynamics of reputation and legitimacy suggests that there may be potential social benefits over time. Sometimes symbolic corporate environmentalism imposes a social energy penalty on society; however, sometimes the social costs may be outweighed by the benefits of dynamic learning and network effects. We need new tools to reveal contingencies about when symbolic corporate environmentalism is particularly damaging and, alternatively, when it even may benefit society.

In this chapter, I present three interlinked models that explain (1) how and why firms that strategically adopt green solutions might invest in more symbolic green solutions than previous conventional analyses have shown; (2) how voluntary investment in green solutions can lead to utility losses; and (3) contingencies predicting the relative importance of social costs and benefits of symbolic corporate environmentalism. I begin with a simple model of the supply of and demand for green solutions based on McWilliams and Siegel (2001) and later expanded by Husted and Salazar (2006). I extend these foundational approaches to account for two critical features of corporate environmentalism.

First, we must recognise that not all green solutions are equal in their impact on the natural environment. We must distinguish between the demand for and supply of green solutions that substantively improve environmental impacts and those that are merely symbolic. Second, although the models are designed to analyse the market strategies of firms, non-market power is pervasive in the corporate environmental domain. We therefore need to adapt the analyses to consider non-market actions by powerful firms, including their ability to manipulate symbolic meanings. I then adapt a model of esteem from Brennan and Pettit (2004) that has not yet been used in the corporate strategy context to show how firms invest in a portfolio of green solutions to maximise their symbolic rather than substantive performance.

Both of these models of firms' decision making hint at a social energy penalty – that is, the loss of social welfare for a constant resource output that is misdirected into symbolic activities. In the second of the three frameworks, I develop a static analysis of the welfare implications of investing in combinations of symbolic and substantive green solutions. If suppliers of green solutions have the power to limit their precise form, there is typically a utility loss compared to when there is full competition for green solutions. Social costs arise from market inefficiency. In the context of voluntary corporate environmentalism, this inefficiency occurs because high-status actors have some control over symbols in the public discourse, thereby limiting the supply of green solutions. When firms voluntarily adopt beyond compliance green solutions, they can choose which types of initiatives to support or practices to implement. I show that this leads to fewer resources being allocated to substantive green solutions than might have been the case if the voluntary initiative had matched consumers' or stakeholders' preferences – and at a higher social cost.

In the third framework, I put the social cost analysis into a more dynamic frame. Corporate control over the supply of voluntary green solutions can lead to social costs. But, as green solutions are institutionalised over time, they can yield positive externalities. As discussed in the third framework, moving from a static to a dynamic analysis allows us to understand how social costs might be outweighed by the positive externalities of diffusing environmental initiatives. The dynamic model introduced in this chapter can help us understand when the social energy penalty might be highest and which factors are most likely to influence it. This third model is the foundation for the empirical studies discussed in the next three chapters.

Strategically investing in green solutions

A key difference between greenwashing and symbolic corporate environmentalism is that whereas greenwashing focuses on communicative practices, symbolic corporate environmentalism arises from any green solution implemented by a firm. Thus, the first step in understanding symbolic corporate environmentalism is to model how managers decide on the quantity and type of green solutions.

Deciding green solution quantity

Milton Friedman (1962) famously questioned the ability of managers to pursue social objectives within the constraints of making maximum profits for shareholders. 'The business of business is business', his argument goes, and so issues such as environmental protection should be left to elected governments that act in the collective interests of society. From this perspective, corporate environmentalism may divert managers away from their more appropriate pursuit of profit maximisation on behalf of shareholders, leading to inefficient resource allocation. A long and passionate debate has ensued about the extent to which firms should undertake voluntary corporate environmental and social initiatives. Even Porter's attempt to 'end the stalemate' (Porter and Van der Linde 1995) between advocates of profit maximisation and those of voluntary corporate environmentalism has been overtaken by hundreds of papers examining the business case for corporate environmentalism.[1]

McWilliams and Siegel (2001) argued that although considerable research attention has been given to whether socially responsible firms outperform other companies that do not meet the same social criteria, more attention should be focused on how managers decide how much a firm should invest in social initiatives. They defined corporate social responsibility (CSR) as 'actions that appear to further some social good, beyond the interests of the firms and that which is required by law' (p. 117). They mention several green solutions that fall within their definition of beyond compliance social actions, such as introducing a recycling programme, pollution abatement technologies and adopting a dolphin-free-tuna eco-label. Thus, green solutions can be seen as a subset of their broader CSR activities.

Adopting a theory of the firm perspective, McWilliams and Siegel (2001: 124) argued that 'there is some optimal level of CSR attributes for firms to provide, depending on the demand for these characteristics and the costs of generating them'. Applying their model implies that there are two major sources of demand for green solutions: consumer demand and demand from other stakeholders, such as investors, employees, NGOs and the community. Consumer and stakeholder willingness to pay for green solutions is dependent on the price of goods and services embodying these attributes, such that the demand for green solutions is downward-sloping.[2] On the supply side, green activities are viewed as a form of investment. Providing green solutions incurs additional incremental cost.[3] Firms need to invest additional resources in a variety of resource domains (e.g., employee skills, changing product and manufacturing processes, and environmental reporting) to be able to produce green solutions (Buysse and Verbeke 2003). The cost function for green solutions is assumed to have the typical properties of being monotonically increasing but with increasing marginal costs of providing additional green solutions.

Given the supply of and demand for green solutions, managers should treat decisions on how much corporate environmental activity to undertake as they treat all investment decisions (McWilliams and Siegel 2001). Through a standard cost–benefit analysis, managers can identify the ideal level of investment in green solutions. McWilliams and Siegel (2001) focused on instances in which CSR attributes are embodied in products and clearly signal a firm's CSR investment. This is the case for many green solutions, such as eco-labelled products and directly traded environmental services. For green attributes embedded in goods or services, the demand for and supply of greening solutions interact to yield an explicit price (or price premium) of the green solution and an equilibrium quantity. However, there also may be less direct trading of greening solutions in the social marketplace. Producers may be rewarded not only directly by a price on green solutions but also indirectly in terms of reputation or other positive social evaluations. Clearly, understanding these 'softer' costs and benefits of green solutions is a more complex analytical task, but it does not challenge the fundamentals of the McWilliams and Siegel model.

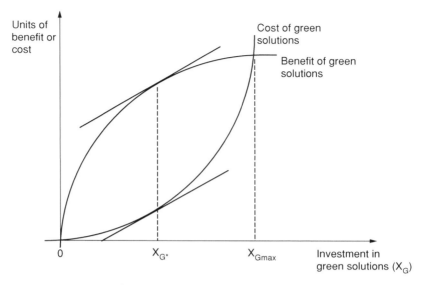

Figure 4.1 Optimal firm investment in altruistic and coerced corporate environmentalism.
Adapted from Husted and Salazar (2006). Costs and benefits are private total costs and benefits incurred by any given firm. Reproduced with permission from John Wiley and Sons.

In a call for researchers to 'take Friedman seriously', Husted and Salazar (2006) built on McWilliams and Siegel's (2001) model and developed an analysis of the conditions under which firms might simultaneously maximise their financial and social performance. They compared the cases of what they termed altruism, coerced egoism and strategy, and they showed 'that it is wiser for the firm to act strategically than to be coerced into making investments in corporate social responsibility' (Husted and Salazar 2006: 75). Husted and Salazar's (2006) model is useful in understanding when firms might be able to maximise both profits and corporate environmentalism. However, achieving this optimal level of strategic corporate environmentalism relies on a number of strong assumptions. Specifically, if we make more realistic assumptions about non-market power in corporate environmentalism as well as the costs and benefits of symbolic as opposed to substantive green solutions, the optimal level of strategic corporate environmentalism at the firm level can yield a social energy penalty.
    Figure 4.1 illustrates Husted and Salazar's (2006) firm-level analysis of the private costs and benefits of producing green solutions.[4] The

firm-level private-cost curve represents the amount spent by a firm for any given level of investment in green solutions. Producing green solutions – such as new clean technologies, emission-reduction initiatives, environmental management systems, environmental reports or eco-labels – requires investments across a number of different resource domains (Buysse and Verbeke 2003). The private cost curve shows the cost of these investments over the long run, and it is subject to the usual microeconomic assumption of decreasing marginal returns of investment. Initial investments may have a relatively high environmental impact for low cost (Hart 1995; Walley and Whitehead 1994), but incremental environmental performance improvement becomes more expensive. At point X_{Gmax} – the point of maximum potential investments in green solutions – the private cost curve becomes vertical, showing that the firm could increasingly invest in green solutions but without seeing any improvement in environmental performance.

The private benefit curve shows the benefits that a firm can capture for any given level of investment in green solutions. Benefits from environmental investments vary depending on the particular green solution, but they might include a wide range of benefits, including product differentiation, reputational improvements, employee loyalty and development of competitively valuable capabilities (King and Lenox 2001; Sharma and Vredenburg 1998). Initially, firms can expect significant improvements due to, for example, an attractive corporate image, but these benefits increase at a decreasing rate because subsequent investments do not generate the same impact in terms of increasing sales, loyalty, image, reputation or learning.

According to Husted and Salazar (2006), an altruistic firm will invest in green solutions up to X_{Gmax}, the point at which the total cost is equal to the total benefits. Up to this point, the firm is always able to find another green solution in which to invest that will yield more benefit than it costs. Rational managers in an altruistic firm may invest up to X_{Gmax} in green solutions but no further. At this point, additional investments are costly but do not provide any more benefit.

Profit-maximising firms will maximise the return on investments in green solutions. This is Husted and Salazar's (2006) 'coerced egoist' case, in which a firm is presented with a set of payoffs for green investment intended to coerce a particular level of environmental performance. Incentives for firms to move beyond zero investment in green solutions include avoiding fines, being sued and threats of

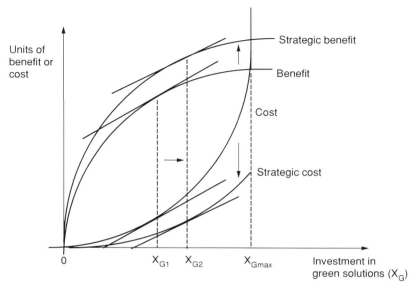

Figure 4.2 Optimal firm investment in strategic corporate environmentalism. Adapted from Husted and Salazar (2006). Costs and benefits are private total costs and benefits incurred by any given firm.

consumer boycotts. The 'coerced egoist' invests in green solutions until the increased marginal benefit of additional investment just equals the marginal cost of that investment. This is shown graphically in Figure 4.1 as point X_{G^*}, where the slopes of the cost and benefit curves are equal and the difference between the curves (i.e., the profit from investment in green solutions) is at its maximum.

Husted and Salazar's (2006) crucial insight is that firms may be able to improve the benefits they can achieve through green solutions and/or reduce the costs of green solutions (Figure 4.2). When firms can appropriate more benefits from investing in green solutions, such as through effective product differentiation, their benefit curve can move upward. Similarly, if a firm is able to innovate and reduce the cost of green solutions, then their cost curve can move downward. In these circumstances, the profit-maximising investment in green solutions increases from X_{G1} to X_{G2}. Thus, strategic corporate environmentalism can lead to a higher investment in green solutions than simply regulating and coercing firms. Society is better off as the investment in green solutions increases by $X_{G2} - X_{G1}$.

Husted and Salazar's (2006) framework provides an elegant and powerful explanation for when strategic corporate environmentalism can be profit-maximising for the firm and increase investment in green solutions for the benefit of society. Their framework has been widely used in explanations for strategic corporate environmental behaviour (see, e.g., the review by Siegel 2009), and it rightly gained considerable traction in explaining when strategic investments in green solutions might pay off. However, their model requires a number of assumptions that are not realistic reflections of corporate environmental decision making. Specifically, changing assumptions about the nature of investments in green solutions, a firm's ability to move the cost and benefit curves, and non-market strategic corporate environmentalism reveal several situations in which there may be a significant loss in green investment compared with the basic strategic corporate environmental case.

First, both McWilliams and Siegel (2001) and Husted and Salazar (2006) effectively assumed that all investment in green solutions is substantive. They assumed that all units of social output produced are additive and qualitatively the same. More social output – in this case, investment in green solutions – is assumed to be always more than less valuable, and all investments are as valuable to society as any another. However, in practice, not all investments in green solutions are the same. Some are merely symbolic and not substantive. Some green investments are at the core of a firm's business and are intended to actually alleviate environmental problems, whereas others are at a firm's periphery and are intended to improve its image and reputation (Bowen 2000b). Society values green solutions that change a firm's core activities more than those that simply affect the periphery, particularly in the dynamic long term (Halme and Laurila 2009). Thus, to the extent that firm investments are diverted into symbolic green solutions aimed at improving a firm's image and reputation, there is a social opportunity cost forgone of investment in more substantive green solutions. Therefore, firms may invest in symbolic green solutions up to the profit-maximising strategic level X_{G2} but invest in substantive green solutions only up to the coerced egoist level X_{G1}. The gap $X_{G2} - X_{G1}$ represents the loss of environmental improvement for society that is misdirected into producing symbolic rather than substantive green solutions.

Furthermore, McWilliams and Siegel's (2001) definition of CSR actions included 'actions *that appear to* further some social good'

(p. 117; emphasis added). A problem with this definition is that some investments in green solutions are aimed entirely at increasing a firm's symbolic performance without an improvement in substantive environmental outcome. Lankoski (2008) termed this a 'false reputation', in which the firm obtains the benefits of a higher level of investment through improved stakeholder reputation but incurs only the direct costs of a lower investment level (plus the costs of the reputation-building activities). If the benefit curve in Figure 4.2 increases by more than the cost curve decreases, then strategic corporate environmentalism will lead firms to profit-maximise at an investment level of less than X_{G2}. The gap between X_{G2} and this new investment level represents a lower level of investment in green solutions than Husted and Salazar (2006) would have predicted because of the divergence between symbolic and substantive green solutions.

Second, Husted and Salazar (2006) recognised the key assumption in their strategic case that firms can indeed move the cost and benefit curves. The altruist or coerced egoist may gain benefits from green investment; however, in the strategic case, benefits are increased or costs are decreased by design. The curves move because the firm has designed a deliberate strategy to appropriate the benefits. In an uncertain and complex world, there is no guarantee that a firm's strategic plans to benefit from green solutions will come to fruition in this way. More important, due to the frequent inability of stakeholders to evaluate the authenticity of green solutions, it is tempting for firms to capture benefits from greening through symbolic rather than substantive investments. A firm's strategy to move the cost and benefit curves by visible communications on green issues is more likely to be successful than those designed to move the curves by changing more opaque internal production or management processes. It also may be less expensive to implement symbolic rather than substantive green solutions. Thus, even if managers intend to adopt a strategic approach, simultaneous changes in communications and internal processes are likely to move the cost and benefit curves more for symbolic green solutions than for substantive solutions. This would open up a gap that represents the additional symbolic investments required to communicate about the substantive green investment. The effect is magnified when there is uncertainty about a firm's environmental performance because the most visible or popular green solutions may be rewarded more than the most efficient ones.

Third, models based on the demand for and supply of green solutions emphasise the market strategies of profit-maximising firms. However, we know that firms also act strategically with respect to non-market strategies (for a thorough review, see Hillman, Keim, and Schuler 2004). Firms respond to calls for environmental improvement and can be highly adept at responding strategically to institutional pressures (Oliver 1991). Strategic responses can be accounted for within the theory of the firm model because firms might choose to comply with norms and produce green solutions to meet stakeholder demand. Managers also might choose to drive a wedge between symbolic and substantive green solutions by buffering, concealing, dismissing or challenging environmental demands. Firms might deliberately produce fewer substantive green solutions by negotiating to define the metrics of green solutions in symbolic rather than substantive terms or by manipulating the language related to green solutions so as to appear to be conforming to stakeholder requirements. Non-market strategies can enable powerful firms to maintain an artificial separation between investment in symbolic and substantive green solutions. This symbolic gap in green output, $X_{G2} - X_{G1}$, can be persistent if a firm has the power to limit the scrutiny of its environmental performance by stakeholders.

Thus, managers can determine an optimal output of green solutions by weighing the incremental costs and benefits of investment in them. Under certain conditions, a firm adopting a strategic corporate environmental approach might produce more green solutions than a firm coerced to do so by stakeholder expectations. Strategic corporate environmentalism can raise green output from X_{G1} to X_{G2}, as shown in Figure 4.2. In the strategic case, a firm's profit is maximised and social welfare is improved compared with the coerced-egoist case. However, recognising that not all green output is qualitatively the same and accounting for non-market power exposes the vulnerability of the strategic case. The standard model neglects a symbolic gap; the output of symbolic green solutions may be much higher than substantive solutions. This may be an unintended consequence of the cost and benefit curves being more responsive to symbolic rather than substantive green solutions. Firms are not able to entirely control the symbolic performance of green solutions because social evaluations, which are so crucial to capturing benefits from green solutions, are made by stakeholders. Stakeholders can misrecognise the legitimacy of green solutions due to the high status of the firms promoting them, which artificially inflates the private benefits of symbolic green solutions. Alternatively, symbolic gaps may be a deliberate strategy adopted by powerful firms to conceal, buffer or bargain with institutional pressures. In any case, the result is that a firm's profit-maximising investment in symbolic green solutions is higher than for substantive green solutions. The additional symbolic output is a loss of green output misdirected into symbolic rather than substantive green solutions; this generates a social cost of symbolic corporate environmentalism.

Designing a portfolio of green solutions

In the previous section, I examine the overall level of investment in green solutions. Here, I focus instead on the decision to invest in a mixed portfolio of green solutions. Whereas others have examined portfolios of environmental investments (see, e.g., Klassen and Whybark 1999), I focus specifically on combinations of symbolic and substantive green solutions. In this section, I integrate ideas from the greenwashing literature (Delmas and Burbano 2011) with an economic analysis of symbolic performance (Brennan and Pettit 2004) to explain how managers decide between investing in symbolic and substantive green activities.

Delmas and Burbano (2011) introduced a useful typology of firms according to their emphasis on communication about environmental performance and their actual environmental performance (Figure 4.3). Greenwashing firms, according to Delmas and Burbano's definition, are those that choose a combination of positive communication about their environmental performance with 'bad' environmental performance (see Quadrant I in Figure 4.3). At the opposite end of the spectrum are 'silent green firms' that achieve good environmental performance but do little to communicate it (see Quadrant IV). 'Silent brown firms' have 'bad' environmental performance and avoid communicating about it, whereas 'vocal green firms' perform well environmentally and trumpet their achievements. This typology is useful because it highlights how decisions related to environmental disclosure are made simultaneously with decisions about environmental performance. Delmas and Burbano's (2011) analysis of the drivers of greenwashing reminds us that symbolic and substantive performances are not mutually exclusive and that firms make investments in their symbolic and substantive performance consistent with their strategic position in the typology. They also argue that these typologies are

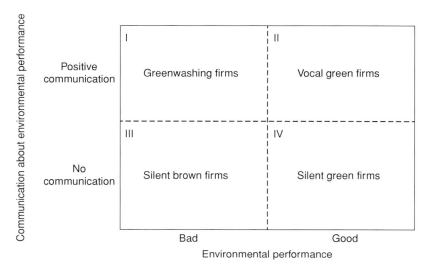

Figure 4.3 Delmas and Burbano's (2011) typology of firms based on environmental performance and communication.
Source: Delmas and Burbano (2011). © 2011 by the Regents of the University of California. Reprinted with permission of the publisher, the University of California Press.

quite stable in the sense that there is sufficient social demand – or at least tolerance – of all types of firms, including those that over- or under-communicate their environmental performance due to drivers in the institutional and market surroundings.

Further unpacking of the typology leads us to examine the pattern of investments underlying each type of firm. Which investments might firms make in particular green solutions to achieve positions in each of the quadrants and why? There are risks and benefits inherent in each of Delmas and Burbano's quadrants, and firms face decisions on how to allocate scarce resources to symbolic and substantive activities. Greenwashing firms may gain reputational benefits from their communications but face the risk of stakeholder sanctions if their poor environmental performance is exposed. Silent green firms may be improving their substantive environmental performance by reducing waste or better controlling their management systems and processes, but they are missing out on the potential reputational or legitimacy benefits of communicating about their good environmental performance. Vocal green firms may be 'walking the talk' on environmental issues and be leaders in their sectors, but there may be risks and heightened scrutiny associated with appearing 'too good to be true' on environmental issues. Furthermore, silent brown firms may not be capturing all they can from potential 'low-hanging-fruit' green solutions.

How can managers decide among these strategies? Given that all green solutions are not qualitatively the same, how can firms decide on the best combination of green solutions? As discussed in Chapter 3, managers implementing green solutions may be trying to mitigate their firm's impact on the natural environment, but they also are usually at least partly trying to improve their firm's symbolic performance as evaluated by stakeholders. How can they decide how to maximise symbolic performance? Brennan and Pettit (2004) provided a powerful analytical framework about how individuals make these decisions. This book has barely caught the attention of management scholars, but it builds an economic analysis of the demand for and supply of esteem that might be applied at the firm level. Here, I apply their framework to explain managers' choices of a combination of green solutions to maximise the extent to which a firm generates positive social evaluations through corporate environmentalism.

Brennan and Pettit's (2004) insight was that positive social evaluations cannot be traded directly like other goods. Building on a long historical literature from moral philosophy, psychology and economics, they developed a model based on esteem – an attitudinal good 'that comes into being by virtue of what people think and feel about the person esteemed: that is, by virtue of their attitudes rather than their actions' (2004: 2).[5] The challenge in maximising esteem is that actively seeking it – through self-promotion, for example – may increase or counterproductively decrease the esteem in which an individual is held. Firms can invest in green solutions but whether or not they gain symbolic performance is determined by the social evaluations of relevant stakeholders. Here, I apply Brennan and Pettit's (2004) framework at the firm level to explain when managers might choose to invest in audience-seeking rather than performance-enhancing initiatives to maximise symbolic performance.

Brennan and Pettit's (2004) approach can be demonstrated by the simple illustration shown in Figure 4.4. Because esteem cannot be traded directly, they argue that individuals can seek esteem by virtually rather than actively demanding it. Managers can directly improve their firm's substantive environmental performance by altering processes, systems and activities to limit impacts on the natural

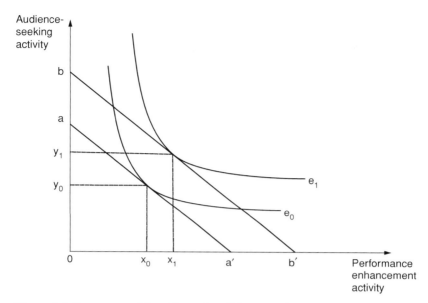

Figure 4.4 Brennan and Pettit's trade-off between investments in audience-seeking and performance-enhancing activity.
Source: Adapted from Brennan and Pettit (2004: 183). Reprinted by permission of Oxford University Press.

environment. But to gain symbolic performance, a firm must make a portfolio of investments to signal its environmental attitude and hope that this is rewarded by increased esteem. A firm can do this by investing in green solutions that focus on substantive environmental performance, what Brennan and Pettit (2004) called 'performance-enhancement activity', by investing in environmental symbols (i.e., 'audience-seeking activity'), or by a combination of both. However, audience-seeking activities are not without cost; it takes time and money to produce environmental reports, join industry schemes, lobby regulators and repaint the headquarters reception area green. As Delmas and Burbano (2011) explained, different firms will choose, on aggregate, different positions in this portfolio space. Greenwashing firms will emphasise audience-seeking activity, whereas silent green firms will invest more in performance-enhancement activities.

Effective esteem for a firm is the esteem due to its investment in substantive green solutions multiplied by its audience size. Therefore, a curve representing combinations of the two activities yielding the same level of esteem likely would be shaped as a rectangular hyperbola, such as e_0 in Figure 4.4. Because the overall effort available to be invested in green solutions is limited, managers can choose from any of the viable portfolio mix of options below and to the left of the budget line aa′ in Figure 4.4. The optimum combination of audience-seeking and performance-enhancing activities for a firm will be where the highest level of esteem can be achieved within the limits of the investment budget – at y_0 and x_0, respectively.

If in a future period a firm allocates more resources to green solutions, then the budget line could move from aa′ to bb′, allowing managers to invest in a wider range of activities. The optimal combination of audience-seeking and performance-enhancement activities would then rise to y_1 and x_1, allowing a firm to achieve the higher level of esteem, e_1. Thus, raising the budget allocated to green solutions can increase a firm's symbolic performance in the form of esteem. However, the extent to which increasing investment in green solutions leads to improvements in substantive performance – that is, a firm's actual environmental impacts – is likely to be lower due to the shape of the esteem curve. The increase in environmental performance-enhancement activity ($x_1 - x_0$) is likely to be less than the green solution budget increase (b′-a′) because some investment is diverted into symbolic activity. This is rational for firms because some communication is necessary to signal environmental attitudes in order to earn esteem. Firms need to invest in labelling, explaining and signifying the material changes they are making to improve environmental performance, even for internally focused practices. As experienced by HSBC, green buildings do not name themselves: at least some effort must be made in developing a shared understanding of the greenness of a solution. This loss in environmental performance due to investments that are diverted into audience-seeking activities is a social cost due to the way esteem is granted in society. These costs can become substantial if firms perceive that their status is threatened and they are tempted to increase their esteem by overinvesting in symbolic activities.

The relative costs of audience-seeking and performance-enhancement activities will vary according to the context. For example, some firms are more visible – perhaps due to their size or branding – thereby reducing the need for and cost of audience-seeking activities. This has the effect of increasing the negative slope of the budget line. Such firms can achieve higher levels of esteem than other firms with the same budget. However, they also will tend to spend more on audience-seeking activities. Similarly, high-status firms face lower audience-seeking costs due to their prominent position in society. These lower audience-seeking costs for high-status firms explain why they invest so heavily in symbolic solutions. Less costly audience-seeking opportunities incentivises firms to invest more and crowd out other alternative voices. High-status firms can publicise their preferred solutions and set the terms of the debate for other less visible or influential firms. Access to a low-cost audience gives high-status firms the strategic advantage of being able to select their preferred green solution, as well as reinforcing their social position through relatively lower costs of investing in esteem.

Consequences of symbolic corporate environmentalism

I previously discussed how managers' investments in green solutions drive symbolic corporate environmentalism. It can be rational for managers in profit-maximising firms to invest more in merely symbolic rather than substantive green solutions because information-poor stakeholders reward symbolic solutions more easily than opaque substantive solutions. Furthermore, it may be tempting for managers in powerful firms to use non-market strategies to buffer, bargain with, influence or control institutional pressures for environmental improvement. Both the McWilliams and Siegel (2001) and Husted and Salazar (2006) models assumed that markets for green solutions are competitive with many suppliers – or at least contestable with one dominant supplier that might be challenged by other firms that can freely enter and exit the market (Baumol 1982). But what if a single firm or small group of firms can control the design of green solutions? What are the consequences of symbolic corporate environmentalism when powerful firms can set the standards for green performance in an industry? In this section, I show how the gap between symbolic and substantive green performance is particularly problematic when a single firm or small group of powerful firms can exert discretionary power over the production of green solutions. Limiting the quantity and form of green solutions produced can impose a social cost on society.

Static analysis of the costs of symbolic corporate environmentalism

The preceding model of investments in green solutions is based on the conventional view of corporate environmentalism. As I outlined in

Chapter 3, this view takes a largely firm-level perspective and focuses on the private benefits to firms of gaining reputation and managing legitimacy through corporate environmentalism. However, as I also outlined in Chapter 3, the critical view places more emphasis on the social costs of corporate involvement in defining green solutions. The critical view frames greening as a control problem and corporate environmentalism as a way for firms to maintain status and authority. Whereas the conventional view assumes that stakeholders will see through blatant attempts by firms to use their status to manipulate green solutions, the critical view highlights how some firms have sufficient prestige to be able to limit the supply of green solutions to those that are acceptable to them. One goal of this book is to bridge the two perspectives by injecting power into conventional analyses of corporate environmentalism. In this section, I model firm power over green solutions as a 'virtual controller' and show how this mechanism can encourage firms to attempt to control the form of green solutions in some circumstances. I then describe the social costs associated with this control.

Symbolic corporate environmentalism is neither always deliberate nor entirely accidental. In an attempt to bridge the conventional and critical views, I introduce a third way – a virtual controller[6] – wherein symbolic corporate environmentalism is a naturally arising outcome of the profit-maximisation decisions (outlined previously) until a firm's control over greening is jeopardised. When there is a credible threat, then firms deliberately exert their authority. Maintaining status and power shapes managers' decisions but does not directly motivate them unless the usual order is threatened. If there is a genuine threat of demands for substantive change, then high-status actors will exert their power to control green solutions. Otherwise, the conventional 'business as usual' continues with firms implementing green solutions to maintain reputation and legitimacy. Thus, the desire for symbolic performance is an important shaper of corporate environmentalism, but whether particular green solutions are motivated by concerns about legitimacy, reputation or status depends on the contextual conditions. Managers typically seek to maximise reputation or maintain legitimacy by implementing green solutions. However, if firms detect that their discretion on environmental issues is being questioned, they might exert their status as powerful social actors to control the green solutions available.

When the virtual controller is triggered into deliberate action, concerns of the critical view about corporate control over rhetoric and resources move to the foreground. If firms are 'backed into a corner' about environmental demands, they can respond by 'voluntarily' adopting green solutions of their choice, thereby preempting regulations that might force them to adopt a solution that they cannot control so easily. The problem is that 'voluntary' initiatives by producers of green solutions may lead to social losses because the preferences of gift givers may not match those of receivers. This line of thinking is inspired by Waldfogel's (1993) analysis of the deadweight loss from gift giving.[7] Gift giving may be a good analogy for corporate environmentalism because much of the investment in green solutions is committed voluntarily beyond immediate legal compliance. Producers incur additional discretionary costs associated with voluntary green solutions, which they assume that consumers – or at least a broader range of stakeholders – value. However, like gift giving, producers often decide the exact form of the voluntary green solution rather than giving cash to stakeholders who can spend the gift on green solutions that match their own preferences. This can be a particularly powerful effect when the intent of the 'gift' is to invest in a green solution that matches the preferences of a firm rather than consumers.

Figure 4.5 adapts Waldfogel's (1993) analysis to show consumers' willingness to pay for green solutions that deliver symbolic compared to substantive performance. Although Figure 4.5 may appear superficially similar to Figure 4.4, there are a few key differences. In Figure 4.5, the analysis is from a consumer's perspective and aims to show how much utility consumers achieve by consuming combinations of symbolic and substantive performance produced by firms. Consumers gain utility and are willing to pay for substantive environmental improvements such as waste reduction or products made with renewable resources, indicated by the horizontal axis. The vertical axis shows consumers' utility from symbolic performance. At first glance, it may seem counterintuitive that consumers may be willing to pay for symbolic performance without substance. Yet, presented with two products identical other than one having a green label or having been produced by a trusted firm, consumers state a willingness to pay for the symbolically greener option. This effect is compounded because consumers may not be able to evaluate the precise substantive performance of a good in any case and therefore use symbolic performance

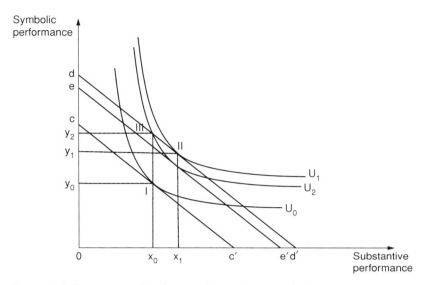

Figure 4.5 Consumer utility from 'voluntary' green solutions.

as a proxy. A more critical view points to consumers' willingness to be reassured by green symbols that can provide emotional reassurance that something is being done about environmental issues without the cost of actually limiting their consumption of natural resources.

Although the curves in Figure 4.5 represent consumer utility rather than firm esteem as in Figure 4.4, the analytical argument is similar. A consumer of green solutions can afford to pay for some combination of symbolic and substantive performance, given by the budget line cc'. Utility from green solutions for a particular individual is a product of symbolic and substantive performance. An indifference curve representing all of the combinations of symbolic and substantive performance that achieve the same level of utility is shaped like curve U_0. If the amount of expenditure to be allocated to green solutions in total is fixed, then a consumer may choose any combination of symbolic and substantive performance below and to the left of the budget constraint cc' in Figure 4.5. The highest amount of utility that a consumer can achieve with this fixed budget is at point I, where the tangent of U_0 meets the budget line cc'.

If a firm voluntarily chooses to improve its environmental performance, this can be modelled as a 'gift' to society and the total expenditure on green solutions can increase. If the voluntary contribution is in the form of a cash donation for environmental improvement, then the budget line would increase to dd′, and consumers could choose any combination of symbolic and substantive performance along the new frontier (dd′). For example, a firm might pay cash into a pollution abatement fund, increasing that fund's budget and allowing the receivers of the cash donation to allocate investment to symbolic and/or substantive environmental improvements according to their preferences. Allocating the additional budget (d–c) would allow consumers of green solutions to reach a higher utility level U_1 at Point II, increasing both substantive and symbolic environmental performance (i.e., to y_1 and x_1, respectively). Waldfogel (1993) pointed out that the cash gift Point II is achieved only when the giver of a voluntary gift is indifferent between gifts. A firm makes a financial donation and then receivers decide how to spend the additional income on substantive or symbolic environmental improvements.

However, voluntary firm contributions to environmental improvement typically are in a specific form other than cash. These 'gifts' reflect the preferences of the giver (i.e., the firm) rather than the receiver (i.e., consumers or stakeholders). Voluntary initiatives may include investments in eco-labelling schemes, membership of industry associations or environmental reporting, as well as direct pollution or waste abatement. As I discuss in the previous section, firms often prefer to voluntarily donate symbolic rather than substantive green solutions to society. In the extreme case of the entire gift being directed to symbolic performance, then consumers would receive $y_2 - y_0$ additional units of symbolic performance for the same budget increase to dd′. Consumers' utility would increase to U_2 (Point III), but this level of utility could have been achieved with the budget ee′. The difference between the budget frontier achieved through a gift fixed by the giver's preferences (dd′) and the lowest budget frontier that could have achieved the same level of consumer utility U_2 (ee′) is a 'deadweight loss'. The loss d–e arises because the preferences of the gift giver do not align with those of the receiver.[8]

Several corporate environmentalism analyses have shown that voluntary environmental initiatives can lead to a welfare increase (i.e., a shift from Point I to Point III). What this analysis adds is that as long as a firm's preferences do not match exactly those of the stakeholders as consumers of green solutions, there is a welfare loss (d–e) associated with firms controlling the exact form of voluntary green solutions (i.e., Point III offers a lower utility than Point II in Figure 4.5). It is worth noting that voluntary green solutions can lead to a loss of utility even if they are not entirely symbolic. Utility will always be less when the supplier chooses the precise form of the gift except in the ideal (and unlikely) case in which the giver happens to select the exact combination of symbolic and substantive performance that would have been selected by receivers given a free choice (i.e., Point II). Overproduction of substantive green performance also could lead to utility losses; however, this is likely to be rare, given the relative costs of symbolic and substantive green investments.[9]

This model uses a conventional economic argument to show the effects that proponents of the critical view have rightly claimed are typically ignored in conventional corporate environmentalism research. Corporate control over the form of green solutions leads to a deadweight loss. The extent of this social cost depends on how strongly the adopting firms are exerting authority over the rhetoric and resources related to corporate greening. Under 'business as usual', firms pursue reputation and legitimacy by optimising the quantity and portfolio of greening solutions, as described previously. However, when there is a danger that their access to resources is under threat, firms use their status – which is often misrecognised as legitimate – to voluntarily step in and offer green solutions. When firms' and stakeholders' preferences are aligned, voluntary corporate environmentalism can increase social welfare. But if these preferences diverge, there is a social loss. This is a vital but so far neglected limitation of voluntary corporate environmentalism.

Dynamic analysis of the social energy penalty

The static analysis shows the likely presence of a deadweight loss arising from firms choosing the precise form of corporate environmentalism. However, this does not imply that greening activities should not be undertaken. As with any intervention in markets, the deadweight loss from adopting green solutions to signal environmental awareness still may be outweighed by economic benefits. From an allocative efficiency point of view, society should be willing to live with the deadweight loss as long as there is a concomitant economic benefit (Nicholson 1992). There may be advantages to diffusing greening solutions – even if there is a social cost associated with them – because adoption of green initiatives can move the whole system to a higher level and enable society to benefit from positive externalities (Conlon, Patrignani, and Litchfield 2012). The question then becomes how to trade off the social costs against the potential benefits of diffusing corporate environmental initiatives.

According to the conventional perspective, the main economic benefit from symbolic corporate environmentalism is that it solves an asymmetric information problem (see Chapter 3, Table 3.1). Stakeholders and audiences for corporate environmental initiatives are in a chronically poor informational state. It is difficult for outsiders to evaluate how green a particular company might be. An efficient way to solve this is to generate a credible and consistent signal of a firm's green performance. Signals such as membership in industry self-regulation schemes, eco-labels, corporate sustainability reports and the like are intended as an informational 'shortcut' for a firm's stakeholders. It is inefficient for each firm to invent an idiosyncratic green club or logo. From an allocative efficiency point of view, it is better to have a consistent symbol that gains value as more firms join the club. The wider the shared meaning or the more recognisable is a representation of a green solution, the more useful it may be as an informational signal.

Increasing returns to adoption arise from two main sources: learning effects and network externalities (Schilling 1998). First, the more firms commit resources to a particular green solution, the more they learn about their own organisational capacity to address environmental issues and how to meet societal expectations more effectively (Banerjee 1998). Learning about environmental issues and potential green solutions is a primary driver of membership in green industry clubs and networks (Delmas and Keller 2005). Furthermore, new environmental standards attract boundary spanners (e.g., consultancy firms and auditors) that help disseminate credible information about the solution from one firm to another, lowering the informational cost associated with uncertain new green solutions to later adopters (Delmas 2002; Jahn et al. 2005). The net result of these learning effects is that the production cost of the next marginal unit decreases as more of the green solution is produced (Wright 1936; Yelle 1979).

Second, green solutions can have a positive network externality: the more firms that adopt a particular green standard, the more recognisable the standard becomes and the higher is the value of the standard to

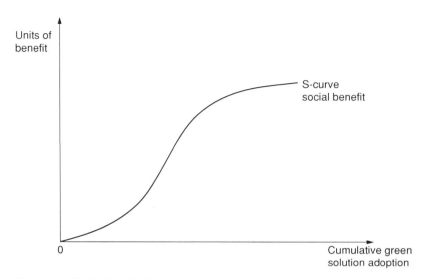

Figure 4.6 Social benefit S-curve.

the next incremental adopter (Arthur 1989; Katz and Shapiro 1985). Prakash and Potoski (2006) explained how green clubs generate scale economies in the production of a club's reputation because a larger membership enhances a solution's visibility to external stakeholders. Evidence from fields as diverse as green buildings, forestry and apparel suggests that the higher the rate of adoption, the more an eco-label is recognised as a credible signal of environmental quality and the higher is the benefit of adoption to the next incremental adopter (Bartley 2003; Chan, Qian, and Lam 2009). Although explanations for these network effects range from vicarious learning to the mimetic isomorphism of neo-institutional theory, the net result is the same. The more a given green solution is adopted, the higher is the potential value to the next adopter of that standard.

The rising economic benefit of adopting green solutions as cumulative green output increases is commonly represented as an S-curve (Figure 4.6). Introduced by Foster (1986), the S-curve represents the increased performance of a new technology over the amount of cumulative effort put into the technology.[10] Technologies need not be technical or manufacturing based, but they can be thought of as 'the general way a company does business or attempts a task' (Foster 1986: 33). In the case of green solutions, the S-curve shows the relationship between the cumulative investment in a new green solution and the incremental value accrued to the next adopter from improved green solution performance. When value is plotted against cumulative adoption in this way, performance improves only slowly at low levels of adoption, then more rapidly as adoption gathers momentum, until value to the next adopter diminishes at higher rates of adoption. There is a social benefit associated with the cumulative production of green solutions if new adopters gain additional performance benefits from the investments of earlier adopters.

We can expect the benefits from previous adopters to increase only slowly at the initial stages because early adopters face considerable uncertainty about the effectiveness of a new technology (Foster 1986). Part of the early cost of a new green solution is the expensive effort required to stabilise shared meanings and establish legitimacy for it. At this stage, there may be several competing solutions and it may not be clear which, if any, of the potential alternatives could eventually establish credibility with stakeholders. Once a leading solution starts to emerge, however, learning effects and network externalities improve its performance and offer increased value to later adopters of the solution. This social benefit applies whether the incremental green output is produced by current producers expanding their corporate environmental initiatives across more of their own activities (e.g., by certifying more plants to an environmental standard such as ISO 14001) or by new firms adopting the solution (e.g., by joining an industry club or eco-label scheme).

In the static analysis described previously, I identify a social cost associated with corporate power to produce green solutions. However, widespread adoption can be allocatively efficient for society because established green solutions economise on the informational costs of demonstrating environmental performance. The question is when the social costs might be overcome by a corresponding social benefit from network and learning effects. Figure 4.7 illustrates this trade-off from diffusing green solutions. The social benefit curve represents the sum of the green solution's standalone value and the social benefit S-curve, whereas the cost curve shows the monopoly costs as the solution gains market share (Schilling 2010). When the social costs outweigh the social benefits, there is a net social energy penalty associated with the green solution. In contrast,

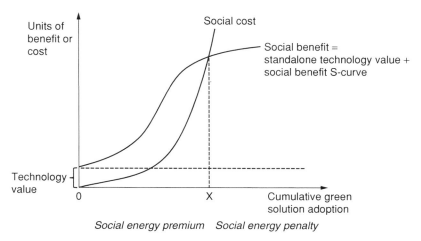

Figure 4.7 Social costs and benefits of symbolic corporate environmentalism. Adapted from Schilling (2010: 85).

when social benefits outweigh social costs, there is a social energy premium.

We typically could expect the social benefit curve to begin at a value above zero for the initial adopter. The first firm produces a green solution to meet its competitiveness, legitimacy or moral responsibility needs (Bansal and Roth 2000), thereby providing a positive benefit for the adopter. Although symbolic corporate environmentalism is regularly criticised for not always having a substantive biophysical impact, symbolic green output should yield a standalone technology value for early adopters. Even largely ceremonial or unsuccessful implementation of a new environmental standard, report or eco-label may improve a firm's information about its own environmental impacts, internal management processes or market. The initial height of the social benefit curve depends on the extent to which producing a particular green solution provides an environmental benefit independent of the number of adopters.

The social benefit curve rises with increased cumulative adoption of green solutions as both existing and new adopters gain value from learning and network effects. Thus, the social benefit at any given level of cumulative output consists of the standalone value of the corporate environmental initiative plus the network and learning externality benefits captured by the next incremental adopter.

Figure 4.7 also illustrates a convex and monotonic increasing social cost curve. It shows the increase in utility loss from the dominance of particular forms of green solution as a new voluntary solution becomes established. In the early stages of adoption, there may be several competing solutions, and each might entail a social cost depending on the extent to which the development of the solution is dominated by powerful, high-status actors. However, as one solution begins to take hold, other alternatives offered by less powerful actors are likely to be squeezed out of contention due to poorer access to political channels and markets. Higher-status firms face lower audience-seeking costs, so they are able to more effectively promote their solutions. This status is often misinterpreted in society so that stakeholders often award even higher esteem to those firms without noticing their relatively lower investments in performance-enhancing activities. One greening solution 'corners the market' and the social cost associated with it becomes more entrenched as cumulative adoption increases, reinforcing the adopters' high status. The technology management literature emphasises random historical events and small differences in initial conditions as the drivers of which technology standard will emerge as the dominant standard (see, e.g., Arthur 1989). However, case studies of the development of self-regulatory mechanisms in the forestry, fair trade and apparel domains have shown the lengths to which powerful actors might go to skew in their favour the membership, certification and verification rules of self-regulatory institutions (Bartley 2003; Renard 2005). Distortions introduced in the early stages of adoption are likely to worsen as other less powerful firms join the scheme. Thus, the tendency towards adopting one green solution that is reinforced by positive network and learning effects also increases the social cost of the standard being dominated by powerful actors in the first place.

Neo-institutional theory provides an alternative argument for why social costs rise at an increasing rate over cumulative output. Tolbert and Zucker (1983) famously argued that early adopters of a new practice do so for technical-efficiency reasons, whereas later adopters are more likely to adopt for legitimacy-based reasons. The first model in this chapter demonstrated that from a single firm's point of view, the profit-maximising level of substantive green solutions produced is likely to be lower than the level of symbolic green solutions. This difference is green output not realised due to symbolic activity. Applying Tolbert and Zucker's (1983) argument, we would expect this firm-level loss in substantive green output to be lower for early adopters but to increase as late adopters implement the solution for symbolic, legitimacy-based reasons. Thus, as more firms adopt a particular green solution, the loss of substantive green output increases at an increasing rate, yielding a convex social cost curve.

In Figure 4.7, as long as the cumulative adoption of a green solution is below the output level X, the standalone, network and learning benefits of adopting the standards for society outweigh the social costs, thereby yielding a social energy premium. At levels lower than X, the benefits of raising awareness, environmental learning and green expectations are higher than the social costs. However, as cumulative output increases beyond X, the social energy penalty outweighs any benefit to society in moving to a higher level of environmental performance – the advantages of the green solution are dominated by too much symbolic versus substantive adoption.

Clearly, the level of X is highly dependent on the shapes of the social cost and benefit curves. The slope of the social benefit curve represents the rate of evolution in green solutions. The technology S-curve literature emphasises how the performance of some solutions improves more rapidly than others (see, e.g., Foster 1986 and Suarez and Lanzolla 2007). In the case of renewable energy solutions, for example, photovoltaic technologies appear to be following a much flatter technology evolution S-curve than wind or geothermal energy, which show sharply increasing performance curves (Schilling and Esmundo 2009). Evidence from the adoption of thermal insulation by homebuilders confirms that decreasing technology cost is a more powerful driver of adoption than either voluntary or mandatory energy-efficiency building codes (Jaffe and Stavins 1995). The social benefit curve will be steeper the greater the extent to which cumulative adoption leads to learning, performance improvements and cost reductions in the green solution.

Similar patterns can be seen in the evolution of less technological environmental solutions. Hoffman's (1999) analysis of the US chemical industry described the painstakingly gradual evolution of self-regulatory mechanisms, particularly Responsible Care, in the period 1960–1993. In contrast, the proportion of FT Global 500 companies that disclosed their carbon performance through the CDP rose rapidly from 46 per cent in 2003 to almost 80 per cent in 2007 (Pinkse and Kolk 2009). A technology management perspective explains how network externalities associated with green solutions vary according to the importance of 'installed base' and complementary goods. If an installed base of a plausible green solution is already available, as in the case of CDP disclosure, firms are more likely to join and adopt the trend rather than go through the protracted negotiation of establishing new institutional norms (e.g., as in Responsible Care). Additionally, the value of both CDP disclosure and membership in Responsible Care depends on the availability of complementary goods, such as stakeholder knowledge and awareness. The adoption of Responsible Care was relatively slow because assets that would enhance the value of participating in it (e.g., consumer awareness) were not yet developed. In contrast, CDP disclosure was offered to firms along with the complementary assets of ready channels to share their participation with a large pool of institutional investors.

The social benefit curve is also likely to be steeper when powerful actors force the institutionalisation of a green solution (Lawrence, Winn, and Jennings 2001). The more that managers perceive regulatory stakeholders to be important to a firm, the more likely they are to adopt an environmental plan (Henriques and Sadorsky 1999). Furthermore, the more that regulatory agencies enforce regulations through inspections, reports of violations and enforcement actions, the greater the potential value in joining a self-regulatory scheme (Short and Toffel 2008). Social force underpinned by intense NGO and media attention also can raise the network externality value of adoption (Büthe and Mattli 2010). Joining an established green solution can offer shelter from media attention, particularly when stakeholders are not fully able to differentiate the environmental performance among firms (Barnett and King 2008).

Thus, the slope of the social benefit curve is a function of a number of factors. A technology management perspective emphasises the rate of performance improvement in the green solution, the importance of installed base and the availability of complementary assets. Other institutional explanations for the shape of the social benefit curve focus on the power of stakeholders to force adoption and the extent to which firms share a common reputation.

The social benefit curve could be quite shallow, reaching its limit at a low level of benefit if significant learning effects or network externalities are not realised from adoption. In this case, the point at which the social cost outweighs the social benefit (see Point X in Figure 4.7) would move to the left. There might be a social energy penalty at quite low levels of output if there are no compensating learning effects or network externalities. For example, social costs are likely to outweigh social benefits if a green solution is not recognised by stakeholders as legitimate (i.e., absence of a complementary asset). Alternatively, there may be a higher social energy penalty if there is insufficient regulatory or media attention to reward coordinated self-regulation (i.e., low network externality to adoption). Both of these situations can be exacerbated if the green solution is of dubious substantive environmental value, moving the entire social benefit curve to a lower standalone technology base level.

The social benefit curve could reach its limit either at low levels of cumulative adoption or at much higher levels. Reaching the limit at low levels would yield an 'abrupt' S-curve, wherein any learning effects or network externality benefits would be exhausted by early adopters (Suarez and Lanzolla 2007). This can occur when a small group of firms comprises the standard-setters for a new green solution. For example, Delmas and Montes-Sancho (2010) analysed the Climate Challenge programme, a voluntary agreement between the US Department of Energy and the largest electricity utilities in the United States. Their analysis revealed how early adopters of the programme experienced higher levels of state political pressure, were more dependent on regulatory agencies, were better connected to the trade association and were more visible. One explanation for this is that early adopters benefitted from complementary assets such as stakeholder interest, coercive force from regulatory agencies and potential spillovers from a collective reputation that underpinned high network externalities of joining the programme. However, late adopters did not have the same network externality benefits because they did not experience the same level of political pressure, visibility and connections with industry associations. At this later stage of the benefit curve, the social benefit curve was flatter. The late joiners invested significantly less in emissions reductions, implying that they adopted for symbolic rather than substantive reasons (Delmas and Montes-Sancho 2010). In the case of an abrupt social benefit curve, the output level at which social costs outweigh the benefits is more likely to be in the flatter, higher region of the benefit curve. In this situation, the social energy penalty is highly sensitive to the extent to which the small group of firms that set the new green standard chooses to exert its monopoly power in defining the green solution.

The opposite of an abrupt social benefit curve is a 'smooth' S-curve, in which the additional benefits of cumulative adoption of a green solution are available only gradually, as output increases. An environmental production technology might require significant investments before performance improvements encourage others to invest. Eco-labels may need to reach a critical level of cumulative adoption before they gain sufficient visibility with customers and therefore be valuable as greening signals for later adopters, particularly if there are several competing labelling schemes. When there is a smooth social benefit curve, more cumulative green output is needed before later adopting firms are persuaded to take advantage of learning and network effects. Indeed, so much cumulative output may be required to generate these effects that the social benefit could be outweighed by social costs at much lower cumulative output levels.

Output level X is typically closer to the origin for a smooth rather than abrupt social benefit curve. This implication is echoed in the technology management literature, as a smooth pace of technology evolution is assumed to lead to an entrenched technological solution that advantages the firms that adopted the solution early (Suarez and Lanzolla 2007). Early adopters can gain benefits from developing their own green capabilities, preempting valuable resources such as a reputation for promoting the green solution, and establishing a green leadership position. These benefits encourage the early-adopting firms to protect the green solution in which they have invested, regardless of actual environmental performance (Foster 1986). Social benefits are limited and the social energy penalty may outweigh them entirely at lower levels of green output.

Whereas the social benefit curve is sensitive to a variety of factors, the social cost curve is primarily a reflection of early adopters' discretionary power. The social cost arises because of the utility loss from high-status actors controlling the precise form of the green solution. The steepness of the cost curve is primarily a function of the discretionary behaviour of powerful firms (Schilling 2010). Power matters in establishing a successful green standard, and the strategic decisions of the standard-setting firm (or another entity) regarding issues including membership criteria, investment protection, and political and commercial strategies drives the extent to which this power imposes social costs (Büthe and Mattli 2010). Because the social cost curve is the cumulative total across all adopting firms reflecting the gap between the profit-maximising level of substantive and symbolic green solutions, the steepness of the curve indicates a firm's ability to generate and protect that symbolic gap. Firms may choose not to exploit the symbolic gap, thereby flattening the overall social cost curve. Some eco-labelling schemes, industry clubs and other self-regulatory mechanisms may be authentic attempts to improve both the symbol and the substance of corporate environmental performance; others are merely symbolic pseudo-certificates that do not reflect the underlying performance. The social cost arises because outsiders may not be able to identify the difference, and firms may have the power to obfuscate this loss in social output misdirected into symbolic activities.

As discussed in Chapter 3, one of the fundamental differences between the conventional and critical perspectives is the assumptions that each view makes about power. Critical views assume that high-status actors in a field have the power to drive a wedge between their communications and signals on environmental issues and their (non-)implementation of substantive environmental improvements. Conventional views, conversely, assume that any differences between corporate green symbols and substantive actions are more benign reflections of imperfect information, implementation or the current state of evolution of environmental expectations.

These two perspectives result in two different shapes of the social energy penalty cost curve (Figure 4.8). The critical view assumes a much steeper cost curve, which crosses the benefit curve at lower levels of cumulative output than a neutral curve (see $X_c < X$ in Figure 4.8). In contrast, the conventional view assumes a much flatter social energy penalty cost curve. The conventional view's social cost curve either does not cross the benefit curve at all or, if it does, then it does so far to the right of X that the social energy penalty is relevant only in extreme conditions.

Thus, the traditional intractability between the critical and the conventional views of symbolic corporate environmentalism can be presented as different sets of assumptions underlying the social energy penalty. The conventional view tends to not be concerned about the social losses arising from the social energy penalty because they typically are assumed to be outweighed by the potential of green solutions to economise on informational and transactional costs. Conversely, the critical view tends to emphasise the costs of the social energy penalty in any analysis of corporate environmentalism because these costs are assumed to outweigh any environmental, learning or network benefits at very low levels of cumulative adoption.

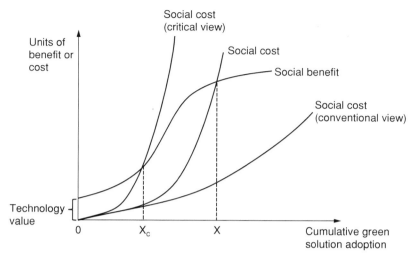

Figure 4.8 Social costs and benefits according to the two views of corporate environmentalism.

Summary of social consequences of symbolic corporate environmentalism

The static analysis demonstrates how differences between a firm's investment in symbolic and substantive green solutions impose a social cost. Green solutions are underproduced compared with Husted and Salazar's (2006) profit-maximising strategic case. This loss of social welfare from underproducing green symbols arises at least partly from the power of high-status actors to influence what is considered an acceptable green solution. Because status operates only as a virtual controller of firm decisions and not as the primary motivation, firms activate their authority to define the form of green solutions only when their position is threatened. Their response when threatened is to adopt voluntary corporate environmentalism; however, these voluntary donations of green solutions may not match the preferences of the consumers of green solutions. The consequence is a loss of social welfare.

A more dynamic analysis reveals when the social energy penalty might outweigh the compensating performance benefits of learning and network externalities. The social energy penalty is particularly damaging in the sense that the social costs outweigh the social benefits at lower levels of cumulative green solution output when (1) the standalone environmental value of the greening solution is low; (2) the standard-setting firms exert their discretionary power in their non-market strategies in managing the green solution; (3) there is a smooth technology evolution curve for the green solution; and/or (4) there are low limits to the social benefits from learning effects or network externalities, even when the green solution is widespread.

In the next three chapters, I provide preliminary evidence from a variety of empirical contexts that examines each of these contingencies in more detail. The dynamic model of the consequences of symbolic corporate environmentalism offers the possibility of understanding when firm-sponsored green solutions might be in the best interests of society – even if they are largely symbolic. Unpacking each of the elements of the model in subsequent chapters sheds light on when we might expect to see a social energy penalty, when it might be larger, how it develops and how we might be able to overcome it.

5 | Study 1: Symbolic gaps in environmental strategies

Conventional corporate environmentalism has become popular in both the academic literature and corporate boardrooms. Since the 1990s, both firms and governments have been moving away from the traditional command-and-control approach to environmental regulation and instead are increasingly reliant on firms to adopt voluntary green solutions that are not direct legal requirements. As managers adopt voluntary environmental strategies, stakeholders such as shareholders, government, NGOs and other actors determine whether a firm has gained legitimacy. An important outcome of corporate environmentalism schemes is 'symbolic performance' – or the extent to which adopting a green solution generates positive social evaluations.

However, as discussed in Chapter 4, a potential problem when firms voluntarily go beyond compliance with environmental regulations is that they might produce more symbolic than substantive green solutions. This leads to a 'symbolic gap' – or the difference between substantive environmental improvements and symbolic performance from corporate environmentalism. Symbolic gaps could arise deliberately as firms exert their discretionary power to produce audience-seeking rather than performance-enhancing green solutions or as an unintended consequence of the lower cost of adopting symbolic green solutions. In either case, firms face the tension that whereas they may gain symbolic performance by adopting symbolic green solutions, they may lose it if the difference between symbol and substance is exposed.

Despite the importance of symbolic gaps, insufficient research has focused on the circumstances under which they are more likely to persist. In this chapter, I argue that powerful firms are more likely to seek symbolic performance and generate symbolic gaps. Symbolic gaps are likely to persist when there is relatively weak monitoring of self-regulation schemes. Large firms have more status, resources and political connections, which often gives them systemic power within fields. We therefore can obtain initial insight into symbolic gaps surrounding firms' environmental strategies by collating all of the available empirical research evidence concerning the relationship between firm size and corporate environmentalism across different contexts.

In this chapter, I develop an argument based on large firms' decoupling and systemic power to explain when symbolic gaps can persist. A meta-analysis of empirical studies on firm size and corporate environmentalism broadly supports three predictions. First, large firms seek symbolic performance through proactive environmental strategy more than small firms. Second, due to decoupling, large firms exhibit a symbolic gap; that is, the relationship between size and self-regulation is stronger for intended strategy statements than for substantive impacts. Third, because large firms have the systemic power to shape the self-regulatory 'game', the extent to which they seek symbolic performance and maintain symbolic gaps is higher in less-monitored fields.

Proactive environmental strategies and power

Firms have adopted corporate environmentalism in response to pressures arising from regulators, NGOs, customers and other actors in institutional surroundings (Bansal 2005; Jennings and Zandbergen 1995). As previously discussed, corporate environmentalism can take many forms, including a wide variety of firm responses to institutional pressures to act on environmental issues including (but not limited to) altering a firm's strategic stance to incorporate greener aims, launching more environmentally sound products, altering materials-transformation processes for environmental benefit, implementing pollution abatement technologies or even simply making an environmental policy declaration. To the extent that these green solutions are an attempt to voluntarily control firms' collective actions on the environment, all of these actions could be examples of industry self-regulation on green issues (King and Lenox 2000).

We know that (1) there is considerable variation in environmental self-regulation across firms, even when institutional pressures are similar (Bansal 2005; Russo and Fouts 1997); (2) legitimacy seeking is a powerful motive for self-regulation (King and Lenox, 2000); (3) self-regulation strategies are laden with signalling and symbolic behaviour (Delmas and Montes-Sancho 2010; Phillipe and Durand 2011); and

(4) self-regulation at the firm level is interrelated with government reg-ulation at the field level (Reid and Toffel 2009). However, we do not yet know much about the field-level contingencies that might influence large firms' self-regulatory strategies or the extent to which they might be symbolic or substantive green solutions.

Scholars have generated an increasing number of empirical studies on the predictors of self-regulation of environmental issues (for a recent review, see King, Prado, and Rivera 2012). These studies typically are aimed at uncovering the triggers of proactive corporate environmental-ism – that is, strategy choices on environmental issues that go beyond basic legal compliance (Hart 1995; Roome 1992). Symbolic gaps have been noticed in the context of self-regulation, particularly in environ-mental reporting (see, e.g., Laufer 2003); in the ceremonial adoption of environmental management schemes, such as ISO 14001(see, e.g., Boiral 2007); and in symbolic participation in voluntary agreements (Delmas and Montes-Sancho 2010; King and Lenox 2000).

As noted in Chapter 4, not all green solutions are equal. Researchers are increasingly becoming aware that proactive corporate environmen-talism measures based on stated intent, environmental initiative imple-mentation, and actual mitigation of environmental impacts tap into different dimensions of environmental proactivity (Branzei et al. 2004; Chatterji and Toffel 2010; Russo and Harrison 2005). However, the link between recognising symbolic corporate environmentalism and the empirical practice of measuring several of its dimensions has not yet been fully exploited. Exploiting differences between dimensions of corporate environmentalism allows us to examine symbolic gaps as firms attempt to gain and protect symbolic performance; they may state proactive environmental intentions or implement environmen-tal initiatives without reducing their actual environmental impact. My elaboration in this chapter is to explicitly consider the role of firm size in maintaining symbolic gaps in corporate environmentalism across different social fields.

Surprisingly little research attention has been given to when and how symbolic gaps persist within fields. Although research suggests that large, visible firms are more likely to respond to institutional pressures (Pfeffer and Salancik 1978), little is known about whether and when they are more likely to generate and maintain symbolic gaps. This oversight is particularly problematic because large firms often benefit from high-status social evaluations (Fombrun and Shanley 1990) and therefore have discretionary power in defining appropriate institutional responses (Phillips and Zuckerman 2001).

Prior studies incorporated aspects of power into explanations of symbolic gaps. For example, Westphal and Zajac (2001) found that powerful CEOs were more likely to only symbolically adopt stock repurchase programmes. Tilcsik (2010) examined how the contest for power within an organisation eventually led to the closing of a symbolic gap. More generally, Boxenbaum and Jonsson (2008) suggested that power relationships within a field may influence the likelihood of decoupling but they did not say how or why. I respond to their challenge by recognising that institutional pressures arise within a network of social relationships (Bourdieu 1990; Wooten and Hoffman 2008) wherein institutional control is based on routine, systemic power that advantages particular groups (Lawrence 2008; Oakes, Townley, and Cooper 1998). Large firms are highly visible and therefore subject to resulting institutional pressures, leading to a tendency to decouple proactive words from actions (Meyer and Rowan 1977). We recall from Chapter 4 that these firms face a lower relative cost of audience-seeking activities and therefore tend to invest more in symbolic activities and earn higher levels of social esteem for equivalent levels of overall investment in green solutions. However, large firms also wield status and symbolic power that individuals misrecognise as legitimate authority to shape the rules of the game. Thus, whereas decoupling arguments explain symbolic gaps as 'rationalised myths' at the firm level, a more power-based approach examines how myths are formed by the powerful and then misrecognised as legitimate within the broader social system (Bourdieu 2005).

In this chapter, I develop a power-based logic to investigate whether and when large firms are more likely to generate and maintain symbolic gaps. This is an important research concern because large firms often are key players in responding to institutional demands and also may have the discretionary power required to separate symbolic from substantive responses (Philippe and Durand 2011). The extent to which large firms have the power to shape the rules of the game and to benefit from symbolic gaps in different contexts has been under-explored. One reason why the field-level determinants of persistent symbolic gaps among large firms have not been adequately addressed so far may be the challenge of data requirements. I overcome this challenge by using meta-analytic techniques to test hypotheses with data from across a wide variety of fields.

The two overarching research questions in this chapter are as follows: (1) Does separating symbolic from substantive performance provide different answers about drivers of corporate environmentalism in large, powerful firms? (2) When can symbolic gaps persist between the likelihood that large, powerful firms will adopt corporate environmentalism through proactive strategic intent, implementation or impact? I argue that the extent to which large firms seek symbolic performance and can maintain symbolic gaps depends on the extent of monitoring within fields. I hypothesise that in highly monitored fields, large firms are more likely to seek symbolic performance but will have more difficulty maintaining a symbolic gap. I test the hypotheses by conducting a meta-analysis of empirical corporate environmentalism studies that capture data from a diverse range of fields. An ancillary empirical contribution of this chapter is that by conducting an across-field meta-analysis, I provide guidance to corporate environmentalism researchers about when large firms are likely to be more environmentally responsive, in both words and actions.

Explaining symbolic gaps: Decoupling and power

A symbolic gap arises when there is a difference between a firm's stated intentions designed to shift social evaluations and its substantive environmental impacts on a given issue within a field. We know that firms may reap legitimacy benefits from gaining symbolic performance and maintaining a symbolic gap. However, researchers have focused less attention on how these benefits are threatened if a symbolic gap is exposed. Firms may gain economic benefit from signalling proactive corporate environmentalism policy statements, but these benefits can be lost if the strategy is perceived as merely symbolic. Institutional theory suggests that persistent symbolic gaps can be explained by *decoupling* at the firm level, whereas a more politicised approach suggests an alternative logic based on *power* within a field.

Decoupling. Institutional theorists focus on organisational legitimacy, defined as 'a generalised perception or assumption that the actions of an entity are desirable, proper or appropriate within some socially constructed system of norms, values, beliefs and definitions'

(Suchman 1995: 574). Maintaining legitimacy can enhance firm survival but also can be challenging when firms are faced with conflicting demands and uncertainty about the efficiency of proposed solutions. Institutional theorists describe this as 'decoupling', in which organisations adopt new practices only ceremonially without necessarily fully implementing them (Endelman 1992; Meyer and Rowan 1977). Within this view, persistent symbolic gaps are explained by decoupling, in which organisations separate their 'talks, decisions and actions' to cope with conflicting institutional demands (Brunsson 1989). Large firms may be more inclined to adopt only ceremonially because they are more visible and need to signal legitimacy (Westphal, Gulati, and Shortell 1997).

Power. However, the typical decoupling logic gives too little attention to systemic power – that is, power that works through routine and taken-for-granted practices that advantage particular groups (Lawrence 2008). High-status firms have the systemic power to shape what is considered to be legitimate within a given field (Deephouse and Suchman 2008). Once new symbols are established, they continue to define what is deemed legitimate and can exert considerable institutional control (Lawrence 2008). Dominant organisations wield their systemic power to generate symbolic power that resides in words, language and symbols valued by community members (Bourdieu 1991). Once established, these symbols are 'misrecognised' as legitimate responses to institutional pressures because the systemic power that privileges high-status organisations is invisible. Thus, persistent symbolic gaps can be explained by misrecognition, wherein less powerful members of a field believe in the legitimacy of symbolic power as well as the legitimacy of high-status organisations that wield it.

Large firms may have more direct political and economic power through their access to more resources, larger numbers of stakeholders (akin to voters) and ability to capture rents from public policy (Hillman et al. 2004). Large firms also are more likely to benefit from higher prestige (Mas-Ruiz and Ruiz-Moreno 2011); hence, the potential to deviate from or define new social norms (Phillips and Zuckerman 2001). Larger firms also are better able to resist external stakeholder pressure (Darnall et al. 2010; Meznar and Nigh 1995). All of these characteristics suggest that large firms are likely to enjoy higher status and therefore systemic power. In this chapter, I build on the features of large firms and develop a power-based logic to contend

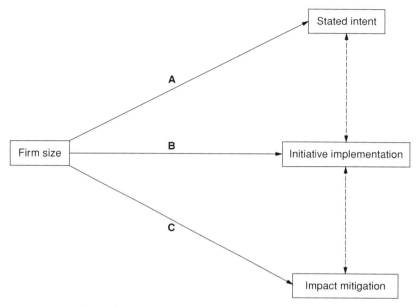

Figure 5.1 Relationships between firm size and corporate environmentalism.

that in more-monitored fields, large firms are more likely to seek symbolic performance but have more difficulty in maintaining symbolic gaps.

Hypothesis development

Figure 5.1 illustrates the relationships between firm size and three different dimensions of corporate environmentalism. The first is 'stated intent' – that is, environmental policies or corporate announcements that communicate a firm's intentions on environmental issues. The second is 'initiative implementation', wherein a firm invests in changing a particular process, product or organisational practice primarily for environmental reasons (e.g., it introduces a recycling scheme or collects environmental information from suppliers). The third dimension is 'impact mitigation', which captures measurable decreases in the substantive impact of the firm on the natural environment (e.g., emissions reductions, waste reductions or reduced energy use).[1] We can expect different effect sizes between firm size and each of these proactive responses within and between fields (i.e., the effect sizes A, B and C in Figure 5.1 are not equal). In the next section, I use decoupling and power arguments to predict when large firms are most likely to seek symbolic performance and can maintain symbolic gaps.

Symbolic performance

The quest for legitimacy has been shown to be a primary driver of proactive corporate environmentalism (Bansal 2005; Jennings and Zandbergen 1995). Larger organisations are likely to be subject to more intense public scrutiny and therefore more likely to signal responsiveness to institutional pressures (Pfeffer and Salancik 1978). Furthermore, dominant players in fields generate and protect symbolic performance, so we would expect large, high-status, established firms to seek to achieve social gains through audience-seeking activities and signalling conformity with social demands. As large firms navigate new institutional pressures, they generate new symbols to signal their conformity, including environmental policies (Henriques and Sadorsky 1996), codes of ethics (Stevens et al. 2005), certification schemes (Jiang and Bansal 2003), and industry voluntary agreements (King and Lenox 2000). These symbols are imbued with value by stakeholders seeking improved environmental performance and thus become legitimate and tradable green solutions. The largest firms are best positioned to use their status to gain symbolic performance through proactive corporate environmentalism because they are perceived as dominant players in a field (Bourdieu 2005).

Several empirical studies of industry self-regulation suggest a positive relationship between firm size and corporate environmentalism. Henriques and Sadorsky (1996), for example, argued that visible firms are more susceptible to public scrutiny or may be called on to act as industry leaders; therefore, they are more likely to possess environmental plans. Similarly, Sharma and Nguan (1999) suggested that larger firms are subject to greater media scrutiny and are forced to adopt a leadership stance on biodiversity conservation to protect their reputation. Hettige et al. (1996) argued that in local economies, large plants are more visible and therefore more susceptible to pressure for clean-up. In a contemporary variant, Delmas and Montes-Sancho (2010) argued that 'big players' – or the largest few firms in each market –

were more visible and therefore more likely to be early entrants into a voluntary environmental agreement.

These explanations for a positive relationship between firm size and proactive corporate environmentalism are based on symbolic performance and the potential effect on brand name and corporate reputation of negative environmental information (Konar and Cohen 1997). The search for legitimacy leads firms to abide by the rules, regulations and norms of the field of which they are a part (Dacin et al. 2007) and to shape their communications so as to demonstrate symbolic performance (Fuller and Tian 2006). Large firms seek to gain and maintain their symbolic performance by performing well in third-party environmental rankings, making positive environmental statements and being awarded environmental certifications (e.g., ISO 14001).

Large firms also are expected to be more proactive in corporate environmentalism because they may have more resources to devote to environmental issues (Russo and Fouts 1997; Sharma and Henriques 2005); they can draw on a broader range of relevant capabilities (Zhu et al. 2007); or they simply benefit from economies of scale in environmental investments (Gray and Deily 1996; Hettige et al. 1996). In larger firms, the investments required to develop symbolic performance in the environmental domain – whether based on changed business practices, new technologies or reporting on environmental issues in a new way – can be distributed across many activities. Larger firms thus are more likely to invest in symbolic performance through proactive corporate environmentalism or, stated differently:

Hypothesis 5.1: There is an overall positive relationship between firm size and proactive corporate environmentalism.

Symbolic gaps

As described previously, symbolic gaps arise from the difference between symbolic and substantive actions on a given issue, operationalised here as between stated intent on environmental issues and either the implementation of particular environmental initiatives or the mitigation of actual environmental impacts. The typical explanation for symbolic gaps is decoupling, in which new practices are adopted only ceremonially without corresponding action. Large firms face complex and conflicting demands from a range of stakeholders on environmental issues, leading them to not only be more likely to respond to institutional pressures but also to increasingly codify their responses (Meyer 2008; Meyer and Rowan 1977). Among firms that decide to adopt a new practice, the larger and more visible firms may be more inclined to conform symbolically to gain legitimacy but disinclined to change practices inside the firm (Westphal et al. 1997). Within the broader economy of esteem, large firms have lower audience-seeking costs and generally invest more in symbolic activities (see Chapter 4). Large firms cope with uncertainty about the efficiency of new organisational practices by decoupling and maintaining a symbolic gap.

Researchers have begun to focus attention on the potential for symbolic gaps in a range of corporate environmentalism contexts. For example, there is an apparent gap among the acquisition of the ISO 14001 certification symbol, implementation of the environmental management standard and actual environmental performance (Boiral 2007; Yin and Schmeidler 2009). Firms that join voluntary environmental programmes have been shown to be no more likely – and, in some cases, they may be less likely – to improve their environmental performance than non-members (Delmas and Montes-Sancho 2010; Rivera and de Leon 2004). Firms use impression management techniques to appear proactive on their website and in their annual reports to influence social evaluations, which may diverge from the substance of their actions (Bansal and Kistruck 2006; Laufer 2003). A core finding in this literature is that the motivation to be legitimate apparently affects the symbols of corporate environmentalism more than the substance of implementation or impact (Rhee and Lee 2003).

Thus, even if firm size is positively related with proactive corporate environmentalism, as captured by stated intent (see A in Figure 5.1), there is not necessarily a relationship between firm size and either the implementation of environmental initiatives (B) or the mitigation of environmental impact (C). I use decoupling to argue that large firms exhibit a symbolic gap, wherein the relationship between size and environmental proactivity is stronger for intended corporate environmentalism statements than for more action-oriented dimensions of corporate environmentalism (i.e., A > B and A > C). Thus:

Hypothesis 5.2: The positive relationship between firm size and proactive corporate environmentalism is moderated by the extent to which firm actions are substantive or symbolic; the relationship is stronger for symbolic stated intent than for substantive implementation or impact.

Symbolic performance across fields

Symbolic performance is valued differently across social systems or fields (Heugens and Lander 2009). To the extent that large firms attempt to gain and maintain symbolic performance through acceptable environmental strategies, we can expect the intensity of their environmental efforts to vary across fields. The question then becomes when, or in which fields, are large firms more or less likely to adopt proactive environmental strategies.

Visible firms experience a higher level of scrutiny from external constituents, which is one reason why visibility is such an important antecedent of organisational behavior (Delmas and Montes-Sancho 2010; Fiss and Zajac 2006). Signalling is most likely when there are active constituents such as third-party rating agencies, ENGOs, well-resourced regulatory agencies and activist shareholders to receive and interpret it. As discussed in Chapter 4, these actors play a key role in sharing information about green solutions. Monitoring is an important complementary asset that can increase the benefits of adopting green solutions to the next incremental adopter. Active stakeholders can directly share learning about green solutions and can underpin network externalities in diffusing green initiatives. Therefore, we expect more attempts to gain and maintain symbolic performance when individuals pay attention to corporate actions. Large, visible firms are more likely to seek and maintain symbolic performance on environmental issues where the potential for monitoring their behavior is high. This leads to the next hypothesis:

Hypothesis 5.3: The positive relationship between firm size and proactive corporate environmentalism is stronger in closely monitored fields.

Symbolic gaps across fields

Firms may gain symbolic performance through the adoption of symbols and language that are recognised and valued by community members. However, the value of this symbolic performance is maintained only as long as community members misrecognise the symbols – and the hierarchical system that produced them – as substance. The ability of large firms to maintain a symbolic gap – wherein the relationship between size and environmental proactivity is stronger for intended corporate environmentalism statements than for environmental impact mitigation (i.e., A > C in Figure 5.1) as hypothesised in H5.2 – will vary across fields. Because the benefits from symbolic gaps are threatened if the discrepancy is exposed, the question becomes: In which fields are symbolic gaps most likely to persist?

The most common answer from the decoupling literature is that symbolic gaps are more likely when there is widespread adoption of a new organisational practice as the new practice gains social legitimacy (Tolbert and Zucker 1983). Other explanations include the extent to which firms are connected with external networks and coalitions (Westphal and Zajac 2001), the stringency of stakeholder demands (Oliver 1991), and other organisational-level variables (Rhee and Lee 2003; Stevens et al. 2005). As responses to institutional pressures become standardised, it is increasingly likely that firms can disconnect their words and actions (Brunsson 2000; Jiang and Bansal 2003). According to this argument, symbolic gaps are most likely to persist in highly monitored fields because large firms cope with complex and conflicting institutional pressures by codifying their environmental responses.

A more power-based approach implies that symbolic gaps between words and actions are most likely when dominant players have the most power to shape the game. The same forces that drive decoupling – that is, contested environmental expectations of firms and uncertainties as to how to address them – are also likely to encourage misrecognition of corporate authority to define appropriate environmental strategies. Large firms are often the high-status, dominant players who seek to develop early voluntary agreement rules, environmental regulations and expectations (Delmas and Montes-Sancho 2010; Hoffman 1999). Given the potentially wide power disparity between large firms and their stakeholders, including regulatory agencies in some cases, there is strong potential for large firms to influence the rules of the new corporate environmentalism game. Large firms also have the resources to enable them to become politically engaged (Schuler and Rehbein 1997). Large, dominant firms 'have the capacity to set the tempo of transformation' (Bourdieu 2005: 202). This can extend beyond political lobbying to influencing which environmental problems are discussed in the public domain and the range of acceptable environmental solutions. These symbols are misrecognised as legitimate in a system that privileges the economic or corporate decision criterion (Ozbilgin and Tatli 2005).

Large firms can maintain symbolic gaps because of their high cultural literacy (Boiral 2007). They benefit from social prestige, mutual forbearance and limited rivalry (Mas-Ruiz and Ruiz-Moreno 2011), and they have the power to influence the accepted symbols of corporate environmentalism (Banerjee 2008). Large firms developed the 'beyond compliance' language in environmental policies, build and maintain voluntary codes of conduct, and often control the entry rules for industry environmental certifications and voluntary agreements (Hoffman 1999; Rivera and de Leon 2004). This effect can be reinforced as leaders in large firms interact with peers within the same high-status group, making them more likely to support one another's strategic positions (Mas-Ruiz and Ruiz-Moreno 2011). It is also strengthened because prestigious firms face relatively lower audience-seeking activity costs and invest more in symbolic green solutions, reinforcing their higher esteem.

As Oakes et al. (1998) noted, the most effective forms of power are those that are associated with little or no visible conflict. Thus, in less-monitored or less-mature fields, the large, high-status firms have higher power over the language and symbols of corporate environmentalism and can invent the grammar of their environmental response. Also, in less-mature heterogeneous fields, resources are dispersed – leading not only to symbolic bargaining to cope with conflicting demands but also to a wide power disparity between firms with high and low status. There is strong potential for high-status firms to influence the rules of the emerging environmental game in less-mature fields because there is an absence of strong monitoring, and stakeholders are actively complicit in accepting corporate solutions to environmental problems as legitimate. High-status firms can wield more institutional control through systemic power in less-monitored fields (Lawrence 2008). In more-monitored fields, monitoring such as shareholder actions and threatened regulatory attention on one firm can influence others in the field to improve their environmental performance (Reid and Toffel 2009).

The potential for large firms to manage the rules of the game and to maintain a symbolic gap is highest in less-monitored contexts, in which active complicity and misrecognition are high. Thus, we should expect the symbolic gap (i.e., A–C in Figure 5.1) to vary systematically, as follows:

Hypothesis 5.4: The moderating effect of the extent to which firms' actions are substantive or symbolic on the relationship between firm size and proactive corporate environmentalism is stronger in less-monitored fields.

Methods

I tested the hypotheses by meta-analysing existing research on the predictors of proactive corporate environmentalism. Testing all four hypotheses within one empirical study would place considerable demands on data collection: I would have needed to gather data on environmental stated intent, initiative implementation and impact mitigation on a large sample of companies across countries, industries and organisational locations during a sufficiently long period to capture issue maturity evolution. Instead, I followed Heugens and Lander's (2009) approach of conducting an across-field meta-analysis. To test H5.1 and H5.2, a research assistant[2] and I gathered all of the available evidence from the empirical corporate environmentalism studies and estimated the aggregate associations of firm size with different dimensions of proactive corporate environmentalism. We then analysed whether there were systematic differences in effect sizes across different data samples, which we assumed to be proxies for different types of fields (i.e., testing H5.3 and H5.4). Meta-analysis enabled us to deploy data from a wide range of fields because it is 'the statistical analysis of the summary findings of many empirical studies' (Glass and McGaw 1981: 21).

The criterion for inclusion in our study was 'any empirical paper which reported on the relationship between firm size and any aspect of proactive corporate environmentalism'. As I described previously, we used a broad interpretation of corporate environmentalism; therefore, our criterion yielded papers focusing on a range of green solutions including investing in specific initiatives, introducing general corporate environmental programmes, being adjudged to have a proactive corporate environmentalism according to third-party ratings, and reducing emissions. Our criterion did not require the firm size and corporate environmentalism relationship to be the main focus of the study;

rather, included papers merely reported on data pertaining to that focal relationship (Hunter and Schmidt 1982).

Meta-analytic techniques

Literature search and inclusion in analysis. We searched the Web of Science, ANBAR, Emerald, ABI Inform Global, JStor, Business Source Premier and Wiley Inter-Science journal indices for articles using the search terms *environmental, environmental performance, environmental responsiveness, green* and *size.* We then tried to partially overcome the 'file-drawer problem' (Glass and McGaw 1981) in which only positive results tend to be published. We sent emails to networks of scholars interested in environmental issues, asking if they had any published or unpublished work that might fit our criterion for inclusion. We sent these requests to the ONE, Social Issues in Management, Business Policy and Strategy, and Organisation and Management Theory listservs of the Academy of Management. In addition, we sent individual emails to all authors identified by our initial searches to solicit further potential articles. Finally, to identify any other conference papers, doctoral theses, or working papers, we searched the Social Science Research Network Working Paper database, author webpages, and the ProQuest Dissertations and Thesis database.

Our entire literature search process identified more than three hundred abstracts of studies that seemed to contain appropriate information. We required three pieces of information to evaluate each study for inclusion in our analysis: (1) some measure of corporate environmentalism, (2) some measure of firm size, and (3) a Pearson correlation coefficient between the two measures – or data that would allow us to calculate such a correlation (Hunter and Schmidt 1982). Corporate environmentalism and firm size often were seen as joint predictors of another variable (usually financial performance). Researchers typically did not specifically examine the relationship between corporate environmentalism and size (but see Darnall et al. 2010 for an exception); instead, size was included as a control variable as a conventional empirical research practice (see, e.g., Branzei et al. 2004, Delmas and Toffel 2008, and Phillipe and Durand 2011). The primary reasons for eliminating studies from our analysis were a lack of descriptive statistics and definitions that fell outside the criterion for inclusion in this study. Table 5.1 lists the studies included in our meta-analysis.

Table 5.1 *Studies included in the meta-analysis*

Study	Corporate environmentalism measure
Ahmed, Montagno, and Fireze (1998)	Intent
Baylis, Connell, and Flynn (1998)	Intent
Christmann (2004)	Intent
Craig and Dibrell (2006)	Intent
Menguc and Ozanne (2005)	Intent
Aragon-Correa (1998)	Implementation
Balabanis, Phillips, and Lyall (1998)	Implementation
Chan (2005)	Implementation
Christmann (2000)	Implementation
Christmann and Taylor (2001)	Implementation
Clemens (2006)	Implementation
Darnall (2006)	Implementation
Dasgupta, Hettige, and Wheeler (2000)	Implementation
Delmas, Russo, and Montes-Sancho (2007)	Implementation
Hartman, Huq, and Wheeler (1997)	Implementation
Judge and Elenkov (2005)	Implementation
Klassen (2000)	Implementation
Klassen and Vachon (2003)	Implementation
Martin-Tapia, Aragon-Correa, and Rueda-Manzanares (2010)	Implementation
Russo and Fouts (1997)	Implementation
Aravind and Christmann (2010)	Impact
Berchicci, Dowell, and King (2011)	Impact
Brammer and Pavelin (2006)	Impact
Clarkson et al. (2011)	Impact
Clarkson et al. (2008)	Impact
Cordiero and Sarkis (2008)	Impact
Kassinis and Vafeas (2009)	Impact
King and Lenox (2000)	Impact
King and Lenox (2002)	Impact
Konar and Cohen (2001)	Impact
Sharfman and Fernando (2008)	Impact
Sharma (2000)	Impact
Sharma, Aragon-Correa, and Rueda-Manzanares (2007)	Impact

Table 5.1 *(cont.)*

Study	Corporate environmentalism measure
Telle and Larsson (2007)	Impact
Brammer and Pavelin (2008)	Intent/implementation
Darnall and Edwards (2006)	Intent/implementation
Hitchens et al. (2003)	Intent/implementation
Judge and Douglas (1998)	Intent/implementation
Lee (2008)	Intent/implementation
King, Lenox, and Terlaak (2005)	Intent/impact
Klassen and Whybark (1999)	Implementation/impact
Branzei et al. (2004)	Intent/implementation/impact
Russo and Harrison (2005)	Intent/implementation/impact
Theyel (2000)	Intent/implementation/impact
Zhu, Sarkis, and Lai (2007)	Intent/implementation/impact

The effect size (i.e., Pearson correlation) reported in the studies varied from −0.22 to 0.46.[3]

Coding. We read and extracted data from the papers using several dimensions: basic identification details; study characteristics (i.e., main aim of study, base discipline, motivation for including size, and measure of corporate environmentalism); methodological characteristics (i.e., date of data collection, sample details, operationalisations used, analysis techniques used, and reliability of measures); and relevant results.

We found a wide range of proactive corporate environmentalism measures, including perceptual measures of environmental performance (see, e.g., Sharma 2000); the existence of corporate environmental policies (see, e.g., Henriques and Sadorsky 1996 and Russo and Fouts 1997); the implementation of environmental initiatives (see, e.g., Bowen 2000b, Klassen 2000, and Theyel 2000); voluntary participation in environmental schemes such as ISO (see, e.g., Potoski and Prakash 2005); and decreasing toxic emissions (see, e.g., King and Lenox 2000). My research assistant and I independently coded whether the corporate environmentalism measure was based on stated intent, implementation or impact according to the definitions outlined in the previous discussion about Figure 5.1 (see Table 5.1). We classified

this information based on the methods used in a paper, often refer-
ring to questionnaires or the precise wording of third-party rankings.
In some cases, studies incorporated more than one type of corporate
environmentalism measure (see, e.g., Branzei et al. 2004 and Russo
and Harrison 2005), in which case we separately recorded effect sizes
based on the different measurement types. In other cases, several published studies seemed to be based on the same underlying dataset (see,
e.g., Darnall, Henriques, and Sadorsky 2008 and Darnall, Seol, and
Sarkis 2009), in which case we recorded the relevant effect size only
once.

We were particularly concerned with asking empirically whether the
estimated effect size between firm size and corporate environmentalism differs across different datasets (i.e., fields) – particularly fields
that are relatively more or less monitored. We distinguished highly-
monitored from less-monitored fields based on national institutional
context, organisational level, issue centrality and issue maturity. The
two assessors coded each study separately, making judgements on the
field and issue context, as follows.

National institutional context. Corporate environmentalism is less
monitored in developing than in developed countries. In developing
countries, governments frequently do not give clear direction to environmental regulators, regulatory agencies lack the capacity to enforce
and monitor compliance with environmental regulations, broader
stakeholder pressures for environmental improvements are perceived
to be weak, and local industry associations encourage less environmental proactivity than in developed countries (Rivera 2010; Shah
and Rivera 2013). Auditing and certification practices can be weaker
in developing countries (Christmann and Taylor 2006). For both formal monitoring by regulatory agencies and informal monitoring by
environmental groups, the media and professional associations are
weaker in less-developed national institutional contexts (Hettige et al.
1996). We therefore can expect a bigger gap between the rhetoric and
reality of environmental strategy in developing countries (Rhee and
Lee 2003). We coded the national institutional context of each effect
size using the World Bank's definition of developed and developing
countries.

Organisational level. Corporate environmentalism is less monitored
at the subsidiary level than at the corporate level. Most environmental reporting and monitoring, including that required for socially
responsible investing, is conducted at the corporate rather than the

subsidiary level (Laufer 2003). The responsibility for developing, maintaining and protecting symbolic performance through environmental reports and industry-club membership related to environmental issues usually resides at the corporate level rather than at each subsidiary. We coded the organisational location of each effect size relative to whether the sample was based exclusively on entire firms (i.e., the corporate level) or on plants/subsidiaries of firms (i.e., the subsidiary level) (Bowen 2000a).

Issue centrality. Corporate environmentalism is monitored more in fields in which environmental issues exhibit high centrality, such as the chemicals and resource-extraction industries, than in other industries. Burke and Logsdon (1996) defined centrality as a measure of the closeness of fit between a corporate social policy or programme and the firm's mission and objectives. When environmental issues are highly central to a firm's activities, we can expect more stakeholder and regulatory attention to environmental concerns (Chatterji and Toffel 2010; Reid and Toffel 2009) and more attempts to protect a firm's environmental reputation (Halme and Huse 1997; Phillipe and Durand 2011). It is difficult to achieve legitimacy through purely symbolic actions in stronger institutional fields such as highly polluting industries (Berrone and Gomez-Mejia 2009). Furthermore, service industries with low issue centrality are 'informationally opaque' in the sense that their responsiveness is difficult to monitor (Ramchander, Schwebach, and Staking 2011). We coded the issue centrality of each effect size relative to whether the sample was based on a high- or low-pollution industry (Halme and Huse 1997).

Issue maturity. Corporate environmentalism is more stringently monitored by experienced stakeholders in mature fields. A firm's environmental strategies evolve and change with altering coercive, mimetic and normative pressures (Bansal 2005; Hoffman 1999). Industry norms and values evolve over time, changing what are considered acceptable activities and bringing in new incentives for appropriate behaviour (Delmas, Russo, and Montes-Sancho 2007). As environmental issues mature as a legitimate concern for firms, environmental performance becomes more salient and increasing numbers of firms are drawn into the corporate environmentalism decision domain (Bansal 2005). Furthermore, the extent of monitoring by third-party rating agencies (e.g., KLD Research and Analytics, Inc.) expands over time, and firms that were poorly rated in the past attempt to improve their environmental impact (Chatterji and Toffel 2010). We coded each effect size for issue maturity relative to whether the sample was based on 'early' data collected before 2000 or 'late' data collected after 2002. This cut-off date was somewhat arbitrary but we used it because there were no effect sizes for 2001 (and, hence, a convenient gap between studies). Experimenting with other dates did not significantly change the results.

We also coded for three study artefacts: (1) the measure of firm size, (2) whether a study was published or unpublished, and (3) whether the study relied on a large sample (defined as more than one standard deviation above the mean sample size). The studies included in the meta-analysis spanned a range of both developing and developed countries (e.g., the United States, Canada, China, Brazil, Bulgaria, Norway, and South Korea) as well as industries (e.g., forestry, chemical, petrochemical, electricity, and manufacturing); however, not all studies focused on a single country or industry. We coded studies that had only unambiguous information on moderators rather than forcing all studies into a subgroup.

Meta-analysis procedure. We conducted the meta-analysis in accordance with guidelines provided by Hunter and Schmidt (1990) and Lipsey and Wilson (2001). This is an effect-size meta-analysis technique that corrects for sampling and measurement error. The main statistics required to undertake the analysis are the Pearson correlation coefficient of the relationship (r) and the number in the sample (n). Our results are based on 70 effect sizes gathered from within 45 studies, with a total sample size of more than 85,000.

We calculated the 95 per cent confidence and credibility intervals for each analysis. Confidence intervals are a familiar method for estimating the extent to which sampling error remains in the weighted effect size, and they can be interpreted using significance-testing methods. Credibility intervals, conversely, indicate whether moderators are operating, which in turn indicates whether the population should be categorised into subgroups (Whitener 1990). We followed Hunter and Schmidt (2004), who argued that credibility intervals are more important than confidence intervals in meta-analysis, and we based our inferences primarily on credibility intervals.

We conducted moderator analyses in three basic ways. First, we calculated the Q statistic, which is an index of how much variability there is within the results (Hunter and Schmidt 1990; Sagie and Koslowsky 1993). Significant Q statistics indicate the possible presence

Table 5.2 *Meta-analysis overall results*

	K	N	Mean r	95% Confidence interval		95% Credibility interval		Q
				Low	High	Low	High	
All studies	70	86,757	0.02	0.01	0.04	−0.16	0.20	0.00
Corporate environmentalism measure								
Stated intent	16	11,326	0.13	0.07	0.18	−0.07	0.33	0.00
Initiative implementation	28	5,247	0.10	0.03	0.17	−0.24	0.44	0.00
Impact mitigation	26	70,184	−0.01	−0.03	0.02	−0.11	0.10	0.00

K = number of effect sizes.
N = total sample size across all included effect sizes.
Mean r = sample-size weighted Pearson correlation coefficient across included effect sizes.

of moderators. We then developed meta-analytic summary data for each moderator subgroup (see Table 5.2) and examined the credibility intervals. Wide credibility intervals that include zero indicated that moderators are likely, which impacted the effect-size estimate (Sagie and Koslowsky 1993; Whitener 1990). However, a more precise method of statistical analysis is weighted least squares multiple regression (Steel and Kammeyer-Mueller 2002). Consequently, we weighted each moderator analysis by sample size in a two-stage multiple regression analysis. In the first stage, we controlled for study artefacts, field context and the measure of corporate environmentalism used. In the second stage, we entered the appropriate interaction effects, determining if they explained significant incremental variance.

Results

Table 5.2 shows the overall findings of the meta-analysis by categorising each effect size according to whether the data related to corporate environmentalism as stated intent, initiative implementation or impact mitigation. The overall relationship between firm size and environmental strategy, which includes all of the effect sizes available, is weak but positive (r = 0.02) and significantly differs from zero at the 95 per cent confidence interval (0.01–0.04).

Table 5.2 shows that studies were distributed across the three different dimensions of corporate environmentalism (i.e., K = 16 for intent, K = 28 for implementation, and K = 26 for impact), demonstrating that there is adequate coverage of effect-size data across the three dimensions. Of note, however, is the average sample size within each type of study, which ranges from 187 for implementation-based effect sizes to 708 for intent-based studies to a high of 2,700 for impact-based studies. This range reflects data availability for the different dimensions – particularly the dominance of impact studies based on Toxic Release Inventory data from the US Environmental Protection Agency (EPA). Based on the confidence intervals, we found support for H5.1's positive relationship between firm size and corporate environmentalism for the dimensions of stated intent (r = 0.13) and implementation (r = 0.10) but not for impact (r = −0.01). We also found support for H5.2, in that the relationship between firm size and proactive stated intent (r = 0.13) is significantly stronger than between firm size and mitigating environmental impact (r = −0.01).

However, the more interesting result was the credibility intervals, which are wide and include zero for all three dimensions; this indicates that the effect size between firm size and each dimension of corporate environmentalism may vary from negative to strongly positive. This variability provided the impetus to test our hypotheses on how the effect size between firm size and corporate environmentalism is influenced by the strength of monitoring in different fields.

Table 5.3 shows the results of our weighted least squares analysis of the 70 effect sizes, each weighted according to sample size. Model 4 shows significantly smaller effect sizes between firm size and corporate environmentalism for studies measuring impact mitigation than in the base case of stated intent. This adds further support for H5.2, which predicted a stronger effect of firm size on symbolic stated intent than on substantive impact.

H5.3 predicted that the positive relationship between firm size and proactive corporate environmentalism is stronger in closely monitored fields. The field-context variables in Table 5.3 show support across the models for smaller effect sizes in studies undertaken in developing compared with developed countries as well as for studies based at

Table 5.3 *Meta-analytic weighted least squares analysis results*

Model number	1	2	3	4	5	6	7
Constant	.08**	.13*	.11†	.14**	.11*	.08	.08†
	(.03)	(.05)	(0.05)	(0.05)	(.05)	(.05)	(.05)
Study artefacts							
Size measure: output	−.00	−.04	−.04	−.01	−.04	.02	−.00
	(.04)	(.05)	(.05)	(.04)	(.04)	(.05)	(.06)
Publication status:	−.00	−.01	−.01	.02	−.02	.07	.06
Unpublished	(.06)	(.06)	(.06)	(.06)	(.06)	(.07)	(.07)
Sample size:	−.08*	−.10*	−.08†	−.04	−.08*	−.05	−.06
Large sample	(.04)	(.04)	(.05)	(.05)	(.05)	(.07)	(.07)
Field context							
National institutional		−.09	−.10	−.11†	−.16†	−.14*	−.33*
context: developing		(.07)	(.07)	(.07)	(.09)	(.06)	(.14)
Organizational level:		−.07*	−.08*	−.05	−.10†	.06	−.01
subsidiary		(.03)	(.03)	(.04)	(.05)	(.05)	(.10)
Issue centrality: high		.02	.02	.04	.019	.02	.03
pollution		(.71)	(.05)	(.05)	(.05)	(.07)	(.12)
Issue maturity: later studies		.01	.02	.05	.037	.05	.14
		(.04)	(.05)	(.05)	(.06)	(.05)	(.09)
Corporate environmentalism measure							
Implementation			.04				
			(.05)				
Impact				−.13**			
				(.04)			
Interactions							
Implementation ×					.07		.29†
developing country					(.12)		(.11)
Implementation ×					.13		.05
subsidiary level					(.08)		(.11)
Implementation × high					−.01		.01
pollution					(.10)		(.14)
Implementation × later					−.01		−.13
studies					(.07)		(.09)
Impact × developing						.09	.26
country						(.15)	(.19)
Impact × subsidiary level						−.26**	−.20†
						(.08)	(.11)
Impact × high pollution						.03	.03
						(.09)	(.14)
Impact × later studies						−.04	−.13
						(.06)	(.09)
K	70	70	70	70	70	70	70
Adjusted R square	.06	.10	.11	.22	.15	.29	.33
F (sig)	1.40	1.02	.96	2.12*	.94	2.19*	1.97*

[a] All coefficients are unstandardised. Numbers in parentheses are standard errors.

† p < 0.10; * p < 0.05; ** p < 0.01.

the subsidiary rather than the corporate level. H5.3 is not supported for high- compared with low-pollution industries or for later studies compared with earlier studies. Thus, H5.3 seems to be supported only when monitoring strength is based on field-level characteristics (i.e., national institutional context and organisational location) and not for issue-level characteristics (i.e., issue centrality and maturity). This was a surprising finding that requires further exploration.

The interaction effects in Table 5.3 were designed to test H5.4: that is, the symbolic gap between stated intent and either initiative implementation or mitigation impact is larger in less-monitored fields. Consistent with our finding on H5.2, we did not find systematic evidence for symbolic gaps for the implementation dimension (i.e., no significant coefficients on implementation interaction effects). Also consistent with our findings on H5.3, we did not find evidence for symbolic gaps based on issue-level characteristics (i.e., no significant coefficients on issue centrality or maturity interaction effects). However, we did find support for H5.4 when symbolic gaps were based on the impact dimension, particularly at the subsidiary level. Thus, symbolic gaps between stated intent and impact mitigation are wider at the less-monitored subsidiary level.

Discussion and implications

The results show broad support for our predictions that large firms seek symbolic performance through proactive corporate environmentalism. Our results showed that large firms exhibit a symbolic gap, wherein the relationship between size and corporate environmentalism is stronger for intended statements than for substantive environmental impact mitigation. The extent to which large firms seek symbolic performance and maintain symbolic gaps is moderated by the extent of monitoring within fields.

Our findings confirmed decoupling expectations of the existence of symbolic gaps but extended contemporary explanations of when symbolic gaps persist. This analysis advances emerging findings about ceremonial adoption in environmental strategies (see, e.g., Boiral 2007 and Laufer 2003) and when organisations decouple (cf. Boxenbaum and Jonsson 2008). The meta-analysis confirms that it does matter whether we measure corporate environmentalism along intent-, implementation- or impact-based dimensions.

This study also made three extensions to the basic decoupling argument. First, the findings indicate that the gap between symbolic and substantive responses is moderated by firm size: that is, large firms are more likely than small firms to state a symbolic responsive intent but are no more likely to substantively mitigate their impact. This effect was included as a control variable in some studies (see, e.g., Westphal et al. 1997) but so far has been held as a widespread assumption rather than a robust empirical finding. The finding provides initial support for one of the core arguments of this book: larger, more powerful firms are more likely to exert their discretionary power to drive a wedge between symbolic and substantive green solutions. This finding also suggests that the generation of substantive and symbolic green solutions is driven by different factors. It turns out that firm size is a determinant of only symbolic and not substantive green solutions.

Second, this analysis expanded the more typical two categories of 'espoused' and 'implemented' (Fiss and Zajac 2006), 'rhetoric' and 'reality' (Rhee and Lee 2003), or 'adoption' and 'implementation' (Kennedy and Fiss 2009) in responses to institutional pressures to the three categories: intent, implementation and impact.[4] The effect sizes between firm size and implementing green solutions differed significantly from substantive impact mitigation but did not differ from stated strategic intent. This finding implies that the likelihood of large firms responding through initiative implementation is closer to symbolic intent than to actual substantive impact. Thus, the findings add weight to recent decoupling research that reminds us that the process of implementation itself may be symbolic (Boiral 2007; Christmann and Taylor 2006) and not the end point in the institutionalisation process (cf. Fiss and Zajac 2006 and Kennedy and Fiss 2009). These findings also reinforce my contention in Chapter 4 that it may be easier for firms to move the private cost curve for symbolic rather than substantive green solutions and that this may be a natural outcome of profit-maximising strategic corporate environmentalism (see Figure 4.2). We need a more nuanced understanding of proactive corporate environmentalism: we must focus more attention not only on whether firms adopt 'beyond compliance' strategies but also on whether and how they are implementing them symbolically (Bromley and Powell 2012; Delmas and Montes-Sancho 2010; Philippe and Durand 2011).

Third, this analysis extended conventional decoupling arguments by giving more attention to power dynamics within fields. For example, Lawrence (2008) encouraged more consideration of 'institutional side effects'. Decoupling proactive corporate environmentalism implies (1) less environmental improvement than might be expected based on stated corporate intentions, or (2) a negative side effect on the natural environment and vulnerable people who might rely on threatened natural resources. Using a power-based logic questions who has the systemic power to gain from decoupling and how this might explain persistent symbolic gaps. We know that less-monitored firms with greater discretionary power are more likely to disconnect proactive strategic intent from implementation actions (Philippe and Durand 2011) and that decoupling can protect local power relationships (Bromley and Powell 2012). Large firms have the misrecognised authority to define acceptable responsiveness as proactive environmental intent rather than impact. Large firms are more likely to adopt symbolic green solutions, setting the norms for other less-prestigious firms to follow. Explanations for symbolic gaps change as we focus more attention on the misrecognition of the symbolic power and status of large firms. I present a deeper analysis of this phenomenon in Chapter 6.

Standard institutional arguments suggest that early adopters do so for efficiency reasons, whereas late adopters are more likely to maintain symbolic gaps as they try to gain social legitimacy (Tolbert and Zucker 1983). Kennedy and Fiss (2009) countered this logic by showing that the lines between efficiency and legitimacy logics are not so clear. I took a different approach and linked decoupling at the firm level with power at the field level. I argued that not only are large firms more likely to adopt symbolic green solutions to gain legitimacy but also that they are the high-status, dominant players in developing institutional responses and expectations. Large firms seek legitimacy by gaining and maintaining symbolic performance; they also can use their status, credibility and connections to shape the rules of the game and protect symbolic gaps between their intentions and substantive performance, particularly in less-mature monitoring contexts. Thus, in early periods, large firms have the latitude to design the symbols of their response. We saw in Chapter 2 that in the early days of environmental awareness, firms such as Chevron gained reputational benefits from environmental advertising campaigns that today would be

dismissed as greenwashing. In later periods, as monitoring intensi-
fies, the symbolic gap between the propensity of large firms to state
proactive intentions and their impacts is less socially sustainable. The
more monitored the field, the more that large visible firms are held
accountable for their actions and not their words and the less valuable
is symbolic performance. This might explain the intriguing strategy
among large firms of addressing substantive institutional pressures
without communicating about these new organisational practices (Fiss
and Zajac 2006). This effect is more likely in highly monitored fields.
However, as discussed in the shift from greenwashing to symbolic
corporate environmentalism (see Chapter 2), closing obvious gaps is
relatively easy compared with the more nuanced task of identifying and
exposing costly, misrecognised symbolic aspects of everyday activities.

The meta-analytic research design enabled me to include empirical
data across fields by accumulating effect sizes from many different
types of datasets. This enabled the exploration of symbolic performance and symbolic gaps at a relatively ignored level of analysis: that
is, across fields. Institutional theorists typically conduct agentic studies
at the individual or organisational level and non-agentic studies at the
field, industry or national level of analysis (Boxenbaum and Jonsonn
2008). This chapter shows an agentic study at the cross-field level by
looking at effect sizes across many organisational fields. An advantage of this approach is that meta-analytic techniques can be deployed
as a method to test previously untested hypotheses rather than only
to aggregate other research studies (Heugens and Lander 2009). This
raised the level of analysis from the firm-level preferred by conventional corporate environmental researchers to the field level preferred
by the critical view.

However, this method is based on the key assumption that each
effect size is indeed drawn from an identifiable field. Clearly, this
method departs from contemporary definitions of fields as defined by
issues rather than by industry classification codes (Wooten and Hoffman 2008). Each effect size in the meta-analysis did not include all
'organisations that partake of a common meaning system and whose
participants interact more frequently and fatefully with one another
than with actors outside the field' (Scott 1995: 56) as would be required
in domain-based definitions of fields. The samples within the meta-
analysis were drawn from populations of firms and did not typically

include other actors within a given field, such as NGOs, professional organisations, regulators and the media. Instead, I adopted a more relational conception of a field (Wooten and Hoffman 2008) and focused on the relative status of organisations within a given social population (Bourdieu and Passeron 1977). Schuler (1996) showed that it may be a firm's relative rather than absolute size that predicts its political activity. Meta-analysis was an appropriate empirical technique for these across-field hypotheses because in any given sample, larger firms tend to have higher social evaluations within the sampled firms (Fombrun and Shanley 1990). This permits the examination of how firm size drives corporate environmentalism across different contexts.

The findings also suggest contingencies related to corporate environmentalism researchers' conventional use of size as a control variable in predicting proactive corporate environmentalism (cf. Branzei et al. 2004 and Delmas and Toffel 2008). Given the paucity of large-sample corporate environmentalism and performance data, it is understandable why researchers routinely include firm size as a control variable. However, this meta-analysis shows that including firm size in all types of corporate environmentalism studies is misleading. This evidence suggests that firm size predicts corporate environmentalism only for intent- and implementation-based dimensions of greening. Future research should control for size only in studies of predictors of symbolic green solutions. Firm size may be irrelevant for predicting substantive green solutions that, after all, are driven by the costs and benefits of the green solutions available (see Chapter 3).

Empirical summary

My answer to the first empirical question posed in this chapter – Does separating symbolic from substantive performance provide different answers about the drivers of corporate environmentalism in large powerful firms? – is 'yes'. The results suggest that larger firms are more likely to attempt to gain and maintain symbolic performance by announcing proactive corporate environmentalism intent in an attempt to gain legitimacy, but they are not more likely to achieve substantive environmental improvements. I also asked: When can symbolic gaps persist between the likelihood that large firms will adopt corporate environmentalism through proactive strategic intent, implementation or impact? The results indicate support for the power of large firms to shape the rules of the game in less-monitored fields. Evidence for such persistent symbolic gaps is a cautionary tale for stakeholders seeking to influence corporate environmentalism who might misinterpret symbolic green solutions as substantive environmental improvement. I argue that large firms can separate their words and actions on environmental issues based on a decoupling logic at the firm level and systemic power at the field level. Large firms may attempt to gain social legitimacy through symbolic performance and decoupling. However, symbolic gaps can persist only when large firms have sufficient systemic power for field members not to question the difference between symbol and substance.

Corporate environmental strategy and the social energy penalty

This chapter focuses on the role of powerful firms in driving symbolic performance and symbolic gaps in proactive environmental strategies. Although the analysis accumulated evidence across many different research studies on one of the drivers of symbolic gaps, I did not address what the consequences of these gaps might be. What do these findings tell us about the social costs and benefits of corporate environmental strategy?

Figure 5.2 illustrates the difference between more- and less-monitored fields in the social energy penalty model introduced in Chapter 4. In less-monitored fields, the social benefit curve is smoother and reaches its limit at a lower level. There is less potential for network externalities because less-monitored fields lack the complementary assets of stakeholder knowledge and awareness that drive the need for standardised self-regulatory schemes. Cumulative adoption does not generate substantial additional benefits to adopting the self-regulatory practice unless there is an audience to legitimise it. Furthermore, there is less force exerted by regulatory agencies, and less intense NGO or media attention driving institutionalisation in less-monitored fields. Less attention means that firms can gain less benefit from sheltering within self-regulatory schemes. Lower monitoring weakens the demand for green solutions and decelerates diffusion.

The net result of a smoother and lower social benefit curve is that the social energy penalty outweighs the potential benefits of standardising green solutions at a relatively lower level of cumulative output

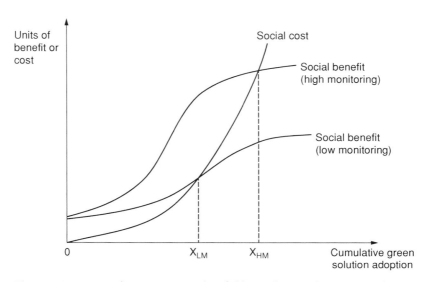

Figure 5.2 Impact of monitoring within fields on the social energy penalty.

(i.e., X_{LM} instead of X_{HM} in Figure 5.2). All else being equal, the social energy penalty is likely to be more of a problem in less-monitored than in more-monitored institutional fields. It is worth noting that this is the case even when firms do not deliberately exert their power over voluntary self-regulation schemes (i.e., when the social cost curve remains the same). Even if firms do not exercise their discretionary power to limit the supply of greening solutions, the point at which the social energy penalty outweighs social benefits is farther to the left for less-monitored fields. Thus, even advocates from the conventional view of corporate environmentalism should seriously consider the potential for social losses from self-regulation in less-monitored fields. The higher likelihood of a social energy penalty should not be ignored simply because it is an unintended consequence of profit maximisation. Control over green solutions generates symbolic gaps and for large, powerful firms, the best strategic approach may be to exploit them if monitoring is weak.

Advancing the power-based arguments, we might expect the social cost curve to be steeper than shown in Figure 5.2. As discussed in Chapter 4, the steepness of the cost curve is primarily a function of the discretionary behaviour of powerful firms. If large firms strategically exert their systemic power, then the social energy penalty might outweigh social benefit at cumulative adoption levels even farther to the left of X_{LM}. Symbolic gaps are most likely when dominant players have the most power to shape the game. All else being equal, the social energy penalty is likely to be more of a problem when powerful firms choose to exercise that power – regardless of the extent of monitoring within a field.

Thus, the social energy penalty can become harmful at lower levels of cumulative adoption of voluntary environmental strategies in less-monitored fields and when powerful firms exploit their systemic power – regardless of the state of monitoring in the field. This begs the question of when and how powerful actors can exert this discretionary power. It is to that question that I turn in the next chapter.

6 | Study 2: Pollution control technology and the production of symbolic capital

Firms engage in corporate environmentalism to the extent that consumers and other stakeholders reward them for doing so. Some rewards may be in the form of economic performance, such as increased profit, revenue or growth. But firms also use green solutions to gain symbolic performance in the sense of positive social evaluations. If we are to understand the market for green solutions, then we must look beyond strictly financial assets to consider the value of all forms of capital. An economist's definition of *capital* usually includes financial or other assets that can be invested along with other factors of production to generate a return. Sociologists, however, have a broader view of *capital*: 'all the goods, material and symbolic, without distinction, that present themselves as *rare* and worthy of being sought after in a particular social formation – which may be "fair words" or smiles, handshakes or shrugs, compliments of attention, challenges or insults, honour or honours, powers or pleasures, gossips or scientific information, distinction or distinctions, etc.' (Bourdieu 1995: 178; emphasis in the original). Although conventional corporate environmentalism scholars are familiar with financial, human and – increasingly – the social dimensions of capital, so far, too little attention has been given to symbolic capital. Corporate environmentalism researchers examine green signals to understand firm reputation and symbols to identify legitimacy, but they have neglected symbolic capital as an indicator of the role of status in greening (see Chapter 3, Table 3.2).

Firms seek symbolic performance by producing cultural symbols. Environmental reporting standards, eco-labels, new technologies, green buildings and job titles are all cultural symbols intended to demonstrate a firm's credibility on environmental issues. Each of these activities has both a material and a symbolic component. The material components of environmental activities are largely within a firm's control because managers design, select and implement green solutions.

However, symbolic meanings evolve within the relational dynamics of a field. Cultural symbols are valuable as signifiers of firm symbolic performance only when others in the field recognise the symbols as valuable. If a symbol is recognised based on the status of the actors who promote it, then the symbol can possess symbolic capital – which, in turn, distinguishes firms associated with it. For example, a new sustainability rating scheme promoted by Dow Jones Indexes (DJI) is imbued with symbolic capital because of the prestige of DJI as the pre-eminent stock exchange index, which in turn is valuable to firms that participate in it. As another example, HSBC's new group headquarters can earn symbolic capital for the firm because it has been awarded an 'Excellent' Building Research Establishment Environmental Assessment Method (BREEAM) rating and because it was designed by the prestigious architect, Lord Norman Foster.

Due to the link between symbolic capital and status, symbolic capital is likely to be most relevant when firms use it to indicate their authority. In Chapter 4, I described 'status' as a 'virtual controller' of firms' environmental decisions. Maintaining power and status shapes managers' decisions but does not directly motivate them unless the usual order comes under threat. However, if firms detect that their discretion on environmental issues is being questioned, they may exert their status as powerful social actors to control the green solutions available. One way they do this is by voluntarily investing in a green solution and ensuring that there is sufficient investment in the shared meanings and representations surrounding that solution to maintain their own high status. If firms can surround a green solution with sufficient symbolic capital, then their authority to define that solution as a legitimate environmental response will not be questioned by stakeholders.

The core question in this chapter is: When and how can actors exert discretionary power over the production of green solutions? The answer, it turns out, is when the field structure allows them the systemic power to generate cultural symbols and when others grant these symbols to be credible indicators of environmental performance. I base the analysis on emerging research that applies Bourdesian analysis to the firm strategy context (see, e.g., Emirbayer and Johnson 2008, Gomez 2010, and Vaughan 2008). Bourdieu explained choices within firms as influenced by the construction, distribution and competition for different forms of capital – that is, economic, social and cultural – across individuals and social field positions (Ozbilgin and Tatli 2005).

A key insight within Bourdieu's approach is that new cultural symbols are most valuable when others in the social field accept that they are legitimate responses to institutional pressures. Constructed cultural symbols can attribute honour, reputation or prestige to individuals or groups, particularly in the view of others in the field who recognise the unequal distribution of power in the field as legitimate (Bourdieu and Thompson 1991). Produced cultural symbols can be granted as a form of symbolic capital, which is a unique form of capital in that it is misrecognised by those who do not see the power structures that construct it (Bourdieu 1990). Symbolic capital is valuable because the context within which it is associated has prestige, whether or not that prestige is warranted.

Explanations of corporate environmentalism so far have under-played the competition for symbolic capital – that is, how actors in powerful positions within a field construct, maintain and manipulate cultural symbols in order to be granted legitimacy by less powerful others (Bourdieu and Nice 1984). This chapter describes how framing corporate investments in green solutions as competition for symbolic capital can enrich our understanding of investments in pollution control technologies. In Chapter 5, I use firm size as a proxy for power within an organisational field; in this chapter, I delve into field structures to explain discretionary power within fields by applying a Bourdesian analysis to the firm context (see, e.g., Emirbayer and Johnson 2008, Gomez 2010, and Vaughan 2008). The chapter extends this new Bourdesian strategy literature by (1) operationalising the types of cultural symbols produced by high-status actors through corporate environmentalism; and (2) providing preliminary evidence on how some firms produce and others grant symbolic capital within a field surrounding a pollution control technology. This is also one of the first empirical studies of CCS demonstration projects, which comprise a new set of technologies designed to radically reduce CO_2 emissions from industrial facilities.

I begin by describing how our understanding of investing in pollution control technology as a strategic response to institutional pressures can be usefully recast as competition for symbolic capital. I then describe the empirical context and methodological approach. The analysis focuses on the types of cultural symbols that firms produce within an emerging and controversial context, the forms of symbolic capital granted by other actors within the field, and the social outcomes of this competition. I argue that the CCS demonstration projects possess symbolic capital because they are produced by high-status firms and granted misplaced legitimacy by others in the field. Casting pollution control technologies within a competition for symbolic capital reveals a social energy penalty on society. I conclude by developing contingencies related to when and how powerful actors can exert discretionary power, as well as discussing the implications for the social energy penalty.

Pollution control technologies and the competition for symbolic capital

Pollution control is the least proactive type of corporate environmentalism (Hart 1995). It includes environmental technologies wherein 'emissions and effluents are trapped, stored, treated, and disposed of using pollution-control equipment' (Hart 1995: 992). Pollution control involves adding 'operations or equipment to the end of an existing manufacturing process, thereby leaving the original product and process virtually unaltered' (Klassen and Whybark 1999). These technologies are widely regarded as costly and inefficient because the necessary investments involve expensive and nonproductive 'end-of-pipe' pollution-abatement equipment (Aragon-Correa 1998; Russo and Fouts 1997). Pollution control investments have the potential to limit the substantive environmental impacts of a company's current activities on the natural environment but have the least potential to underpin an adopting firm's competitive advantage.

Given that pollution control is a costly green solution with little scope to gain competitive benefits, the question becomes: Why would managers choose to voluntarily adopt them? The answer lies in the potential for pollution control investments to demonstrate a firm's legitimacy on environmental issues. We know that some green solutions will be costly and are adopted only to maintain social legitimacy (Bansal and Roth 2000; Okereke 2007). This may be the case particularly with voluntary CO_2 emission reduction investments. Although there may be win-win opportunities from carbon management innovation within the overall economic system (Stern 2007), incumbent carbon-intensive firms may face substantial costs during the transition to a low-carbon economy (Helm and Hepburn 2009). The primary reasons why such incumbent firms would voluntarily adopt pollution control investments are to signal awareness of CO_2 emission reduction concerns and to gain symbolic performance.

Pollution control may be expensive for individual firms. But from a regulator's point of view, it may be better to encourage pollution control than no green solutions at all. Although governments may not mandate pollution control investments, they may encourage them through incentives such as project subsidies. Public subsidies for pollution control technology typically are positioned as a solution to market failure: governments provide funds to stimulate innovation, productivity and ultimately economic growth. However, such public investment can be a double-edged sword. Choosing technological winners early can be useful as a way to scale up incremental improvements of existing technologies (Hargadon 2010) but also can worsen lock-in to the current technological system (Unruh 2000; Vergragt, Markusson, and Karlsson 2011). Individual firms can benefit from being the 'chosen ones' and therefore have an incentive to position themselves and their technologies as legitimate solutions to a public policy problem. Given the mixed incentives and uncertainty surrounding new energy technologies, we should expect symbolic and legitimacy-seeking behaviour around pollution control investments – even when the technology also might deliver substantive environmental improvements.

Similar to all green solutions, subsidised technology investments have a symbolic component. Managers may be unsure about which action to take and therefore decide to participate in a government-supported voluntary scheme to show that they are 'doing something'. Institutional theory is useful here because it emphasises how a search for legitimacy leads firms to abide by the rules, regulations and norms of the field of which they are a part (Dacin et al. 2007). However, as discussed in Chapter 5, competition for legitimacy does not occur on a level playing field because high-status firms have the systemic power to shape which symbols and technologies are considered legitimate within a given field (Deephouse and Suchman 2008). Once new cultural symbols are established, the symbols continue to define what is deemed legitimate and they can exert considerable institutional control (Lawrence 2008).

A promising way to inject power into the competition for legitimacy relative to pollution control investments is to revisit the writings of French sociologist Pierre Bourdieu (see, e.g., Bourdieu 1990, 1995, and 2005). Bourdieu highlighted how the search for legitimacy leads dominant organisations to use their capital endowment and privileged field position to demonstrate and produce cultural symbols and to use their authority to benefit from symbolic capital. Dominant organisations wield their systemic power to produce and reproduce symbolic power that resides in words, language and symbols valued by field members (Bourdieu and Thompson 1991). Once established, these symbols become a form of symbolic capital that is 'misrecognised' as legitimate responses to institutional pressures because the systemic power that privileges high-status organisations is invisible. As discussed in Chapter 5, as firms navigate new stakeholder pressures, they generate new cultural symbols – including codes of ethics, environmental policies and certification schemes – to signal their institutional conformity. These symbols are imbued with value by stakeholders seeking improved environmental performance and thus become a legitimate and protectable form of symbolic capital.

Given the importance placed on legitimacy-seeking corporate behaviour in neo-institutional theory, it is surprising that so little attention has focused on symbolic capital. In rare exceptions, Oakes et al. (1998) illustrated the importance of symbolic capital in their analysis of business planning in cultural organisations, and MacLean, Harvey, and Chia (2010) analysed the power of corporate directors, showing how individuals' symbolic capital helped them ascend to the pinnacle of corporations in the United Kingdom and France. Ezzamel and Burns (2005) also used symbolic capital at the individual level in their investigation of competition between finance managers and buyers/merchandisers in implementing a new control system. Zeitlyn (2003) used symbolic capital to understand how participating in the 'open source movement' enhanced the reputation of software developers. Fuller and Tian (2006) shifted the production of symbolic capital from the individual level to the firm level and suggested that it may have a role in firm-level corporate social responsibility strategy. However, the production and reproduction of cultural symbols by firms, as opposed to individuals, has not yet been operationalised coherently. We need a systematic way to describe the types of cultural capital that firms produce and reproduce within emerging social fields. This could help us to understand how powerful firms generate symbolic capital and performance.

The aim of this chapter is to explore data from a pollution control empirical context to shed light on (1) which cultural symbols are generated by powerful actors surrounding voluntary pollution control technologies, (2) who grants these cultural symbols as symbolic capital, and (3) when can we expect the social energy penalty costs for those environmental technologies to be highest? To answer these questions, I investigate how dominant organisations produce cultural symbols and how others grant symbolic capital within the emerging and socially controversial field of CCS demonstration projects.

I present findings from a discourse analysis of more than 1,200 publicly available documents that mention CCS demonstration projects both planned and underway in the United States, Australia, Canada and the European Union, to which approximately US$7.5 billion of public money has been committed. CCS is an intriguing research context because of the substantial reduction in CO_2 emissions that the technology potentially could deliver in the future. Although CCS technologies are largely proven, it is not yet clear who will pay for the CO_2 emissions reductions. Projects are routinely announced and then subsequently delayed or withdrawn. So far, audience-seeking commitments to this green solution far outweigh emissions-reduction performance from the technology. The following analysis shows how firms produce three types of cultural symbols – that is, emblems, credentials and kin – that are variously granted legitimacy by others in the discursive struggle over a new pollution control technology. The CCS demonstration projects can be understood as a form of symbolic capital, wherein governments grant legitimacy to a firm's response to climate change by awarding substantial, visible subsidies. However, this symbolic activity is not without cost and it imposes a social energy penalty on society. I conclude the chapter by identifying factors that underlie a firm's discretionary power to raise the social cost of corporate environmentalism.

Empirical context: CCS demonstration projects

Publicly funded CCS demonstration projects are an instructive example of government involvement in stimulating new pollution control technologies.[1] CCS comprises a family of new technologies that is almost universally relied on in future greenhouse gas (GHS) mitigation and stabilisation scenarios (Pacala and Socolow 2004). 'CCS technology' can be thought of more accurately as a chain of technologies designed to separate CO_2 from industrial sources, transport it to a storage location, and isolate it from the atmosphere for the long term. Proven CCS technologies have the potential to reduce CO_2 emissions from large industrial sources and coal-fired power stations by approximately 85 per cent, depending on the type of noncapture plant being displaced (Intergovernmental Panel on Climate Change 2005). According to the International Energy Agency, widespread deployment of known CCS technologies could account for 20 per cent of the needed global emissions reduction by 2050.

However, CCS is an expensive technology and is not yet fully operational on an integrated, commercial scale. Establishing the viability of CCS will require public subsidies in the short term; however, similar to other new energy technologies, the public funding committed to the projects eventually will be dwarfed by corporate investments (Huberty and Zysman 2010; Mowery, Nelson, and Martin 2010). The governments of the world's eight largest economies ('the G8') announced twenty large-scale CCS demonstration projects by 2010 with a view to deployment by 2020. Post-combustion capture of CO_2 from flue gases is a classic end-of-pipe technology, so it is unlikely that investments in installing CCS equipment will reap benefits for power producers unless there is aggressive carbon pricing (Hart 1995). Each of the CCS technologies requires significant energy input. If this energy comes from fossil-fuel-based sources, the capture process incurs an 'energy penalty' – or a decreased power output per unit of fuel input (House et al. 2009). Because there are currently few incentives for substantive action on CCS, including a relatively low carbon price, this field continues to be shaped by widespread symbolic behaviour.

The social field surrounding CCS demonstration projects is still emerging and is rife with controversy and contestation. Hansson and Bryngelsson (2009) noticed an 'interpretive flexibility' wherein some experts view CCS as an incremental innovation and others view it as a way to break current energy lock-in in the long run. Buhr and Hansson (2011) found significant differences in how CCS projects are framed by both proponent firms and governments. Although the CCS technologies are promising overall, there are recognised uncertainties about their viability, affordability and effectiveness (Shackley and Gough 2006). The technology is controversial and public acceptance may be a significant barrier to deployment (Ha-Duong, Nadai, and Campos 2009). CCS technology subsidies comprise only one potential policy option among many – including carbon pricing, conservation and direct regulation – for combatting climate change, so there is social competition over solutions (Helm and Hepburn 2009). Firms, governments and civil society organisations are actively communicating in a competition to influence technology development, policy mechanisms and subsidy choices (Meadowcroft and Langhelle 2010). This is a particularly compelling field to analyse because each stage of the CCS chain – that is, capture, transport and storage – has different technological options, technology maturity, cost implications and industry players (Bowen 2011).

A recent increase in research efforts places CCS technology investments within a broader political (see, e.g., Meadowcroft and Langhelle 2010 and Perrow 2010), sociotechnical (see, e.g., Stephens and Jiusto 2010), and innovation (Praetorius and Schumacher 2009) systems. A parallel literature is being developed on how and why firms differ in their climate change innovation and carbon management strategies (see, e.g., Kolk and Pinkse 2010 and Okereke, Wittneben, and Bowen 2012). Some studies include industry perspectives in panels of experts on CCS (see, e.g., Dapeng and Weiwei 2009 and Hansson and Bryngelsson 2009) and have started to examine CCS as a commercial investment decision (Bowen 2011). However, although there is significant potential for symbolic actions in the field surrounding this emerging and controversial pollution control technology, the effort that CCS project proponents devote to producing and manipulating cultural symbols related to these publicly subsidised projects has not yet been fully examined.

Methodology

My research aim was to investigate how dominant organisations produce and reproduce cultural symbols, as well as their consequences, within an emerging field surrounding a pollution control technology. Cultural symbols are meaningful only within the relational field that (re)produces them (Bourdieu and Thompson 1991); therefore, we need to investigate them within broader organisational, institutional and field structures. In the case of CCS demonstration projects, the field – or all 'communities of organisations that participate in the same meaning systems, are defined by similar symbolic processes, and are subject to common regulatory processes' (Scott and Meyer 1994: 71) –

consists of globally distributed and interconnected firms and governments investing in the projects as well as the organisations that interact with them. This definition posed considerable challenges for collecting and analysing data, and it effectively ruled out surveying or interviewing a meaningful selection of globally distributed key informants. I therefore adopted a two-stage data collection and analysis approach. First, I developed initial insights on the field structure by conducting a limited, preliminary set of interviews within one jurisdiction. Based on these interviews, I then used secondary data to compare symbols around CCS projects in multiple, globally interconnected jurisdictions.

Stage 1: Preliminary interviews in the Canadian CCS context

To understand the field positions and relational dynamics of actors associated with CCS demonstration projects, I conducted eighteen informal interviews with key informants in Canada. I talked with representatives of six companies involved in Canadian projects that had been allocated public funding; two companies that might be candidates for CCS adoption but that did not receive public funding in the first round; two companies that have CCS investments outside of Canada but that are not currently involved in Canadian CCS projects; four industry associations or research consortia; two energy and environmental NGOs; and the main provincial government department responsible for overseeing CCS investments.[2]

I examined the practitioners, practices and discourses related to CCS to provide a sense of the field structure in the Canadian context (Tatli 2011). Practitioners in the CCS field – including energy-policy professionals from industry and government – interact closely and are physically connected in proximity to one another through the 'plus 15' walkway that connects corporate towers in Calgary. Practitioners participate in dense interpersonal relationships networks, facilitated by mobility among people in technical roles in industry and publicly funded research groups. The practices surrounding CCS emphasised political engagement and investment in research. Discourses about CCS showed a shared sense of awareness of high public scrutiny and that 'something must be done' about carbon emissions, as well as a shared faith that technological and entrepreneurial solutions eventually will emerge to develop lower carbon energy sources.

Together, these characteristics suggest a highly concentrated field with a shared interest in protecting the ability to exploit carbon-intensive natural resources. As in Tatli's (2011) analysis of the diversity management field, there seemed to be a gap between the discourse and the practice of CCS. The discourse emphasised the need for entrepreneurial solutions to the carbon emission challenge, whereas the practices emphasised political access, lobbying, and long-term basic research and engineering investment. This disconnect in the Canadian CCS field provided the impetus to examine communications related to global CCS demonstration projects.

Stage 2: Analysis of CCS demonstration project communications

After gaining a sense of the field structure in one jurisdiction, I broadened the analysis to leverage the enormous amount of information on globally distributed CCS demonstration projects in the public domain. I conducted a discourse analysis of firm and government communications on CCS demonstration projects and climate strategies based on realist ontology (Fairclough 2005). I analysed the 'communicative practices of [field] members . . . for the ways that they contribute to the ongoing (and sometimes rather precarious) process of organising' (Mumby and Clair 1997: 181). This was an appropriate research approach because firms use symbolic devices to appear proactive on their websites and in their annual reports, which may diverge from the substance of their actions (Bansal and Kistruck 2006; Laufer 2003). I used announcements, reports and websites as a source of symbolic organisational texts (Lamertz and Heugens 2009) and as a basis for discourse analysis (Caruana and Crane 2008).

The sample includes all of the major CCS demonstration projects that were both planned and underway in the United States, Australia, Canada and the European Union in 2010. Governments in these four jurisdictions had committed approximately US$7.5 billion of public money to CCS demonstration projects since 2008. Although CCS demonstration projects were being planned or discussed in other locations – notably China, Norway and the United Arab Emirates – this sample captured the majority of large-scale global projects. The sample included all CCS demonstration projects that had been awarded more than US$100 million (US$50 million in Australia) of public funding by 2010. I derived the list of projects from a variety of sources, including the CCS Project Database at the Massachusetts Institute of Technology (MIT Energy Initiative 2010), reports to the G8 on the status of full-scale demonstration projects (International Energy Agency 2009, 2010), a survey of CCS technologies (Innovation Norway 2009), and official announcements on energy policy and stimulus-package investments.

Table 6.1 lists the twenty-three projects included in the study with their country of origin, primary project partners, allocated public funds and project design choices. The last two columns show the current phase of the project as of June 2010, according to the WorleyParsons asset lifecycle model (International Energy Agency 2010); the phases range from identify, evaluate and define to execute and operate. As shown in Table 6.1, only one of the twenty-three projects reached the 'execute' stage of detailed engineering and project management. All of the other projects were in various stages of planning, with start-ups for the facilities planned mostly in 2014 and 2015.

Firms involved in the funded CCS demonstration projects include coal mining companies (e.g., Xsrata Coal and Rio Tinto) and large electricity utilities (e.g., Vattenfall, American Electric Power, and TransAlta), especially those with extensive assets in coal-fired power plants. Several oil and gas firms (e.g., Shell, ExxonMobil and Marathon) were also involved in the projects as either point-source emitters at oil upgrading or refining facilities or as the partners responsible for CO_2 compression and injection. The CO_2 capture technology industry is dominated by energy equipment manufacturing firms that have expertise in boilers, plants, turbines, and so on, including Alstom, Siemens, Mitsubishi and GE. Other firms specialise in capture technologies (e.g., Powerspan) and pipeline construction (e.g., Enhance), although no large companies specialise exclusively in CO_2 storage services or long-term stewardship (Hertzog 2009).

The main data sources were archival and Internet-based documents related to the projects and the companies' broader carbon management strategies. For each project, my research assistants collected four main sets of documents: (1) the official government announcement of the project and any press releases by the project partners near the same date; (2) web pages and environmental or sustainability reports published by any of the project partners that included mention of CCS technologies; (3) the top twenty Google hits from a search on the

Table 6.1 *Carbon capture and storage demonstration projects*

Project name	Country	Main project partners	Industry	Public funds (US$)	Facility type	Project design	Phase in 2010	Planned start-up
ZeroGen	Australia	ZeroGen Mitsubishi	Government Equipment manufacturing	CCS Flagships Program part of $1.7bn	Syngas-fired power plant	• New build • IGCC • Storage TBD	Evaluate	2015
Wandoan	Australia	Stanwell Xstrata Coal GE	Power generation Mining Equipment manufacturing	CCS Flagships Program part of $1.7bn	Syngas-fired power plant	• New build • IGCC • Saline aquifer or EOR	Identify	2015
Collie South West Hub	Australia	Griffin Energy BHP Worsley Verve Energy Wesfarmers Perdaman	Power generation Mining Power energy Mining/Fertilizers Fertilizers	CCS Flagships Program part of $1.7bn	Various sources: coal-fired power plant, fertilizer plant	• Retrofit • Transport/storage hub • Storage TBD	Identify	2015
CarbonNet	Australia	State of Victoria	Government	CCS Flagships Program part of $1.7bn	Various sources, transportation network	• Retrofit • Transport/storage hub • Storage TBD	Identify	2015–2019
Gorgon	Australia	Chevron ExxonMobil Shell	Oil and gas Oil and gas Oil and gas	Western Australia Funding $52m	LNG production	• New build • LNG processing and injection • Depleted gas field	Execute	2014
Alberta Carbon Trunk Line	Canada	Enhance Energy Northwest Upgrading	CCS specialist Chemicals	Alberta CCS Fund $480m	Fertilizer plant and oil sands upgrader	• Retrofit • Gasification • EOR	Define	2012

Project	Country	Partners	Sector	Funding	Facility	Technology	Stage	Date
Quest	Canada	Shell Canada, Chevron Canada, Marathon Oil Sands	Oil and gas, Oil and gas, Oil and gas	Alberta CCS Fund and Federal Contribution $775m	Scotford oil sands upgrader	• Retrofit • Post-combustion • EOR or storage	Define	2017
Project Pioneer	Canada	TransAlta, Epcor/Capital Power, Alstom	Power generation, Power generation, Equipment manufacturing	Alberta CCS Fund $425m	Coal-fired power plant (Keephills 3)	• New build • Post-combustion • EOR or storage	Evaluate	2015
Swan Hills	Canada	Swan Hills Synfuels	CCS specialist	Alberta CCS Fund $278m	Syngas-fired power plant	• New build • In situ coal gasification • EOR	Evaluate	2015
Boundary Dam	Canada	SaskPower, SNC Lavalin	Power generation, EPC	Saskatchewan Government and Federal $228m federal	Coal-fired power plant	• Retrofit • Oxycombustion • EOR	Define	2013
Futuregen	USA	US Department of Energy, Private coal producers and users	Government, Mining, Power generation	$1.073bn	Coal-fired power plant	• New build • Pre-combustion • Saline aquifer	Evaluate	2018
AEP Alstom Mountaineer	USA	AEP, Alstom	Power generation, Equipment manufacturing	CCPI/ARRA $334m	Coal-fired power plant	• Retrofit • Post-combustion • Saline aquifer	Evaluate	2015

(cont.)

Table 6.1 (*cont.*)

Project name	Country	Main project partners	Industry	Public funds (US$)	Facility type	Project design	Current phase	Planned start-up
Plant Barry	USA	Southern Energy Mitsubishi	Power generation Equipment manufacturing	CCPI/ARRA $295m	Coal-fired power plant	• Retrofit • Post-combustion • Saline aquifer or EOR	Evaluate	2012
Texas Clean Energy Project	USA	Summit Power Seimens	EPC Equipment manufacturing	CCPI/ARRA $350m (and $100m tax credits)	Coal-fired power plant	• New build • Gasification • EOR	Evaluate	2012
W.A Parish	USA	NRG Energy Fluor Corp	Power generation EPC	ARRA $154m	Coal-fired power plant	• New build • Post-combustion • EOR	Evaluate	2013
Hydrogen Energy California Project	USA	BP Rio Tinto	Oil and gas Mining	ARRA $308m	Hydrogen Fueled power plant	• New build • IGCC and hydrogen production • EOR or storage	Define	2015
Antelope Valley	USA	Basin Electric Powerspan Burns and McDonnell	Power generation CCS specialist EPC	ARRA $100m	Lignite-fired Boiler	• Retrofit • Post-combustion	Evaluate	2012
Jaenschwalde	Germany	Vattenfall Alstom	Power generation Equipment manufacturing	EERP $222m	Lignite-fired power plant	• New build and retrofit • Oxyfuel post-combustion • Storage TBD	Identify	2015

Location	Country	Company	Sector	Funding	Plant type	Details	Stage	Year
Porto-Tolle	Italy	Enel Ingegneria e Innovazione S.p.A.	Power generation	EERP $123m	Coal-fired power plant	• New build • Post-combustion • Offshore saline aquifer	Define	2015
Rotterdam	Netherlands	E.ON Electrabel	Power generation Power generation	EERP $222m	Coal/biomass power plant	• Post-combustion • Offshore depleted gas field	Identify	2015
Belchatow	Poland	PGE EBSA Alstom Dow	Power generation Equipment manufacturing Chemicals	EERP $222m	Lignite-fired power plant	• New build • Post-combustion • Saline aquifer	Identify	2015
Compostilla	Spain	ENDESA Generacion Foster Wheeler	Power generation EPC	EERP $222m	Coal-fired power plant	• New build • Oxyfuel saline aquifer	Define	2015
Hatfield	UK	Powerfuel Power Shell UK Kuzbassrazrezugol	Power generation Oil and gas Mining	EERP $222m	Power plant	• New build • IGCC • Offshore gas field	Define	2014

IGCC = integrated gasification combined cycle

EOR = enhanced oil recovery

LNG = liquefied natural gas

CCPI = Clean Coal Power Initiative

ARRA = American Recovery and Reinvestment Act, 2009

EERP = European Economic Recovery Plan

project and partner names; and (4) other useful materials on public funding of CCS projects, including industry publications, newspapers and reports. This wide net captured not only specific communications about CCS projects but also broad contextual discourse about CCS relative to other solutions to climate change, business strategies and corporate environmentalism.

After organising the materials and eliminating duplicates, research assistants converted the 1,202 documents into pdf files and uploaded them into Atlas.ti, a qualitative data analysis package. Of the approximately fifty documents for each project, many were quite similar. For example, the dataset contained as many as ten slightly different versions of a given project announcement from different corporate, trade publication, national newspaper and government sources. I kept these similar documents in the database because they had some core elements in common (e.g., the same quotations from project representatives) but different interpretations and presentations of the project information.

I conducted the analysis using Atlas.ti v. 6, which allows direct coding of pdf documents (Muhr 2009; Muhr and Friese 2004). Because Bourdieu's symbolic capital within fields is an already established conceptual framework, I broadly followed Miles and Huberman's (1994) deductive method of coding. The initial coding scheme included the flagging of different types of cultural symbols as well as descriptive codes for project, country, firm, industry, and data source. I began with a general code for discourse on CCS that was designed to capture 'compelling narratives about what a technology is, what a technology might become and why it is needed and preferable to competing technologies' (Lounsbury and Glynn 2001).

In successive rounds of interpretive coding, I refined the codes into types of cultural symbols, giving particular attention to when cultural symbols were mentioned by actors who were not the primary producers of the symbols. I also interpreted the quotations coded as 'discourse' in the first round by (1) adding codes for managerial perceptions of climate change; (2) dividing the framing of CCS technology into positive, negative or neutral; and (3) coding for Bansal and Roth's (2000) competitiveness, legitimation and responsibility motives that I noticed in the Stage 1 interviews. I added new codes to capture the use of euphemisms (e.g., 'clean coal') about the national interest, the recent economic downturn (e.g., 'getting us through these difficult times') and company size or dominance. Finally, I searched for patterns in the data by cross-matching types of cultural symbols with the various descriptive and discourse codes. Through this iterative process, I analysed how symbolic capital appears and is relevant across the dataset. I investigated similarities and contradictions by refining the codes and explanations for how symbolic capital is produced and granted by various actors in the global CCS demonstration project field.

Results

The analysis suggested two main sets of findings: (1) on three types of cultural symbols produced by organisations, and (2) on the granting of symbolic capital by others in the institutional field.

Cultural symbols produced by organisations

In the first round of interpretive coding, I identified all quotations that fell within Bourdieu's (1995: 178) definition of 'capital' that was provided previously. Within this broad coding, I identified the subset of nonfinancial, cultural symbols that firms seemed to be using to confer status or prestige on themselves or others. In subsequent rounds of coding, I refined the types of symbolic capital found in the materials into the general categories of 'emblems', 'credentials' and 'kin' (Table 6.2). These labels were inspired by Bourdieu's original explanations of cultural capital at the individual level (Bourdieu and Nice 1984; Bourdieu and Thompson 1991). However, refining, applying and operationalising the types of cultural symbols that firms – rather than individuals – produce and reproduce in this field is a primary contribution of this chapter. Identifying the cultural symbols produced by dominant organisations is the first step in analysing how discourses within the field grant them as symbolic capital.

Emblems. I defined 'emblems' as distinctive badges with symbolic meaning used to confer prestige and reputation on their owners. Emblems are the most overt form of cultural symbols. Examples in the data included technology awards and corporate prizes for socially responsible behaviour. The primary function of these awards is to support their recipients' reputation for sound environmental or social practices. HTC Purenergy, for example, uses the 'prestigious' Deloitte Technology Green 15 Award to support its position as 'Canada's

Table 6.2 *Types of cultural symbols*

Category	Theme	Illustrative examples and companies
Emblems	Awards	• 'HTC Purenergy, Canada's National Champion of CCS technology, is a winner of the prestigious Deloitte Technology Green 15 Award'. (HTC, technology) • 'Alstom Power received an Emerging Technology Award for its Oxyfuel pilot plant project' (Alstom, equipment manufacturing) • Canada's Top 100 Employers; Canada's Most Earth-Friendly Employers; Canada's 50 Best Corporate Citizens (Epcor, power generation)
	Trademarks and patents	• ECO2® ammonia-based post-combustion carbon dioxide capture technology (Powerspan, technology) • Flex-Burn™ carbon capturing circulating fluidized-bed technology (Foster Wheeler, EPC) • 'Mitsubishi Heavy Industry's CO_2 recovery technology is KM-CDR Process™ . . . that uses the company's proprietary KS-1 solvent for CO_2 absorption and desorption' (Mitsubishi, equipment manufacturing)
	Technologies	• 'Alstom is a global leader in energy technology and brings expertise in the Chilled Ammonia carbon capture process' (Alstom, equipment manufacturing) • 'As a major player in gasification, Foster Wheeler has the necessary in-house expertise located in our major engineering design centers around the world' (Foster Wheeler, energy services) • Press announcement of 'the first commercial-scale application of its kind in the US' attended by the State's Lieutenant Governor (Powerspan, technology)

Table 6.2 *(cont.)*

Category	Theme	Illustrative examples and companies
Emblems *(cont.)*		• '...one of the world's first fully-integrated CCS facilities for a coal-fired power plant' (TransAlta, power generation)
	Projects	• 'When this project is commissioned, it will be a trade symbol' and 'we want to build a flagship project which puts Collie on the map' (Perdaman, chemicals)
		• 'This is the first major integrated retrofit in Poland and we are very pleased to be able to work on this unique opportunity... This project will benefit from... our position as leaders in clean power production' (PGE, power generation)
		• 'We are delighted to be working with Shell in our vision to be the first commercial-scale coal-fired power generator with carbon capture in the world. Success in this project would be enormously significant for UK and EU energy policy...' (Powerfuel, power generation)
		• 'The EU endorses Spain's CCS project by investing Euro 180m... Endesa contributes to the EU's project with its technological and institutional capacity to validate CCS technology' (Endesa, power generation)
		• 'I am delighted that Doosan Babcock in partnership with HTC Purenergy has been chosen to conduct this project... This illustrates that Doosan Babcock is at the cutting edge of carbon capture technology' (Doosan Babcock, equipment manufacturing)
		• 'Western Australia has international recognition for its CCS plans through the Gorgon Project, which... is the biggest project in the world' (government of Western Australia)

(cont.)

Table 6.2 *(cont.)*

Category	Theme	Illustrative examples and companies
Credentials	Rankings	• '... recognized on numerous occasions by important players in the capital markets such as the Dow Jones Sustainability Index as the most advanced company in its sector world-wide in this field' (Endesa, power generation) • 'According to the Carbon Disclosure Project (CDP), Endesa obtains the highest rating among the world's electricity companies in the fight against climate change. The CDP is the most prestigious index for evaluating companies' activities and strategies in this area' (Endesa, power generation)
	Accreditation	• Global Reporting Initiative scores (BHP, mining; E.ON, power generation; Epcor, power generation) • ISO 14001 (Shell, oil and gas; Dow, chemicals; Verve Energy, power generation) • UN Global Compact (Endesa, power generation; E.ON, power generation; Alstom, equipment manufacturing) • 'Australia's Greenhouse Challenge Plus Program providing reporting of project emissions and greenhouse gas reduction measures' (BHP, mining) • 'Epcor Tower will be certified to a Leadership in Energy and Environmental Design (LEED) Silver standard or higher' (Epcor, power generation)
	Heritage	• 'TransAlta has close to 100 years of experience with power generation... We are proud of our history as a leader in sustainable energy production' (TransAlta, power generation) • 'Our experience comes from our 117-year heritage of designing, servicing, and improving steam-generating equipment' (Foster Wheeler, EPC).

Table 6.2 *(cont.)*

Category	Theme	Illustrative examples and companies
Kin	Industry associations	• International Council on Mining and Metals (BHP, mining) • International Utilities Alliance (Endesa, power generation)
	Research consortia	• Electric Power Research Institute (Basin Electric, power generation) • 'Griffin Energy is a long-term supporter of research into geo-sequestration through its affiliation with the Centre for Coal in Sustainable Development' (Griffin Energy, power generation) • 'CIUDEN is part of the European Energy Research Alliance (EERA), and represents Spain in the International Energy Agency-GHG Program' (CIUDEN, governmental administration agency) • 'Since 2006, Endesa has spearheaded project CENIT CO_2 (Strategic National Consortium for Technical Research on CO_2)... Spain's foremost R&D effort in the fight against climate change... The Minister of Science and Innovation described CENIT as 'a transformational instrument''' (Endesa, power generation)
	Scientific experts	• 'In the United States, Alstom is working with researchers at the prestigious Massachusetts Institute of Technology (MIT) to share expertise in capturing and sequestering CO_2' (Alstom, equipment manufacturing) • numerous co-authored technical papers on Foster Wheeler's website (Foster Wheeler, EPC) • 'Since 2002, GE has provided – and gained – insight on climate change by serving as an industry expert to the Intergovernmental Panel on Climate Change (IPCC)' (GE, equipment manufacturing)

(cont.)

Table 6.2 *(cont.)*

Category	Theme	Illustrative examples and companies
Kin *(cont.)*	Government partnerships	• 'The Department of Energy was among the first to recognize the significance of Ramgen's efforts and their early and ongoing support has been critical to our success. Their insights and financial support have enabled Ramgen to work to develop needed solutions to the combined goals of energy security and Climate Change'. (Ramgen, compression technology) • 'In addition to the scientific and technological criteria, the European Commission took into consideration the advanced stage of the project and the cooperation between public and private institutions' (Endesa, power generation) • 'We are pleased to have partners in the Government of Canada and the Government of Alberta to join us in this important initiative... The advancement of Project Pioneer will depend on visionary partnerships' (TransAlta, power generation)

National Champion' in CCS technology. Among the technology and service companies, there was a tendency to use technological language – in particular, trademarks and patents – to signal their 'leading-edge' and, hence, high status in green solutions. Project participants used CCS technologies as a discursive device to position themselves as 'global leaders', 'major players' and 'first movers'.

Organisations also used the CCS demonstration projects as an emblem of their environmental reputation. Project participants emphasised the 'significance', 'recognition' and 'endorsement' received for their projects. Because the first CCS projects were unlikely to have a short-term positive economic payoff, participants attempted to attach prestige and symbolic value to their 'vision' for 'flagship projects'.

Organisations attached value to their selection for participation in these projects through language such as 'winning' project funding or 'being rewarded' for technological leadership. Announcements were couched in terms of 'delighted' and 'pleased' to be associated with nationally important projects and the reflected prestige that, for example, 'illustrated that Doosan Babcock is at the cutting edge of carbon capture technology' (see www.doosanbabcock.com).

The names of the CCS public funding programmes and the demonstration projects contributed to conferring status on project participants. The Australian commonwealth government, for example, named its initiative the 'CCS Flagships Program'. Government programmes also were symbolically connected with other socially desirable outcomes, including domestic economic stimulus and green jobs such as the 'American Recovery and Reinvestment Act' and the 'European Economic Recovery Plan'. Politicians invoked prestige and leadership in how they named and described corporate involvement in the projects. In his speech announcing Project Pioneer, Stephen Harper, the Prime Minister of Canada, said:

The aptly named 'Project Pioneer' will reduce carbon emissions from the plant by a million tonnes a year . . . it will be the first of its kind in the world! . . . I'd also like to take a moment to acknowledge the workers here at the Keephills plant who will make this project a reality. Like the 19th-century coal miners and the 20th-century wildcatters who gave birth to the Alberta energy industry, history will remember you as the pioneers who transformed the industry in the 21st century, as the pioneers who kept Alberta at the forefront of the global energy market, as the pioneers who contributed to a prosperous future for all of Canada! (Government of Canada website, October 14, 2009)

Credentials. Credentials are qualifications or documents that entitle the bearer to credibility – in this case, for their environmental performance. Bourdieu and Nice (1984) showed how credentials, such as educational qualifications, help to establish and maintain privileged positions for individuals in social contexts. As shown in Table 6.2, firms attempted to demonstrate their credentials as legitimate contributors to efforts to reduce environmental impacts. Similar to individuals, firms produced cultural symbols that often were substantively remote from the CCS project but were intended to signal their status within the field. Just as individuals gain privileged social positions through substantively disconnected 'qualifications', firms touted LEED-certified corporate headquarters and a long and established corporate history as status symbols of their credibility on green issues.

Organisations prioritised cultural symbols by ritualistically repeating accreditation to global standards, including ISO 14001, the UN Global Compact, and the Global Reporting Initiative (GRI), in annual sustainability reports. Some firms went as far as to repeat major sections of their reports in GRI format in order to transparently produce their 'A+' rating. Firms communicated not only about their own credentials but also about the reputation of those conferring the credentials by pointing out that the ranking agencies are 'the most prestigious' or are designed by 'key players'. These examples show evidence of the simultaneous production and granting of symbolic capital by insider organisations in this field.

I overlaid the types of cultural symbols with Bansal and Roth's (2000) three motivations for environmental investments, particularly competitiveness and legitimation. As shown in Table 6.1, there is a wide variety of firms involved in CCS projects, each with its own motivation to become involved with the technology. First, there are coal mining companies and large electricity utilities. For these firms, CCS is an additional cost imposed on their operations from social demands for environmental improvement. These large point-source emitters, often euphemistically called 'coal users', positioned CCS as necessary for legitimation and maintaining their licence to operate. One example follows:

We know that our ability to continue to operate and our capacity to grow is linked directly with our capacity to responsibly manage and limit our impacts on the environment and be responsive to changing public, government and business attitudes . . . The challenges are huge and we are tackling them in part by pursuing new technologies such as capturing carbon dioxide and storing it permanently underground. (Epcor, power generation)

The emblems and credentials deployed by these firms were less directly related to CCS as a technological solution and more to establishing legitimacy on broader corporate citizenship and environmental responsibility. Given that these firms were unlikely to gain short-term economic advantage through CCS projects, their symbolic activities focused more on the value of transparency (e.g., participation in the GRI or CDP) and the credibility and high quality of their disclosures.

They appropriated cultural symbols from a broader corporate citizenship discourse to signal their status within the narrower CCS field. For example, Epcor (an electricity utility and coal user) emphasized its awards as being in Canada's Top 100 Employers, Canada's Most Earth-Friendly Employers, and Canada's 50 Best Corporate Citizens. In the language of Brennan and Pettit's (2004) *Economy of Esteem* (see Chapter 4, Figure 4.4), these firms experienced a steeper budget line due to their high visibility on carbon-reduction issues, thereby leading them to invest relatively more in audience-seeking, legitimisation activities.

In contrast, firms that specialised in capture technology, equipment manufacturing and project management showed competitiveness motives for involvement in CCS projects, as in the following examples:

We are seeing significant development in the area of carbon capture and storage as our clients seek to minimise the economic impact of reducing emissions. Our Business Solutions group is set up to support our clients in this objective. (Foster Wheeler, energy services)

At this year's summit, the advisory board provided valuable input on commercial, technical and policy-related opportunities for GE in the key emerging fields of biofuels, carbon capture and storage, and energy efficiency. (GE, equipment manufacturing)

The emblems and credentials employed by these firms emphasised technology awards, trademarks and patents. For example, Alstom, an equipment manufacturer, showcased its Emerging Technology Award for its Oxyfuel pilot-plant project. The technology, equipment and project management providers face a lower relative cost – and possibly even a commercial opportunity – from CCS as a green solution, which flattens the budget line in Figure 4.4 and makes them more likely to invest in implementing CCS projects and substantive reductions to CO_2 emissions.

Of note here are the oil and gas companies that were sometimes involved in projects as point-source emitters at oil upgrading or refining facilities and sometimes as the technical services partners responsible for CO_2 compression and injection. These firms face the competitiveness opportunities of CCS through their expertise in compression, injection and geological mapping as well as the legitimacy-based threats related to emissions from their chemical plants and final petroleum-based products. The analysis indicated that these firms' use of emblems and credentials were generally more similar to the indirect legitimacy-seeking of the point-source emitters. The manner in which the oil and gas firms emphasised less proximate cultural symbols from the broader corporate responsibility discourse suggests that the legitimation threats of climate change outweigh the potential competitiveness benefits of implementing CCS for these firms. CCS is, after all, only a small part of their overall portfolio of green solutions. These are large, visible firms in a high-impact industry. The potential opportunities of lower costs of performance-enhancement activity are outweighed overall by their audience-seeking activities (i.e., the budget line in Figure 4.4 is steeper). This leads them more towards legitimation and symbolic green solutions.

Kin. Kin are distinguished by belonging to a class or group with common attributes, often related through common ancestry or experience. In this third category of cultural symbols listed in Table 6.2, prestige is gained through 'not only their land and instruments of production but also their kin and their clientele, the network of alliances, or, more broadly, of relationships . . . ' (Bourdieu 1995: 178). Firms highlighted their associations with 'prestigious' scientific experts and 'transformational' research consortia. They also signalled memberships in industry associations, demonstrating how they are prominent and responsible members of their industry sector – regardless of the direct relevance of a particular association for CCS. Almost all of the firms highlighted the importance of their relationships with government and their role as influential partners in combatting the common social problem of GHG emissions.

Similar to emblems and credentials, the type of kin displayed in organisational communications broadly matched a firm's competitive opportunities in CCS. Firms that presented CCS as a commercial opportunity highlighted their interactions with kin that could reinforce their technological solutions, such as scientific experts who would help deliver performance-enhancing activities. Foster Wheeler, for example, highlighted on its corporate website several technical papers written by in-house research groups about CCS and other technologies presented at conferences. Firms that were undertaking CCS for legitimation reasons, conversely, focused on their connections with industry associations and broader research consortia. Peabody Energy joined a number of research partnerships to 'participate', 'evaluate' and 'support' CCS development. The company also demonstrated its 'clean

generation' activities on its website by stating that it joined the Pow-
ertree Carbon Company LLC, 'a consortium of twenty-five major US
power companies funding six major reforestation projects along the
Lower Mississippi River' (see www.peabodyenergy.com).

In some cases, legitimation firms' actual research and development
(R&D) in CCS was functioning as a symbolic green solution: pur-
ported investments in developing the technology did not seem to be
aimed at swift deployment of CCS technology. For example, Griffin
Energy, an Australian power generator, claimed in June 2010 on
its website that 'Griffin Energy is committed to a sustainable future
through its significant investment in research and new technology'.
On further inspection, however, it is clear that this was not in-house
R&D; rather, it was in an 'affiliation with' and 'funding for' the Cooperative Research Centre for Coal in Sustainable Development (CCSD).
However, the CCSD finished its work in June 2008. In this example, the company was using affiliation with a CCS research group as
an audience-seeking symbol long after any substantive investment in
research had ended.

Granting symbolic capital

The previous section described how different types of organisations
produced and reproduced different types of cultural symbols. In particular, firms that stood to gain the most from CCS technologies emphasised cultural symbols that were the most closely connected with commercial opportunities (e.g., patents and connections with scientists).
Firms driven more by a legitimation motive focused on symbolic value
from more general environmental awards, accreditation, research consortia and industry associations. Yet, not all cultural symbols are forms
of symbolic capital. Symbolic capital is recognised depending on the
relational positions and discourses around cultural symbols within a
specific field. Cultural symbols underpin symbolic capital when viewed
as symbols of legitimate domination by field members, most often by
the dominated members (Bourdieu 1995). Thus, the next step is to
analyse the discourse surrounding CCS projects to see who grants
legitimacy to various cultural symbols, particularly those produced by
high-status organisations in the field.

Bourdieu (1995: 58) analysed the outcome of a social game as
depending on the deal, the cards held, the players' skill, and 'the

competence which [sic] enables the strategists to make the best use of this capital'. To the extent that large, established energy industry incumbents are experienced and skilled in energy-policy discourse, these dominant players have significant power to shape the symbolic game. This influence can extend beyond political lobbying to the environmental problems that are discussed in the public domain and the range of acceptable green solutions. CCS project proponents are granted misrecognised authority to define technical fixes that perpetuate the current fossil-energy system as legitimate responses to climate change in a system that privileges corporate discourses.

During the coding process, I tracked arguments that were used for and against CCS as a solution for climate change and public funding of CCS demonstration projects. The field of opinion captured within the data included the pro-CCS orthodoxy, such as arguments for continued access to low-cost coal reserves for energy production, job creation, technology export potential, and energy security. Anti-CCS heterodoxy arguments consisted mostly of concerns about CCS as inefficient and uneconomical, technically uncertain, crowding out investments in other renewable alternatives, and subsidising large polluters. By careful analysis of who was using each argument and which actors prioritised the various types of cultural symbols, I found several examples of others granting symbolic capital to the CCS project proponents.

Governments routinely legitimised an incumbent firm's preference for CCS as a technological solution to climate change by emphasising national competitiveness arguments for CCS, even when the arguments were economically questionable. Australia, for example, does not have a strong manufacturing industry; therefore, no Australian technology manufacturer has specialised in CCS technologies, particularly the lucrative capture technologies (Innovation Norway 2009). The Australian government committed $AUS2.4 billion to support CCS projects and claimed in its press release that this would 'boost Australian technology' (Kerr 2009). Yet, the two short-listed CCS projects in Australia's CCS Flagships Program rely on technologies from Japan (i.e., Mitsubishi in the ZeroGen Project) and the United States (i.e., GE in the Wandoan Power Project). The government's discursive positioning grants misplaced legitimacy to an industry association's claim that 'Australia has the expertise and technical capacity to play a leading role in exporting technology to developing countries'.

The Australian government is not alone in granting legitimacy to CSS as a green solution by awarding project subsidies. The previous analysis of cultural symbols described how firms used their participation in publicly funded (and, hence, government sanctioned) demonstration projects as a valuable and rare emblem of their reputation on climate change issues. Government representatives, unions and the media grant these emblems as symbolic capital by associating a project proponent's claim to support the national interest by investing in CCS projects. They misrecognise a project proponent's authority to define an appropriate green solution by not seeing the power structures that prioritise an incumbent firm's corporatist discourse. This explains the consistent emphasis by both firms and governments on how CCS projects support the national interest by providing jobs, future export opportunities, and leading-edge technologies; fulfilling international obligations; and supporting economic recovery. Discourse around public subsidies for CCS demonstration projects collectively promotes a firm's authority to define appropriate GHG reduction solutions.

Furthermore, I did not find discussion of more radical responses to climate change, such as dramatically changing Western lifestyles or an immediate ban on the extraction and use of fossil fuels in the materials. Even critical reports about CCS by NGOs, such as Greenpeace's *False Hope* (2008), present primarily economic arguments against CCS based on deployment timing, inefficiency, risk and liability. This illustrates how NGOs and others that are disadvantaged by the symbolic order reinforce the narrow field of opinion boundaries by legitimising dominant economic arguments by using them. This is a particularly important limitation in the discourse because the habitus (or ways of being) of the early participants disproportionately influence the value of symbolic capital over time (Bourdieu 1995). We know that incumbent firms are often the dominant players that seek to develop early voluntary agreements, environmental regulations and expectations (Delmas and Montes-Sancho 2010; Hoffman 1999); this analysis serves as a reminder that powerful firms also shape the boundaries of the debate.

In another example, the CDP – an independent, not-for-profit organisation that holds the largest database of primary corporate climate change information in the world – grants legitimacy to a firm's reproduction of cultural symbols by awarding points for complete corporate climate change disclosures. This encourages firms to include climate change credentials, emblems and kin, whether or not they affect their substantive environmental impacts. Symbolic capital is granted by the NGO's scoring system and is further embedded as industry analysts, consultants and academic researchers use the CDP scores.

It is not only governments and NGOs that grant legitimacy to a firm's CCS-related emblems, credentials and kin. These cultural symbols also are reinforced by a firm's attempts to obfuscate the extent to which investment in CCS is a genuine attempt to solve the climate problem. Project proponents share incentives to maintain the value of symbolic capital with other actors because their political and symbolic interests are aligned (Levy and Egan 2003). Governments and incumbent firms in coal-intensive energy systems have a common political interest in symbolic CCS demonstration projects. What is needed in these economies is a demonstrable response to climate change: '[W]hat is valued is activity for its own sake, regardless of its strictly economic function, inasmuch as it is regarded as appropriate to the person doing it' (Bourdieu 1995: 175). When interests are aligned in this way, governments and firms are more likely to 'understand the fundamental principles of the strategies' (ibid.: 65).

Examples in the data revealed how governments rewarded firms for politically motivated project-selection choices rather than those based more strictly on efficient CO_2 reduction. Engineering models show that CCS projects based on pre-combustion of natural gas have a much lower energy penalty than post-combustion based on coal. Yet, the UK government stated a political preference for funding post-combustion pilot projects based on coal to protect jobs and current industry players, even in the face of a proposed more efficient pre-combustion proposal in Peterhead, Scotland (Bowen 2011; Scrase and Watson 2009). Similarly, the Australian government is complicit in its support for the politically important mining industry in Victoria through its emphasis on transportation and storage projects rather than more radical solutions (see Table 6.1).

Governments grant further authority to project proponents by agreeing to long and drifting project timelines. FutureGen in the United States, for example, was once due to be operational by 2012; current plans predict a start date of 2018. During this hiatus, companies in the FutureGen Industrial Alliance can benefit through association with this US Department of Energy–promoted project without the constraints of irreversible commitments, serious planning and immediate investment.

Promised projects at the end of long timelines dampen public scrutiny of this proposed green solution in a social field. The project is a form of symbolic capital through which the interests of both powerful parties can be served.

The analysis suggested three core insights on the granting of symbolic capital in CCS demonstration projects. First, the data revealed a narrow field of opinion, wherein critics inadvertently legitimised dominant economic discourses and related cultural symbols by reproducing them. Second, governments supported the symbolic capital of incumbent firms, particularly by connecting them to symbols of national interest even if they were not economically justified. Third, the aligned political interests of incumbent firms and governments, particularly in coal-heavy economies, led them to collectively misrecognise the legitimacy of subsidy-receiving incumbent firms to promote CCS as a solution to climate change. This resulted in negotiating symbolically rather than economically or technically preferred CCS project designs.

Discussion and implications

This chapter investigates how dominant organisations produce cultural symbols and how others grant symbolic capital in the field surrounding a new pollution control technology. This analysis is the first to systematically examine the production of cultural symbols related to CCS projects, and it highlights how governments grant symbolic capital to firms by providing legitimating public funding for pollution control investments. Orthodox discourse on CCS describes current public funding as inadequate (Stephens et al. 2011), yet firms are benefitting from their involvement in these projects as valuable symbolic capital. The CCS projects have an additional symbolic value because the context they are associated with is seen as prestigious. Firms are skilled at protecting the symbolic capital around CCS projects by emphasising government support for the projects and how they are supporting the national interest.

This analysis is important because dominant organisations have the systemic power to limit the field of opinion on CCS as a solution for climate change. The authority of dominant firms to limit the range of solutions to climate change to include only those scenarios involving widespread deployment of CCS is misrecognised as legitimate, and it gives the false impression that firms and governments are committed to urgently mitigating GHG emissions. Meadowcroft and Langhelle (2009: 289) succinctly summarised the strategic stance of incumbent energy firms as 'CCS when absolutely necessary; but surely it's not necessary quite yet'. The public places misrecognised confidence in firms' reassurances about CCS as a solution for climate change that does not require radical changes to the current energy or economic system.

This study echoes the concern within technology policy research that public investment in a limited range of government-sanctioned energy technologies could waste resources and limit the efficiency of finding substantive solutions to climate change (Mowery et al. 2010). The extension here is that large-scale public investment in choosing winning technologies limits not only innovation and the development of new solutions but also the social conversation about a wider range of solutions, which is dominated by actors in powerful field positions. Thus, the social energy penalty can be seen as a part of the dangers of 'big push' technology programmes, in which the interests of incumbent firms and governments might be highly aligned and are granted unwarranted prestige by an unquestioning public.

Conventional corporate environmentalism research explains the investment in green solutions as a quest for legitimacy or reputation within an institutional field (see Chapter 3, Table 3.1). This chapter extends this approach by emphasising power dynamics within a field, particularly systemic power that comes from position within a field and permits the dominant players to produce and reproduce cultural symbols as indicators that they are fulfilling their proper social function. The Bourdesian approach is fundamentally relational (Ozbilgin and Tatli 2005). Future research on corporate environmentalism should remember that corporate strategies are also relational: gaining symbolic performance through green solutions depends on not only the capabilities and opportunities facing individual firms and governing bodies but also on the links between them and others in the institutional field. There is further potential to extend previous treatments of symbolic capital in the organisational literature (see, e.g., Fuller and Tian 2006) to show that firms use emblems, credentials and kin to signal their responsibility on environmental issues. One way is to directly ask actors within fields about the extent to which they perceive various cultural symbols or organisations as legitimate indicators of a responsible environmental investment. However, such an analysis would be inherently problematic because it is difficult for actors within fields to see the underlying relational power dynamics surrounding them.

The primary theoretical limitation of this study is that it focuses generally on symbolic capital within a social field and not on other key elements of Bourdieu's theory, notably habitus (Emirbayer and Johnson 2008; Gomez 2010). Although this is a common problem in organisational applications of Bourdieu's ideas (Oakes et al. 1998; Swartz 2008), there is still considerable value in applying his theoretical frame in the CCS context. This chapter also focuses on 'big D' rather than 'small D' discourse in the analysis of publicly available documentation on CCS demonstration projects (Eriksson and Kovalainen 2008; Fairclough 2005). Others may find it beneficial to explore the microprocesses of discourse construction on CCS technologies by connecting with current research in energy policy (see, e.g., Hansson and Bryngelsson 2009 and Stephens and Jiusto 2010).

Empirical summary

CCS technologies have been positioned by international agencies, governments and incumbent energy firms as vital in reducing substantive CO_2 emissions. Yet, despite announcements of billions of dollars in public funds, concrete plans to demonstrate and deploy the technologies are routinely postponed to the future. My analysis shows that although public funding provided to firms to develop CCS demonstration projects may be necessary due to the unfavourable economics of early-stage pollution control technology development, both governments and firms are symbolically using CCS demonstration projects to signal their corporate environmentalism.

The first empirical question I sought to answer in this chapter was about which types of cultural symbols are generated by powerful actors around voluntary pollution control technology investments. The analysis showed that cultural symbols produced within this field can be categorised as emblems, credentials and kin. I then speculated about which types of cultural symbols are most likely to be used by firms that are motivated by legitimation rather than competitiveness motives. In answer to the second question about who grants these cultural symbols as symbolic capital, the analysis provided examples of how governments, unions, the media and even NGOs grant cultural symbols as symbolic capital. Third, I asked when we can expect the social energy penalty costs related to those investments to be the highest. This is not easy to answer empirically because of the difficulty in directly measuring the social energy penalty. However, the findings do suggest some conjectures on the social energy penalty when they are cast in the social energy penalty model from Chapter 4, and it is to this that I turn in the next section.

Pollution control technologies and the social energy penalty

Pollution control technologies are usually costly for firms; therefore, managers voluntarily adopt them only if they perceive potential to improve their symbolic performance. This leads firms to produce and reproduce at least three types of cultural symbols – emblems, credentials and kin – in an attempt to generate positive social evaluations. The problem is that these symbols are misrecognised by those less powerful in the field, who mistakenly grant them as symbolic capital. Thus, generating and protecting symbolic performance is not without social cost. Maintaining the system requires 'social energy' (Bourdieu 1995: 195) in the forms of discursive effort, willful ignorance and endless reconversion of economic capital into symbolic capital (and back). Engineers define the incremental fuel required to operate a plant with CCS compared with one without as an 'energy penalty' (House et al. 2009). Analysing the discourse surrounding CCS demonstration projects suggests a social analogue: that is, a 'social energy penalty'. One way to think about the social energy penalty is as the additional symbolic efforts required to maintain a social outcome or the loss of social welfare for a constant resource output that is misdirected into symbolic activities. The cost of symbolic practices related to CCS investments is a social energy penalty wherein excessive investment and attention are placed on CCS as a politically preferred technological solution.

   The most obvious elements of the social energy penalty are the time and money committed to producing and appropriating emblems, credentials and kin by dominant players of a social field. Firms invest substantial discursive effort into positioning their activities as responsibly supporting the modern energy needs and lifestyles. High-status players build and institutionalise prestigious associations, accreditation agencies and awards as 'organised exhibition[s] of symbolic capital' (Bourdieu 1995: 180). They participate in advanced technology demonstration projects as a point of corporate pride and to confer status on themselves by showing that they can do it (ibid.: 185). Governments in heavily coal-based economies are granting legitimacy to demonstration projects by providing hard subsidies and soft support by connecting the projects to national pride and to the public interest. Thus, both public and private CCS project participants are complicit in wasting social energy in inefficient and nonproductive practices.

The social energy penalty also includes willful ignorance – by both dominant and marginal players in the field. From within, firms cannot separate symbolic from economic capital or economic from noneconomic arguments because the two are 'perfectly interconvertible' (ibid.: 178). Even apparently altruistic motivations for undertaking CCS projects, such as contributing to national technological leadership, may be misconceived economic arguments for firm survival. All firm activities have both a material and a symbolic component. Outsiders cannot discern the difference between substantive and symbolic work; they only see whether dominant players are fulfilling their 'socially defined proper function' (ibid.: 175). The narrow field of opinion also means that the effectiveness of CCS as a substantive solution for climate change among the whole universe of potential solutions is 'socially repressed' (ibid.: 176). Radical solutions to climate change are dismissed as heretical, whereas CCS is promoted and perpetuates lock-in to our high-carbon energy system. This collective willful ignorance reproduces the system of status and domination that obscures economic incentives, thereby wasting social energy.

A third dimension of the social energy penalty is the endless reconversion of economic capital into symbolic capital (and back). In the case of CCS demonstration projects, firms convert public funding into cultural symbols by emphasising the prestige of the project and their technological leadership. Other actors in the social field misrecognise the authority of project proponents to produce a legitimate reputation for environmental responsibility, converting it into an economically valuable social licence to operate. Although the different forms of capital may be perfectly interconvertible, the conversion process is costly.

We can understand the impact of symbolic activities by powerful firms on the social energy penalty using the model from Chapter 4. In

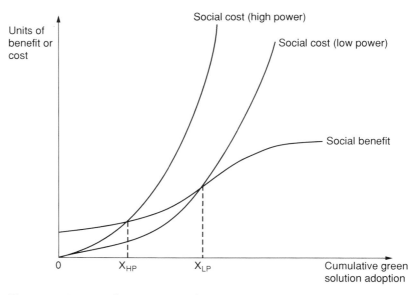

Figure 6.1 Impact of power within fields on the social energy penalty.

the case of investments in CCS, we expect the social benefit curve to be smooth and to reach its limit at a relatively low level (Figure 6.1). The Global CCS Institute's most recent Status of CCS Report highlights the enormous and long-term investments needed to improve CCS technology and make it cost competitive with other carbon-reduction technologies (Global CCS Institute 2011). Numerous industrial-scale pilot projects are needed not only to refine the technology but also to provide on-the-job learning for technicians, engineers and managers; to test emerging legal and regulatory systems and familiarise regulators with the technology; and to develop industry partnerships and provide opportunities for real community engagement (Global CCS Institute 2011: 46). Cooperation and learning among international project proponents is not well enough coordinated for strong learning or network effects (de Coninck, Stephens, and Metz 2009), leading to a smooth curve. Furthermore, ten large-scale integrated projects were put on hold or cancelled in 2010 due to the financial crisis, uncertainty about national climate policy, and/or reprioritised investment (Global CCS Institute 2011). Learning from pilot programs is likely only when projects proceed through to the operation or execution phases.

Identifying and evaluating projects may be useful for firm reputation but will not lead to dramatic technology-performance improvements. Given the weak learning and network effects, there are few additional benefits available to the next incremental adopter.

Chapter 4 discusses the fact that the social cost curve is primarily a reflection of early adopters' discretionary power. Figure 6.1 illustrates the difference between the social cost curves for fields in which powerful actors exert their systemic power to a greater or lesser extent. The social energy penalty becomes salient at lower levels of cumulative investments in green solutions when actors can exert higher discretionary power (i.e., $X_{HP} < X_{LP}$ in Figure 6.1). Analysing the field structure and cultural symbols surrounding CCS demonstration projects suggests several preliminary conjectures about when the social energy penalty is more likely to become an issue at cumulative output level X_{HP} than at X_{LP}. Understanding the discourse, practitioners and practices within a field (Tatli 2011) can suggest contingencies for when the social energy penalty might be relatively larger.

First, with regard to discourse, the analysis revealed that both governments and NGOs granted firms authority to define appropriate CO_2 mitigation solutions by prioritising the pro-CCS orthodoxy. Powerful firms produced cultural symbols around their involvement in CCS projects, and others granted legitimacy to their efforts by conforming and reinforcing a narrow field of opinion about CCS. Powerful incumbents exerted discretionary power, thereby limiting the voluntary supply of green solutions to include CCS as a technological solution. We therefore can expect the social energy penalty to be higher when there is a narrow field of opinion due to the lack of competition for solutions and thorough examination of radical alternatives. Linking this with contemporary institutional theory, we also might expect the social energy penalty to be higher when the most powerful actors in the field – in this case, incumbent firms and governments – hold complementary rather than conflicting institutional logics.

Second, the analysis revealed that practitioners in the Canadian CCS field were connected in dense networks within Calgary's energy-production cluster and quite mobile among firms, technical roles in industry and research groups, and even between industry and government. More broadly, the CCS fields examined – in the United States, Australia, Canada and the European Union – are relatively concentrated and dependent on government support. Thus, firms are more likely to prefer an ongoing, long-term relational approach to their political activities and to be more politically active (Hillman et al. 2004). The social energy penalty is likely to be higher when the power structure is more concentrated and the field is dominated by high-status actors.

Third, with respect to practices, we might expect a higher social energy penalty when firms adopt pollution control technologies for legitimation rather than competitiveness motives (Bansal and Roth 2000). A good indicator for the presence of a high social energy penalty is when the emblems, credentials and kin prominent within a field surrounding a technology are based on nontechnical criteria. This indicates that more social effort is being dedicated to signalling legitimacy to stakeholders such as local communities, NGOs and the public rather than signalling competitive benefits to shareholders. Another indicator might be whether it is common to delay or extend project deadlines, which is particularly tempting for reluctant, incumbent and powerful actors who only need to be seen as planning something to gain valuable legitimacy.

For similar reasons, we expect the social energy penalty to be higher in fields dominated by technology users (who face a cost of adoption) rather than technology developers (who can see the commercial opportunities in developing the technology). The social energy penalty may be higher when practice is driven by firms that are not likely to gain economically from CCS technologies, as in the coal-rich economies of Canada, Australia and the United States. A firm's symbolic practices in these contexts are less directly related to CCS technologies (e.g., awards for general corporate environmental performance rather than for developing specific technologies); the conversion is less likely to reap direct economic benefit, thereby wasting more social energy.

Funding sources are also likely to affect the social energy penalty. Many CCS projects are reliant on government subsidies, which are often awarded to the most symbolically and politically astute firms. The CCS field is dominated by large public–private consortia consisting of established firms within an industry (cf. Mowery et al. 2010). This might allow firms to exert their systemic power because observing individual actor behaviour within collective initiatives is difficult. Joint initiatives require a coherent, shared set of cultural symbols, which further tempts firms to invent new symbols to signal their environmental responsibility. Thus, the social energy penalty may be higher when green solutions are provided through government subsidy or public–private consortia.

Overall, this analysis suggests that the social cost curve will be more vertical when fields are characterised by narrow discourses, complementary institutional logics, concentrated practitioner networks, actors with motives of legitimation rather than competitiveness, technology users rather than technology developers, project-development consortia, and reliance on government subsidies. Clearly, these suggestions need to be empirically tested and may turn out to be somehow idiosyncratic to CCS investments. That said, it does seem clear that we need to take more seriously the power dynamics surrounding pollution control technology investments. In the absence of unambiguous economic performance incentives, the temptation to generate and protect symbolic capital can lead firms to exert their discretionary power, thereby making a social energy penalty more likely. This is even more likely when the established order comes under threat and firms exert their status to act on green solutions rather than being driven by reputation or legitimacy.

Figure 6.1 shows that the social cost of symbolic behaviour related to pollution control technologies can outweigh the benefits of adopting them at low levels of cumulative output (X_{HP}). This is the case even when there is a standalone environmental value of the technology (i.e., where the social benefit curve crosses the vertical axis above zero; see Chapter 4, Figure 4.7). It is probably reasonable to assume a positive standalone technology value for most pollution control technologies because the purpose of adopting them is to store, reduce or eliminate unwanted pollutants. However, the extent to which CCS technology offers standalone environmental benefits is controversial. Questions remain about whether it is technically feasible to capture and bury sufficient carbon to impact the overall atmospheric concentration of CO_2, the long-term implications of storing CO_2 underground, or – indeed – whether CCS is publicly acceptable. Problems in any of these areas would threaten the standalone technology value of CCS, lowering the entire benefits curve in Figure 6.1 and driving X even farther to the left. The jury is still out on CCS as a green solution, but it is possible to imagine that the standalone technology value will be so low – and the learning and network effects due to delaying and ceremonially planning projects so weak – that it could be an example of social cost outweighing social benefit from the very first project. This also could be the case for other pollution control technology investments surrounded by a 'perfect storm' of discourses, practitioners and practices within a field permitting the promotion of environmentally questionable technologies by powerful actors.

In this chapter, I ask when and how actors can exert discretionary power, and I provide answers by examining the field structure and cultural symbols surrounding an illustrative pollution control technology. I examine the symbolic practices of twenty-three CCS demonstration projects across four different jurisdictions, providing a broad view of symbolic performance across these contexts. However, the analysis focuses on one field – that is, CCS demonstration projects. Other technologies are developed within a context of several overlapping fields, each with actors embedded within their own meaning systems. It is to this context that I turn in the next chapter.

7 | *Study 3: The evolution of measurement and performance standards*

How do we know if firms are improving their environmental performance? Researchers with the conventional perspective tend to assume that performance-based environmental standards – such as LEED green building certification or membership in the Dow Jones Sustainability Index – signify improved environmental performance. They also routinely evaluate the substantive impacts of firm activities by counting their emissions, water use, energy efficiency and other dimensions of their environmental footprint. A more critical perspective explicitly recognises that measurement involves firms investing in collecting, measuring, comparing, reporting and narrating a story on their environmental impacts.

Measurement systems, technologies, processes and reporting documents have both a material and a symbolic component. Environmental measurement systems are diverse and socially contested. New measurement standards can eventually provide credible indicators of corporate environmentalism. But, in the early stages, firms may be uncertain about which measurement norms to follow to be able to demonstrate their environmental legitimacy. Over time, a single or narrow set of measurement, accounting and disclosure standards becomes established as the norm. The final set of measurement standards that is integrated into existing institutional fields and ultimately valued as comprising credible signals of a firm's corporate environmentalism depends on the relational dynamics and meaning systems within institutional fields.

This process is currently unfolding around corporate carbon accounting and disclosure standards. Some firms are learning to report their carbon management initiatives, going so far as to track CO_2 emissions through the value chain at the product level and then disclosing this information on consumer product labels. Firms face the challenge of developing new measurement capabilities and technologies within the 'ongoing experiment' of emerging carbon markets (Callon

2009: 537). Conventional corporate environmentalism research often assumes that carbon disclosure is based on measurement that is materially accurate, consistent over space and time, and transparent (see, e.g., Thomas, Repetto, and Dias 2007). However, in this early stage of the evolution of carbon disclosure standards, norms and shared meanings are not yet stable (Hoffmann and Busch 2008). Both voluntary and mandatory symbolic performance standards relative to carbon accounting and disclosure are still evolving.

In Chapter 5, I defined an 'institutional field' as including 'all organisations that partake of a common meaning system and whose participants interact more frequently and fatefully with one another than with actors outside the field' (Scott 1995: 56). Fields are held together not only by similar regulatory processes – whether they are strongly or weakly monitored (see Chapter 5) or dominated by a concentrated, powerful elite (see Chapter 6) – but also by actors sharing similar symbolic processes (Scott and Meyer 1994: 71). Fields are held together by how actors think about classification systems, specify what is taken as similar or different, confer identities on themselves and other actors, and determine what is remembered and recorded (Douglas 1986). New measurement standards challenge existing meaning systems and what is perceived as legitimate in the field. New symbols and norms that become integrated into the field are likely to be those that are consistent with the existing meaning systems and relational dynamics of the field.

In the early stages of new measurement and classification systems, there is still uncertainty and contestation about which systems will ultimately become established. However, because of the potential value of shared recognition, learning effects, and the motivating complementary asset of stakeholder interest, there are likely to be network externalities associated with the adoption of a common set of standards. This begs the question: How do we end up with a particular measurement and disclosure system gaining momentum and becoming the dominant design? What determines the extent to which new environmental disclosure standards prioritise symbolic rather than substantive performance criteria? Ultimately, when is there likely to be a higher social energy penalty associated with new symbolic performance standards?

In this chapter, I investigate the practitioners, practices and discourses surrounding the evolving carbon measurement and disclosure.[1]

I am primarily interested in how the distribution of actors and meaning systems around a new measurement technology leads to an emphasis on symbolic rather than substantive corporate environmentalism. Firms need to develop new norms on measurement and disclosure that are acceptable indicators of their environmental responsiveness. However, they are in the process of doing this within a broader social conversation on understanding the science of climate change, reducing GHG emissions and an emerging international governance regime. At this early stage, carbon measurement and disclosure is not fully standardised. The question is: Which of the various disclosure norms will eventually dominate? Or, in the language of the model in Chapter 4: Which of the many potential S-curves will the new symbolic performance standards follow? What are the implications of this for the social energy penalty? My analysis shows that the answer depends on the distribution of discourses, interests and power across subfields identified by different practitioners and practices. Furthermore, the eventual shape of the S-curve will have a significant impact on the potential social energy penalty arising from new measurement standards.

Carbon accounting as a new measurement standard

Carbon accounting is a system of measurement technologies designed to gather data on CO_2 emissions, collate it, and communicate it – both within and between social entities. In this, I follow Bebbington and Larringa-Gonzalez (2008: 698) in broadening a narrow view of carbon accounting from 'the valuation of assets (such as granted pollution rights) and liabilities (if an organisation is obliged to cover their emissions)' to 'the diverse ways in which accounting is involved in the broader process of change associated with global climate change'. In the next decade or so, we can expect carbon accounting processes, norms and procedures to be standardised, resulting in a core set of dominant designs. However, the norms currently around carbon accounting are not yet settled, so there is considerable uncertainty about which measurement and reporting conventions will become widely adopted and become the eventual standard.

Carbon accounting technologies are evolving at the scientific, organisational and nation-state levels. Carbon accounting has many similarities with other accounting systems: it is a quantitative record of a particular unit that is established according to measurement rules and procedures and then communicated within and beyond measuring entities. However, accounting for carbon also differs from other accounting systems in that it is directly tied to emerging GHG regulatory or voluntary schemes and in that the value of the unit recorded is not monetary unless translated through the price of carbon on a commodity market. The carbon accounting system is also unusual in that it is evolving within the context of innovations in developing consensus on scientific facts and with the engagement of experts from a variety of unconventional sources (especially NGOs) (Callon 2009). Investment in carbon accounting is an example of corporate environmentalism in that firms commit resources to measuring, disclosing and reporting their carbon performance either as a precursor to enhancing their performance in managing carbon emissions or as an audience-seeking signal to interested stakeholders.

Economists analyse carbon markets as a set of technical questions for solving market failures by including externalities, focusing on the costs and benefits of various instruments to incorporate environmental costs (Hepburn 2006). Yet, there is increasing recognition that these markets are developed through 'a laborious and ongoing process of construction of spaces for calculation and transaction, of accounting systems that determine both who is accountable and how and what to count and not to count' (Lohmann 2009: 500). These constructions, as well as the design of carbon measurement and accounting arrangements, are themselves a strategic activity (Callon 2009). The evolution of carbon accounting provides an opportunity to observe how the interests, positions and meaning systems of multiple actors influence the design of a new measurement standard.

The Intergovernmental Panel on Climate Change's (IPCC) Guidelines for National Greenhouse Gas Inventories (IPPC 2006) emphasise that 'good practice' carbon accounting procedures should be transparent, complete, internally consistent, comparable and accurate. Five volumes of guidelines cover the detailed procedures for measurement and reporting of GHG inventories designed to meet these principles. The national inventory guidelines are a foundational carbon accounting technology that provides a governance context and motivation for the development of carbon counting and accounting. However, Callon (2009) questioned the attainability of these theoretical principles by constructing markets as 'problematic networks' crossing arbitrary divisions among economics, politics and science. Similarly, the IPCC's apparently scientific and neutral national GHG inventory procedures are evolving within a highly politicised environment, wherein each measurement principle has different implications for who wins and who loses in the new carbon accounting regime (Kolk, Levy, and Pinkse 2008).

Carbon accounting is a 'stem issue' (Callon 2009) that is problematised in different ways across a wide range of actors involved in developing a new measurement technology. Each of the IPCC's measurement principles is theoretically desirable. However, each is prioritised differently within the discourse across three arenas in which organisations vie for power to devise carbon accounting methodologies and systems. The first arena includes scientific organisations struggling with ways to identify GHG emissions, capturing their existence at the molecular level, and modelling their atmospheric impacts. The second arena includes traditional professional accounting actors and firms that are experimenting with ways to set up carbon accounting systems within and across organisations to record carbon decision-relevant data. The third arena includes policy makers, industry associations, NGOs and lobbyists who are devising carbon accountability systems and inventories across countries to collate GHG emission data and make them verifiable and comparable.

Each set of practitioners interacts with one another, 'participates in the same meaning systems' and 'is defined by similar symbolic processes' (Scott and Meyer 1994: 71). As discussed in Chapter 6, Bourdieu (1995) emphasises the recursive relationship between the distribution of actors' interests and capitals within a field and discourses that legitimise particular activities. According to this view, the particular measurement standards that eventually become institutionalised are those that are consistent with the meaning systems, discourses and practices of the most powerful actors in the field – even if that power is not fully acknowledged. We know that much corporate environmentalism eventually is about symbolic rather than substantive performance. But questions remain on what influences the extent to which new measurement standards are based on symbolic rather than substantive criteria. In this chapter, I explore an answer to this question by focusing on the field structure and discourses about performance criteria surrounding the emerging issue of carbon measurement and disclosure.

Research approach

To explore the current state and likely future evolution of the carbon accounting domain, we hosted an 'Accounting for Carbon' workshop at the University of Oxford.[2] We invited representatives who participate in the science, reporting and governance of carbon accounting to highlight the contentious conversations within their domain, and we facilitated an across-arena exploration of how to address current carbon accounting challenges in the United Kingdom. Participants included senior scientists and executives from a national measurement and standards-setting laboratory, accounting professionals and academics, representatives from early-adopter firms, participants in professional consortia and joint projects that are designing the reporting frameworks, and NGO and policy representatives.

We designed the workshop so as to draw out the controversies, implicit assumptions and dominant discourses within each field. A team of note takers recorded the details of focus group and larger group discussions. During the workshop, we analysed interactions among participants within and between the three carbon accounting arenas. Afterwards, we supplemented and reinforced our findings by conducting interviews with some of the participants and by gathering secondary data. Similar to the CCS project described in Chapter 6, our analytic goal was to identify 'compelling narratives about what a technology is, what a technology might become and why it is needed and preferable to competing technologies' (Lounsbury and Glynn 2001). The carbon accounting technologies under investigation varied from scientific measurement technologies to corporate carbon reporting to national GHG inventories. We gave attention to how members of each arena discussed the issues among themselves and particularly to how they explained their carbon accounting approach to actors in other arenas.

With Bettina Wittneben, I previously analysed and published most of the results section that follows in an accounting journal (Bowen and Wittneben 2011). However, I subsequently realised that the material can be usefully recast in a Bourdesian frame to further advance the implications. Specifically, Tatli's (2011) operationalisation of Bourdieu's conception of a field by examining practices, practitioners and discourses is similar to our original coding scheme but it has the advantage of systematising our earlier ideas. Therefore, I structure the findings in the next section around the practices, practitioners and discourses within our workshop and interview data.

Three fields in carbon accounting

Our conversations with participants on the current state of carbon accounting in the United Kingdom suggest that there are at least three arenas in which organisations vie for power in devising carbon accounting methodologies and systems. The first field consists of scientific organisations charged with measuring GHG emissions and modelling their atmospheric impacts. The second field includes traditional professional accountants and firms involved in setting up firm-level carbon accounting systems to record carbon decision-relevant data. The third field includes policy makers, industry associations, NGOs and lobbyists in the broader governance system that are leading efforts to collate GHG emission data and make data verifiable and comparable across firms and countries.

Table 7.1 outlines the primary differences and similarities among three subfields related to the emergence of a new environmental measurement technology. The three fields of 'counting carbon', 'carbon accounting' and 'accountability for carbon' are not entirely separate from one another. Some boundary-spanning practitioners include NGOs and environmental consultancies that bridge the science, reporting and governance fields; some professional accounting practitioners have crossed over into the transnational governance arena (Suddaby, Cooper, and Greenwood 2007). Nevertheless, delineating some boundaries wherein the discourse, practices, practitioners and symbolic processes are more similar among actors within rather than between fields is useful for understanding the evolution of a new set of social technologies (Tatli 2011).

Practices and practitioners

The central issue connecting actors in the first field is the science of counting carbon in a physical or chemical sense. When we use 'carbon' in our accounting systems, we are – in effect – using only a proxy for actual emissions of a range of GHGs.[3] The trade in the proxy of carbon might not always match the tonnes of CO_2 equivalent emitted. The central mission of practitioners in the counting carbon field is

Table 7.1 *Three carbon accounting organisational fields*

	The counting carbon field	The carbon accounting field	The accountability for carbon field
Level of analysis	Molecular	Plant, corporate, product	Global social system
Origin of carbon problem	Physical, chemical, biological processes	Industrial production processes	Geopolitical entities
Practices	Calibration of atmospheric emissions; chemical equivalences	Assessment of organisational effort; ensuring a level playing field; carbon commoditisation	Allocation of emission-reduction responsibilities across jurisdictions and generations; mitigation of emissions and reducing limits over time; enhance best practice in emission reductions
Practitioners	*International*: e.g., International Organisation for Standardization (ISO); Intergovernmental Panel on Climate Change (IPCC) *National standards*: e.g., UK, National Physical Laboratories (NPL); USA, National Institute of Standards and Technology (NIST) *National geo-science*: e.g., USA, American Geophysical Union (AGU); EU, European Geosciences Union (EGU); UK, British Geological Survey (BGS)	*Specialised*: e.g., World Resources Institute (WRI); Climate Disclosure Standards Board (CDSB) *General accounting*: e.g., International Accounting Standards Board (IASB) *Accounting firms*: e.g., Deloitte, PricewaterhouseCoopers *Professional associations*: e.g., Association for Manufacturing Excellence (AME); Institution of Chemical Engineers (IChemE)	*Transnational*: e.g., UNFCCC Secretariat; European Commission for the EU ETS; International Carbon Auction Partnership *National*: e.g., UK, Department of Energy and Climate Change; USA, Environmental Protection Agency *Sectoral*: e.g., Corporate: International Emission Trading Association (IETA); *Not-for-profit*: Gold standard by WWF

Source: Adapted from Bowen and Wittneben (2011).

to focus closely on the underlying science of counting carbon in a physical sense. As MacKensie (2009) stated, to design a functioning carbon market system, we must develop a science of 'making things the same'.

Practitioners in the counting carbon field include international agencies such as the IPCC and the ISO. These organisations develop recognised standards, for example, regarding calibration (e.g., ISO 17025) and GHG equivalences (IPCC 2001). These international agencies are supplemented by national organisations responsible for ensuring accurate measurements and standards (e.g., the National Physical Laboratory in the United Kingdom) and geoscience organisations that promote scientific understanding of atmospheric emissions (e.g., the American Geophysical Union). All of these practitioners have in common a focus on the physical, chemical and biological origin of the GHG emissions problem, including CO_2, and they are trained and qualified in the physical, biological and ecological sciences.

The primary practices in the carbon counting field involve calibrating atmospheric emissions and developing our understanding of molecular-level issues, such as the chemical equivalences of different GHGs (MacKensie 2009). Scientific knowledge in this domain, and the organisational structures such as the IPCC designed to validate and publicise it, are continuously evolving (Callon 2009). Workshop participants from this organisational field identified controversies surrounding particular practices, including which chemical substances should be counted towards GHG inventories and how to measure emissions from sources that are difficult to measure (e.g., land use). Practitioners in this field professed a confidence in their technical practices – they believed that most of the necessary scientific measurement technologies are already available. However, they seemed less confident about their legitimacy to engage in practices related to prioritising the development of particular measurement technologies. They emphasised that the measurement techniques to prioritise for development should be guided by scientific curiosity and technological potential. They also acknowledged their reliance on the availability of funding and the importance of maintaining relationships with funders to access resources to explore new measurement techniques.

Organisations in the second organisational field are connected through efforts to develop or adapt carbon accounting systems within firms to record carbon management data. Firms, investors and securities regulators are demanding new quantitative and qualitative reporting standards within accounting systems as they become interested in assessing organisational efforts to manage GHG emissions risk (Cook 2009; Lash and Wellington 2007). As public pressure mounts to address climate change and therefore reduce emissions, organisations in this field are under regulatory and PR pressure to record, communicate and reduce carbon from the production of goods and services across the value chain.

Key practitioners within this field include specialised carbon accounting organisations such as the World Resources Institute (WRI), which developed the standardised GHG Protocol, and the Climate Disclosure Standards Board, which brings together businesses, environmental organisations and leading professionals to enhance best practices in carbon accounting and reporting. Consultants within accounting firms such as Deloitte LLP and PricewaterhouseCoopers are active practitioners in this domain as they seek to shape, develop and build competitively valuable capabilities for helping firms learn about new carbon accounting requirements (Engels 2009). Standards organisations such as the International Accounting Standards Board (IASB) seek to integrate carbon concerns into current accounting practices through their economic-based regulatory approach (Cook 2009; Suddaby et al. 2007). Professional associations, including the Association for Manufacturing Excellence in the United States, are participating in this field by educating their corporate members about emerging carbon accounting requirements and collating best practices. Other practitioners in this field include managers within organisations that are now expected to report carbon performance, ranging from large, visible and publicly listed firms, to those European firms required to report emissions within the European Union Emission Trading System (EU ETS), to local authorities whose emissions performance is increasingly monitored in the United Kingdom.

The key practices of actors in this field are to develop consistent assessments of organisational effort on climate-related issues so as to ensure a level playing field among firms, industries and trading systems and over time. The focus is on accounting for carbon emissions as they arise through industrial production processes, whether at the plant, corporate or even product level. Within this field, carbon is commoditised so as to facilitate trade and to better understand trade-offs in firm-level decision making about GHG emission risks (Lohmann 2009).

Controversial frontiers within this field include whether to extend the scope of carbon accounting beyond direct emissions (Scope 1) and indirect electricity-use emissions (Scope 2) and the optional reporting of other indirect GHG emissions across supply chains (Scope 3) (Ranganathan et al. 2004; World Business Council for Sustainable Development/World Resources Institute 2001). There are active conversations in this field about the pros and cons of different carbon accounting methods, the extent to which carbon accounting should be voluntary or mandatory for different types of firms, and the integration of both qualitative and quantitative GHG emissions data within existing managerial and financial accounting systems (Cook 2009). All of these practices are contested within the carbon accounting field, and they are interconnected with both the carbon counting and accountability fields. The carbon accounting field is drawn together through practices that address how to provide for social demands for increased GHG emission performance transparency at the firm level.

Table 7.1 lists the characteristics of the third organisational field, based on how accountability for carbon is allocated in the current system of governance. The third field consists of governmental organisations and NGOs contesting the issue of allocation of CO_2 emission reductions responsibilities across jurisdictions and generations. Practitioners in this field reside in transnational organisations such as those administering the EU ETS and the International Carbon Action Partnership (ICAP). For example, ICAP governs the emission reductions by signatories to the treaties and transmits experience and knowledge from expert consultations back to the international climate policy process. National organisations include practitioners in the Department of Energy and Climate Change (DECC) through initiatives such as the Carbon Reduction Commitment Energy Efficiency Scheme in the United Kingdom and the recent entry of the US EPA into the mandatory GHG emissions reporting domain. Key actors in this field include the three agencies negotiating commensurability standards for carbon trading – that is, the International Emission Trading Association, the International Swaps and Derivatives Association, and the European Federation of Energy Traders (MacKensie 2009). The field incorporates experts from NGOs such as WWF, which initiated the development of the Gold standard for premium quality carbon credits (Lohmann 2009), and the Prince of Wales Accounting for Sustainability Forum, which is seeking to develop a Connected

Reporting Framework (Hopwood 2009). This field is also populated by many market designers, carbon traders and brokers, lobbyists and members of advocacy NGOs seeking to influence the design of carbon trading schemes, such as the EU ETS (Braun 2009).

Practices in this organisational field address how the accountability for carbon is allocated across nations, industries and time (Giddens 2009). Actors in this field measure, monitor, and hold GHG emitters accountable for their activities, enforcing these practices when they fail to deliver on their commitments (Newell 2008). The accountability field is drawn together by practices that commoditise carbon so as to quantify national CO_2 emissions inventories and allocate mitigation responsibilities. In contrast with the carbon accounting field, however, the focus is not only on the ability to commoditise carbon to facilitate trade and the production of national inventories but also to realise actual and decreasing caps on the amount of carbon traded over time. Within this field, the origin of the carbon problem is widely understood to reside in the historical industrial-development trajectories of developed and developing countries (Giddens 2009). The challenge is to devise a set of governance systems that can ensure actual scientifically measurable cuts in GHG emissions and enforce consequences on those actors who do not take appropriate mitigation actions. Although national carbon inventories are not based on collating carbon accounts from firms, there is an important interaction between the carbon accountability and accounting fields about the extent to which governments have the information to hold industry accountable for emissions.

Each of the three fields shown in Table 7.1 consists of different practitioners who enact different practices within the overall emerging technology of accounting for carbon. Our conversations with members of these fields showed that the narratives around what carbon accounting is, why it is needed, and why particular types are preferable to others also varied across the different fields.

Discourses

As noted previously, the IPCC's (2006) guidance on the development of carbon measurement technologies states that carbon accounting procedures should be transparent, complete, consistent, comparable and accurate. Table 7.2 defines each of these desirable characteristics

Table 7.2 *Discursive priorities of measurement criteria across three carbon accounting fields*

Criterion	Definition	Counting carbon	Carbon accounting	Accountability for carbon
Accuracy	Accuracy is a relative measure of the exactness of an emission or removal estimate. Estimates should be accurate in the sense that they are systematically neither over nor under true emissions or removals, so far as can be judged, and that uncertainties are reduced so far as is practicable.	High	Low	Medium
Transparency	Transparency means that the assumptions and methodologies used should be clearly explained to facilitate replication and assessment by users of the reported information.	High	Low	High
Completeness	Completeness means that all sources and sinks and gases are included for the full geographic coverage.	Medium	Low	High
Consistency	Consistency means that an inventory should be internally consistent in all its elements over a period of years.	Low	Medium	High
Comparability	Comparability means that estimates of emissions and removals reported should be comparable among entities. For this purpose, agreed methodologies and formats for estimating and reporting should be used.	Medium	High	High

Source: Definitions are adapted from IPCC (2006).

for the eventual dominant design of this new environmental measurement technology. In the discussions among practitioners invited to our workshop, it became apparent that there is a definite incongruence among the three fields in the discursive priority placed on each characteristic (see Table 7.2).

Practitioners in the counting carbon field insisted on the importance of measuring CO_2 and other GHGs accurately. Because some of these calculations are more easily attainable than others, an indicator of certainty is necessary to attach to the results of the emission calculations. GHG emission calculations vary highly in uncertainty: whereas the calculation of CO_2 emissions from the burning of a particular fossil fuel is fairly straightforward, methane emissions from cattle can vary by breed, feed and other factors, presenting challenges for the accuracy and certainty of calculations. Within this field, the consistency across calculations is not viewed as such a high priority because it is recognised that emissions cannot be easily compared across GHGs – even by using a common unit such as a CO_2 equivalent (Bruce, Yi, and Haites 1996; Shine et al. 2005; Smith and Wigley 2004; Vine et al. 2003). Measurement technologies improve and develop over time so that using the same measurement technique year after year is less important than transparency in describing methods.

The dominant discourse in the field of carbon accounting is based on comparability and commensuration derived from market logic. 'Comparability' refers to the extent that emissions are based on agreed methodologies and formats so that equivalent entities and activities will generate equivalent carbon accounts. Comparability is important for external reporting so as to maintain a level playing field between organisations within and between sectors. Underlying comparability is 'commensuration', defined as 'the transformation of different qualities into a common metric' (Espeland and Stevens 1998: 314). Commensuration is a social and political process but it is vital to maintain the ability to quantify and trade (Kolk et al. 2008). Indeed, practitioners in this field are adept at maintaining distance between 'traders' conceptual, largely electronic universe of "abstract", simplified and fungible carbon credit numbers and the "concrete", diverse, particular, highly complex, often obscure local projects that produced them' (Lohmann 2009: 506). Although this discourse is far removed from the underlying substantive environmental impacts of economic activities, it is this distance that can help maintain consistency and an aura of certainty.

The casualty, of course, is accuracy as the discursive focus on agreeing shared reporting methodologies becomes farther removed from measuring the underlying true emissions. For example, it has become common for firms to report improvements in their own Scope 1 emissions relative to output over time but without accurately reporting overall emission increases. Furthermore, even commonly used firm-level indicators, such as a firm's production output, are not necessarily accurate, thereby casting doubt on the accuracy of relative emissions measures. There is less conversation in this field about transparency and completeness than there is about establishing credibility through an apparently high degree of comparability and competence to self-report carbon emissions.

Similar to the discourse regarding CCS demonstration projects described in Chapter 6, more radical policy options, such as mandating emissions standards, are largely absent from the dominant discourse in the carbon accounting field. The conversation is about increasingly elaborate and coordinated carbon accounting frameworks. Broader solutions to the environmental impacts of economic activity are routinely underplayed within the technicalities of and conversation about designing new environmental disclosure standards.

Finally, discourse in the accountability for carbon field prioritises consistency across carbon inventories through transparent, complete and comparable procedures (IPCC 2006). Only consistency can make it possible for emissions by nations and economies to be compared over time, supporting answerability and enforceability practices around CO_2 emissions. This so-called commensuration project (Kolk et al. 2008; Levin and Espeland 2002) is vital in allocating responsibility and accountability. That the recorded emissions are indeed accurate is important to grant legitimacy to the system and to satisfy various stakeholders; however, accuracy is defined in a weaker sense in this field than in the counting carbon field. The IPCC guidelines describe accuracy as 'relative' and should reduce uncertainties 'as far as is practicable'. Lacking the exactness of the counting carbon field, this discourse is less concerned with the 'true value' of emissions estimates and with precision as a measurement principle. Moreover, 'given the current state of scientific knowledge . . . the inventory uncertainties are high compared with the demands given by the inventory applications, even if they are prepared according to the guidelines and good practice (IPCC 2001)' (Rypdal and Winiwarter 2001: 107). The dominant discourse in this field focuses less on accuracy and more on reducing unknowns to consistent probabilistic scenarios compared with a constructed 'business as usual' (Bebbington and Larrinaga-Gonzalez 2008; Lohmann 2009).

Thus, there is an inherent discrepancy among the three fields in how they give discursive priority to the IPCC's measurement criteria of accuracy, transparency, completeness, consistency and comparability. Although accuracy is scientifically valuable, it may come at a high cost to both the development of measurement techniques and the reporting efforts of organisations. There also is a risk that accuracy that is too strongly enforced will make company reports difficult to analyse and interpret (Hopwood 2009). In fact, a market system requires the consistency and commensurability between emissions, both within and across companies, prioritising comparability (MacKensie 2009). The problem is that ensuring comparability with existing accounting standards can lead to 'very strange results' when applied to the new carbon emission instruments (Cook 2009). Understanding the different discursive priorities placed on consistency across fields can help us understand the IASB's unsuccessful support of the International Financial Reporting Interpretations Committee's interpretation of emissions rights. The very features desired by carbon market designers to improve carbon accountability (i.e., prioritising consistency and comparability) led to 'public outcry' in the carbon accounting field because they diminished the overall importance of accuracy and indicators of substantive GHG reductions (Cook 2009: 457).

Discussion and implications

In this chapter, I extend Callon's (2009: 540–541) reminder that 'calculative equipment, whether it serves to establish equivalences between chemical entities (for example, to measure their effects on global warming), to price goods, to organise encounters between supplies and demands (auctions or other mechanisms), or simply to measure emissions, is . . . the subject of stormy debates and lies at the heart of structuring carbon markets'. I focus on how three related fields prioritised the dimensions of accuracy, transparency, completeness, consistency and comparability in the development of a set of new environmental measurement technologies designed to measure and disclose firm performance. The three fields can be distinguished by their practices based at the molecular, the organisational and the societal levels, respectively. Practitioners within each field describe different emphases among these principles. Most discursive effort about carbon accounting within corporate environmentalism is about symbolic comparability, methodologies and formats for consistent reporting. The accountability challenge is to find an acceptable way to make carbon accounting work without lowering accuracy so much that the performance measurement system is completely detached from substantive emissions performance.

Practices within the three carbon accounting fields demonstrate the complex nature of measuring, reporting and effectively communicating GHG emissions. The science of how emissions are measured is still evolving, the social practice of accounting for carbon within organisations is still contested, and the effectiveness of a global carbon governance system has not been proven. Some argue that current systems of carbon markets are overly costly and ineffective (Wittneben 2009); others contend that the sheer notion of setting up a carbon market is inherently flawed (Lohmann 2010). Both critiques arise from the potential of the symbols around new environmental disclosure standards to become detached from substantive CO_2 emission reductions.

If a carbon accounting system is to have any substantive impact on reducing carbon emissions, accuracy must be taken more seriously within corporate environmentalism. The problem is that in the short run, developing carbon accounting systems 'accurate' to several decimal places may be counterproductive. Additional focus should be on understanding tolerances around current best estimates of carbon performance. We need to be explicit in recognising that in current corporate carbon accounting practice, accuracy is low and uncertainty is high. Initial enthusiasm for corporate environmental reporting and high tolerance levels allow companies to begin reporting their carbon performance relatively easily (Bumpus 2009). However, this uncertainty should be recognised and reported. For example, corporate environmental disclosure could move towards providing indicators of uncertainty or tolerances in carbon reporting, not only point indicators. Bebbington and Larringa-Gonzalez (2008) provided a useful distinction between the accounting challenges of risks as contrasted with uncertainties arising due to climate change. Firms that have already begun to invest in environmental management and disclosure may be developing risk management competences through established accountancy tools (e.g., sensitivity analysis and hedging); however, the dominant worldview in corporate environmentalism does not give adequate attention to measurement uncertainty. This is a particular problem in a new and emerging measurement technology because neglecting uncertainty measures from the outset can become embedded within the eventual dominant design, creating an artificial and unfounded social confidence in the system that can be difficult to change.

Another implication of this analysis is that we should be wary of locking-in measurement and performance standards too early. Much of the current contestation in the carbon accounting field is about which elements of carbon measurement and disclosure will eventually be retained in the dominant design. Which of the many potential future S-curves will prevail? Standards can develop significant inertia over time, and an initial period of lower accuracy and higher tolerance for the development of different carbon disclosure standards may lead to measurement and reporting innovations, which could place carbon disclosure standards on a preferred social benefit curve in the long run. This dynamic is compounded given the tendency to closely focus on market design in the early stages of market development but then to take market-design decisions as given once the market has begun (Callon 2009). Lessons from early experiences in other accounting domains demonstrate that we may not need accurate accounting in the short run but rather that controllable accounting that can evolve over time (Suzuki 2003). Inevitably, developing more consistent and comparable global accounting standards is a political process, and it may be easier to maintain constructive conversations with 'losers' in the carbon market if the standards are not locked-in prematurely (Biondi and Suzuki 2007).

At this early stage of carbon accounting technology development, it is perhaps inevitable that there should be different discursive priorities across the three coexisting fields. The question then becomes: Which, if any, of the measurement criteria are most likely to be entrenched as important as new measurement standards become institutionalised? The answer will depend on the distribution of interests and power within the system. Scientists, who prioritise accuracy, are dependent on funding from government and other sources and are hindered by the constraints of the current scientific climate of ideas. In contrast, practitioners in the accountability field value the desirability of

completeness, consistency and transparency but they depend on political will to be able to promote these objectives. In 2009–2012, the
enthusiasm for the climate change political agenda deflated with the
demise of the Kyoto Protocol and prolonged economic pressure from
the financial crisis, limiting political interest in governing carbon
emissions.

The actors with the most interest in and power to develop current
carbon disclosure standards are those in the carbon accounting arena.
Firms may not have the scientific expertise of the counting carbon
practitioners or the force of answerability of the accountability field.
However, they do have the financial resources, industry networks,
relationships and accounting expertise to be able to invest in new
carbon disclosure technologies. Accounting associations, management
accounting consultancies, firms and industry associations are routinely
afforded the legitimacy to develop new measurement standards. As
a result, it is hardly surprising that the eventual dominant design
will focus on criteria related to comparability rather than accuracy.
Members of the other fields may be reassured that there is at least an
ongoing conversation about developing carbon disclosure standards:
some corporate environmentalism may be better than no environmentalism. But resources will be invested in improving the comparability
and consistency of standards as part of audience-seeking for carbon
performance rather than the accuracy, transparency or completeness
required to drive substantive performance-enhancement. A firm's voluntary 'gift' of carbon accounting information may not match stakeholders' preferences, leading to a utility loss.

Over time, measurement standards based on comparability rather
than accuracy, transparency or completeness become embedded as
the normal and legitimate way to report carbon performance. Politicians may eventually reengage with the carbon management agenda,
but 'there is a tension between the incentives for individual minds to
spend their time and energy on difficult problems and the temptation
to sit back and let founding analogies of the surrounding society take
over' (Douglas 1986: 55). The founding analogies – that is, the early
labels adopted to describe who and what is noticed, remembered and
recorded – become a vital element of the eventual dominant design.
Although all of the actors involved in new carbon measurement technologies may have been driven initially by social concerns, the distribution of practices, practitioners, discourses, interests and power

can lead to performance standards that are quite separate from the underlying substantive environmental impacts. Once this happens, 'all the advantages lie with joining the corporate effort to make founding analogies do the work, and very little advantage lies with the privateer working under his own flag' (Douglas 1986: 51). Once a symbolic gap has emerged in a measurement and performance standard, significant social energy is required to close it.

Empirical summary

The evolution of new carbon measurement and disclosure standards incorporates a wide range of activities conducted by scientists, accountants and policy makers. Carbon accounting technologies are evolving in three interconnected arenas: (1) the scientific knowledge of how to recognise and count carbon dioxide emissions, (2) the accounting effort to collect and record this information at the organisational level, and (3) the policy arena of devising accountability systems such as national GHG inventories that use and compare these data. All of the actors are drawn together by the stem issue of developing carbon accounting that is transparent, complete, consistent, comparable and accurate (IPCC 2006). However, the relative importance of each measurement criterion varies across the three carbon accounting fields (see Table 7.2).

In this chapter, I ask how we end up with particular measurement standards gaining momentum and becoming the dominant design over time. To answer this question, I argue that organisational fields are held together not only by regulatory processes (as explored in previous chapters) but also by common meaning systems and shared symbolic processes. New institutions such as performance standards must fit within these fields to be accepted as legitimate. Therefore, the eventual performance standard that establishes itself as the dominant design is likely to be consistent with the meaning systems and symbolic processes of a field. In the case of carbon accounting, scientists prefer measurement systems that are accurate and transparent, accountants prefer standards that are comparable, but the governance field prioritises measurement that is internally consistent, transparent and complete.

This helps to answer the second question in this chapter: What determines the extent to which a new environmental disclosure standard is based on symbolic rather than substantive criteria? Even if individual actors are drawn to the carbon accounting domain by an authentic desire to make a substantive difference in the GHG emissions problem, there are inherent dynamics in fields that prioritise the interests and meaning systems of some actors over others. This chapter investigates the distribution of practices (i.e., what people do), practitioners (i.e., who they are), discourses (i.e., what they talk about and consider important), and power (i.e., who has the interest and resources to effect change) across the carbon accounting domain. Performance standards are more likely to be based on symbolic criteria when powerful actors prioritise comparability and reporting formats over other substantive indicators, including accuracy, transparency and completeness of disclosures. These standards become embedded with time as early labels and institutions are understood to be the normal and legitimate way to measure and report environmental impacts.

Environmental disclosure standards and the social energy penalty

Corporate environmentalism requires firms to collect, measure, report and narrate their environmental story so that they can generate positive social evaluations. New measurement systems need to be developed that incorporate green features, classifications and activities that firms have not previously communicated. Standardising these new performance indicators should benefit society as credible indicators of corporate environmentalism and as a way to hold large, high-status organisations accountable. Yet, this chapter shows the influence of interacting discourses, practitioners, practices and power in institutional fields on the shape of the performance standard S-curve. What do these findings reveal about the emergence of new measurement and disclosure standards and the social energy penalty? Or, more specifically, when is there likely to be a higher social energy penalty associated with new measurement standards?

Figure 7.1 shows the now familiar model of the trade-off between the social costs and benefits of corporate environmentalism. In this case, the figure compares the benefits of a given performance standard that is based on substantive as opposed to symbolic criteria. As discussed in this chapter, some discourses about new carbon measurement and disclosure standards prioritised criteria such as accuracy and

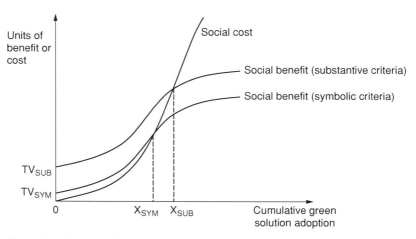

Figure 7.1 Impact of a standard's criteria on the social energy penalty.

completeness (i.e., substantive criteria), whereas others emphasised comparability, agreed methods and formats (i.e., symbolic criteria). Figure 7.1 explains why the shape of the S-curve, as well as the resulting social energy penalty, depends on the extent to which the underlying measurement criteria are based on substantive or symbolic indicators.

The social cost curve in Figure 7.1 is upward sloping because – as with other contexts examined in previous chapters – early entrants in developing new measurement standards have status and power. Accountancy firms possess the emblems, credentials and kin to facilitate the development of new carbon accounting rules; firms have the authority to voluntarily decide which set of standards, if any, they will choose to adopt. As discussed in previous chapters, the steepness of the curve depends on the discretionary power of early adopters. In the carbon accounting context, there are more actors, fewer concentrated practitioner networks, and less reliance on government sponsorship of a particular technology standard than in, for example, the CCS demonstration projects case described in Chapter 6. Therefore, the social cost curve is upward sloping but relatively neutral, as shown in Figure 4.8 (see Chapter 4).

However, simply because there is a more diffuse power base for the development of the measurement technology, it does not mean that there will be no social energy penalty. I show in this chapter that in the case of carbon accounting, widely distributed practices, practitioners, discourses and interests lead to prioritising symbolic comparability over substantive completeness or accuracy. Emphasising different measurement criteria leads to different social benefit curves. Figure 7.1 shows two social benefit curves: the upper one reflects a symbolic performance standard based on substantive criteria and the lower one is based on symbolic criteria. Both curves exhibit the same S-curve shape: performance standards can benefit from network externalities and learning effects whether they are based on substantive or symbolic criteria. A new carbon accounting system will become more valuable the more that others adopt it and the more recognised it becomes. Consultancies, professional accountants and industry associations will disseminate learning on the new symbolic performance standard. However, analysis of the discourses surrounding new carbon accounting technologies reminds us that standardised environmental management and disclosure do not necessarily lead to ensuring substantive GHG emission reductions. The extent to which generating and disclosing better carbon management data provides an environmental benefit independent of the number of adopters is reflected in the performance standard's standalone technology value (TV) – that is, the initial height of the social benefit curve.

Carbon accounting is a way of narrating a carbon performance story aimed at generating positive social evaluations, and such stories do not necessarily correspond with emission reductions. Investing in carbon measurement and disclosure can be merely symbolic rather than a serious attempt to mitigate substantive environmental impacts, particularly for the largest firms. Institutional isomorphism reminds us that ceremonial adoption of carbon accounting can appear highly comparable, but it may not be particularly accurate or yield substantive mitigation impacts. Furthermore, institutional theory suggests that the more that carbon accounting procedures are negotiated and bargained within the organisational field, the higher the likelihood is that new systems will be decoupled from a firm's technical core. But, as I argue in Chapter 4, even largely ceremonial implementation of a new environmental standard may improve a firm's information about its own environmental impacts, internal management processes and market. There is positive standalone technology value from a new performance standard, even without considering whether other firms have implemented it (i.e., $TV_{SYM} > 0$ in Figure 7.1). The first firm reports its carbon performance to meet its own needs, whether for competitiveness, legitimation or responsibility reasons (Bansal and Roth 2000).

The problem from society's point of view is that the primary driver to develop a carbon accounting system is the need to measure and mitigate GHG emission levels. If there were no GHG emission problem, there would be no need to allocate societal resources to developing CO_2 inventories and markets. The standalone technology value of an emerging performance standard is much higher for standards based on the extent to which it encourages substantive CO_2 reductions over time (i.e., $TV_{SUB} > TV_{SYM}$). Measurement standards have the most standalone value when measures are 'fit-for-purpose'. If society's goal is to mitigate the actual GHG emissions generated by human activities, then the social benefit of standards based on substantive criteria will be higher than those based on symbolic criteria at all levels of cumulative adoption, as shown in Figure 7.1.

Therefore, the most immediate answer to the question of when there is likely to be a higher social energy penalty associated with new measurement and performance standards is this: when the standard is based more on symbolic than on substantive underlying criteria. Because of the lower standalone technology value of standards based on symbolic criteria, the cumulative standard adoption level in which the social costs outweigh social benefits is reached sooner for standards based on symbolic measurement criteria than for those based on substantive criteria (i.e., $X_{SYM} < X_{SUB}$). In the specific case of carbon accounting, the social energy penalty is likely to be higher if actors within the carbon accounting arena adopt a set of standards that prioritise consistency over accuracy.

The carbon accounting context shows the social energy penalty in action: high-status scientists, politicians and professional accounting firms are expending considerable communicative effort in seeking legitimacy for their preferred measurement system. The discourse within each field prioritises different criteria. The problem is that in the absence of a powerful, connected and concentrated elite (as described for the CCS demonstration project case in Chapter 4), the eventual dominant design for the standard is likely to be the one most acceptable – or least objectionable – to the actors most engaged in the process. Weak standards based on largely symbolic criteria can be much more versatile than specific standards based on substantive criteria. Thus, there may be a natural tendency towards performance standards based on symbolic rather than substantive criteria in diffuse institutional fields. The social energy penalty may be higher where high-status actors from different social sectors – for example, scientists, politicians and business leaders – are trying to use the same environmental practice to achieve different objectives.

It seems likely that carbon accounting will continue to grow in importance as new emission-reduction regimes are set up and existing regimes are linked. Various stakeholders will give increasing attention to an organisation's carbon budget, which must be measured, reported and conveyed. As we embark on this course of reporting GHG emissions, new systems of measurement, accounting and disclosure will become norms for credible environmental performance. Policy makers and progressive business leaders need to consider how much effort and attention is invested in improving consistency within complex carbon accounting regimes in relation to substantive GHG emission reductions over the course of the regulatory process. Without sufficient attention to substantive criteria, we could end up on a standardisation path that prioritises particular symbols, reporting practices and disclosure norms that may be disconnected from their underlying environmental value. Such symbolic corporate environmentalism can be costly to society because once those norms are established, it can be difficult to change them – regardless of their usefulness in remedying environmental problems. Over time, the social benefits of measurement and disclosure are outweighed by the social costs, which occurs all the more quickly if the standard is based more on symbolic than substantive criteria.

In Chapters 4, 5, and 6, I used a variety of empirical studies from different contexts to explore the contingencies related to when the social energy penalty is likely to be highest. I unpacked the various implications of the model presented in Chapter 4, particularly on what might influence the shapes of the social costs and benefits of corporate environmentalism curves. Analysing different contexts has allowed me to manoeuvre each of these curves one at a time. However, none of the studies attempted to directly measure the social cost or benefit curves. In the next chapter, I address the empirical challenge of how the social costs and benefits of symbolic corporate environmentalism might be measured.

8 | *Measurement and methods*

In this book, I build the case that symbolic corporate environmentalism can result in both social costs and benefits. In Chapters 5, 6, and 7, I provide preliminary evidence for parts of the model. Although these chapters support the idea that there may be a social energy penalty and that the severity of this penalty depends on a variety of field- and firm-level variables, I did not directly test the model. Quantifying more precisely the social costs and benefits of symbolic corporate environmentalism remains an empirical challenge for future researchers. In this chapter, I provide speculative outlines of how to estimate the social costs and benefits of symbolic corporate environmentalism. I describe key dimensions of the social cost and social benefit curves, drawing on research from other areas for inspiration about how to estimate them when needed. The overall aim of this chapter is to inspire others to test elements of the model in the future and to suggest relevant bodies of theory that have addressed analogous measurement problems in the past.

Estimating the social cost curve

Symbolic corporate environmentalism imposes both direct and indirect costs. Firms incur direct costs when managers allocate resources to symbolic green solutions. Some are deliberate investments in reputation building to conceal, buffer or bargain with institutional pressures; others may comprise an unintended consequence of strategic corporate environmentalism.[1] Regardless of whether symbolic green solution investments are deliberate, these direct costs are incurred directly by a firm and represent a diversion of societal resources towards manipulating symbols rather than managing substantive environmental impacts. Indirect costs, conversely, are costs that result from the field- and firm-level dynamics surrounding symbolic corporate environmentalism.

Estimating the social cost curve involves both the direct and indirect costs of symbolic corporate environmentalism.

Direct costs of symbolic corporate environmentalism

My starting point for examining symbolic corporate environmentalism was to extend the emerging academic literature on greenwashing (see Chapter 2). Revisiting the definitions of greenwashing in Table 2.2 provides a sense of the corporate activities that are involved in greenwashing and therefore a baseline level of the costs that such activities might incur. The direct costs of symbolic corporate environmentalism include, at a minimum, those associated with marketing, advertising, communications, reporting and disclosure of a firm's green investments. As discussed in the conceptual models in Chapter 4, these costs are in addition to those related to substantive environmental improvement. But I also argue that symbolic corporate environmentalism is broader than simple greenwashing, in that it includes the shared meanings and representations related to all of the changes made by managers within firms that they describe as primarily for environmental reasons – not only the deliberate, disclosure-based practices. Simply adding up the cost of deliberately symbolic communicative activities would underestimate the direct cost of symbolic corporate environmentalism.

In the CCS demonstration projects study described in Chapter 6, I analyse the cultural symbols related to an environmental technology. This had the advantage of moving beyond the signals and symbols usually considered in the conventional perspective on corporate environmental strategy to include additional costs associated with generating and protecting symbolic capital. There are direct social costs associated with the time and money committed to producing and reproducing emblems, credentials and kin by members of a social field. The critical perspective emphasises the direct cost of building, institutionalising and participating in organised exhibitions of symbolic capital by dominant actors. The conventional perspective acknowledges direct costs associated with reputation building to generate symbolic performance. The first element of the social cost curve is the direct cost of a firm's investments in emblems, credentials and kin.[2]

Emblems are distinctive badges with symbolic meaning used in this case to confer prestige on their owners for sound environmental performance. In some cases, estimating the cost can be as simple as recording the membership fee to earn an emblem. For example, The Sustainability Consortium – a collaboration to improve the sustainability of consumer products over the life cycle and supply chain – offers a Tier I corporate membership for $100,000 per year. Part of the benefit of this level of membership is that members 'will also be recognised as being in the forefront of sustainability efforts around the globe'.[3] Many of the more than fifty household-name companies listed as Tier 1 members reproduce The Sustainability Consortium's logo in their own environmental or sustainability reports and websites as an emblem of their environmental performance.

Firms also invest in their own emblems and symbols to signal their environmental performance through, for example, reports and websites. Boiral's (2013) analysis of more than 1,200 images from twenty-three sustainability reports from firms in the energy and mining sectors revealed an overwhelming tendency to show images and symbols far removed from actual environmental impacts. The average cost of preparing and developing a sustainability report is approximately $112,000 at current prices and can take as many as 4.5 person-years to complete (Guimond and Nagle 2001). The same survey showed that 45 per cent of the time cost is incurred by internal environment, health and safety departments and an additional 24 per cent by outside consultants. The communications departments – which shape, position, and present emblems of environmental performance – incur 25 per cent of the cost.

Credentials are qualifications or documents that entitle the bearer to credibility – in this case, for their environmental performance. The most widely recognised certificate in the corporate environmentalism domain is the ISO 14001 standard. The cost of this certification for a single plant – excluding the cost of organisational changes that firms may have to implement to attain the standard – is estimated at US$50,000 to US$200,000, depending on plant size and the environmental management system already in place (Delmas 2002); furthermore, it can cost US$5,000 to US$10,000 per year to maintain (Bansal and Hunter 2003). Multiplying this amount by at least fourteen thousand certifications worldwide represents a total direct cost of US$1.4 billion or more. In the construction sector, certifying a new building to the USGBC's LEED Silver standard adds 2 to 6 per cent to the cost of a building (Morris 2007), including 2 per cent for commissioning, documentation and fees to verify compliance with the standard (National Environmental Monitoring Conference 2003). Again, multiplying by the 10 billion square feet of building space covered by the scheme (USGBC 2012) and a modest construction cost of US$120 per square foot for commercial buildings yields a direct cost of acquiring LEED credentials of approximately US$2.4 billion.[4]

In another example, companies including BASF and Nestlé proudly claim on their sustainability websites that they are recognised for their collaboration and transparency by participating in schemes such as the CDP. There is no fee to display the CDP logo on a company's website, but there is considerable investment in terms of staff time and expertise to fill out the increasingly detailed CDP investor questionnaire. A recent benchmarking survey revealed that large companies have, on average, 3.6 employees providing centralised support on sustainability issues and that much of their time is expended in responding to surveys and completing certification processes to maintain credentials (Hause 2008). This is in addition to the one hundred or more employees sometimes needed to collect and manage data in support of the environmental function within a firm.

There is evidence that companies are becoming adept at the credentials game, but it also incurs costs. For example, the CPA-Zicklin Index of Political Accountability and Disclosure scores S&P 500 companies in the United States on their political spending and whether they disclose it (Center for Political Accountability 2012). A comparison of the 2011 and 2012 scores reveals several companies that have made spectacular improvements in their scores. Costco raised its score in one year from 3 to 85 out of 100; The Walt Disney Company raised its score from 12 to 67; and Capital One Financial raised its overall score from 20 to 63. It is difficult to imagine that these companies achieved orders-of-magnitude improvements in the underlying transparency of their political lobbying. It is more likely that having scored poorly in the first year of the Index, they invested staff time in understanding how the Index was constructed, completing questionnaires, and altering some of their practices that strongly influenced their scores. These companies were rewarded in 2012 by being certified as strong improvers and leaders in their sectors. Similar strategic manipulation of ratings scores has been observed in credentials such as the LEED green building standards (see, e.g., Corbett and Muthulingam 2007). There are direct costs associated with these credential games.

More advanced credentials cost more. For example, the GRI developed a comprehensive sustainability reporting framework that rates the extensiveness of a firm's sustainability disclosures from C to A+. The incremental cost of preparing a report eligible for the GRI's A+ credential compared with a C level based on data already collected by a firm is approximately 9 to 12 per cent of the reporting cost.[5] This is purely the cost of a symbolic credential because the difference between a C and an A+ GRI rating is the extensiveness of disclosure – not improved substantive impact or even environmental management practices implemented by the firm.

Kin are distinguished by belonging to a class or a group with common attributes, often related through common ancestry or experience. It costs time and money for firms to maintain relationships within the environmental domain in order to send the message that they are part of the environmentally sound family. Bradford and Nagel (2002) found that, on average, large US companies are members of eleven sustainability organisations, interest groups and/or trade associations. The dues and memberships for these associations cost, on average, US$277,000 each year at current prices, plus the average fifty-eight person-days invested in participating in these organisations. The CCS demonstration project study (see Chapter 6) also highlighted the importance of relationships with politicians and scientific experts. Data related to political donations and contributions to academic science are available across industries in most developed countries, although estimators need to separate out the fraction of those costs dedicated to green solutions.

Estimating the direct costs of symbolic corporate environmentalism is perhaps the most straightforward of the estimation challenges presented by the model. An analysis would likely proceed in three steps. First, the emblems, credentials and kin used by a firm to generate symbolic performance on environmental issues should be listed. Second, the direct cost of each should be estimated at the firm level and multiplied up to the appropriate level of analysis, whether at the field, industry or economy level. These two steps would likely lead to an overestimate because certain aspects of direct costs may be the cost of substantive green solutions and not merely symbolic. Some of the cost of acquiring green credentials (e.g., the LEED Silver standard) may be substantive changes to the building design or construction needed to qualify for the certification. Similarly, some of the time and money invested in memberships and associations may be for learning or net-working opportunities, as well as for the symbolic value of being a member. Thus, the third and most challenging step in estimating direct costs of symbolic corporate environmentalism is to separate the purely symbolic fraction of investments in emblems, credentials and kin. Estimating this nebulous factor is an empirical challenge but one worth examining – perhaps first at the firm level – to appreciate the scale of direct costs of symbolic corporate environmentalism across the entire economy.

Indirect costs of symbolic corporate environmentalism

The empirical studies presented in this book indicate a less tangible set of costs arising from symbolic corporate environmentalism that is not fully accounted for in current research. The analyses suggest at least three sets of indirect costs: those resulting from inertia, lock-out and misrecognition.

The conventional technology management and standards literature acknowledges that inertia among standards, once they are established, can become socially costly. Inertia cost is the cost to regulatory author-ities, to the state, or – more broadly – to society of trying to change industry practice after a particular standard is established (Büthe and Mattli 2010). This was most evident in the carbon accounting study (see Chapter 7), as voluntary disclosure standards are becoming nor-malised and may be difficult to change later through formal regulation. Because early voluntary standards become embedded as social norms, later attempts by regulators to formalise, standardise or enhance the standards become more costly because regulators and the regulated must reverse what has already been done. For example, the USGBC's LEED certification standards may or may not be the best way to certify green buildings. However, builders and consumers in the United States are likely to continue to adopt them for a considerable period because of the sunk cost in their development and the inertia that reinforces a de facto standard over time.

A more strategic set of costs consists of lock-out costs – that is, costs arising from the proprietary nature and control over standards such as entry and membership criteria (Büthe and Mattli 2010). Lock-out costs also include the cost of distortions from introducing modifications and updates after particular norms are established.

For example, in its LEED 2012 guidelines for green buildings (later renamed LEED v.4), the USGBC proposed strengthening its criteria for awarding points for using green wood to 'FSC or better.' The previous guidelines recognised wood certified to the less demanding SFI standard. Changing to 'FSC or better" would exclude 75 per cent of North America's forests that currently are environmentally certified. This change of LEED certification rules by its members imposes an additional cost on future certifiers who must source more expensive FSC-certified wood. It also imposes a local social cost in doemestic forestry areas as demand for SFI-certified wood falls (Abusow 2012).[6] Whereas inertia costs are borne by outsiders trying to change an already established standard, lock-out costs are imposed by insiders who can control the membership and entry rules. Lock-out costs reflect who is in and who is out of negotiations about shared meanings, which often are dominated by powerful incumbents.

The third set of indirect costs encountered entails misrecognition costs, wherein society members grant misplaced authority to powerful actors to design legitimate responses to environmental challenges. The CCS demonstration project study described in Chapter 6 demonstrated that large, established energy industry incumbents have the skill, connections and experience to shape the early symbolic game involving a pollution control technology. The carbon accounting study described in Chapter 7 emphasised how once early shared meanings are adopted, significant social energy is required to change them. Although it is easier to let the powerful take the lead in self-regulation, there are opportunity costs associated with green solutions that might have emerged had the discourse not been so narrow. Within the critical perspective, misrecognition costs arise from wilful ignorance and the incremental emotional and social energy needed to change how people think about established institutions. The extent of these costs is closely connected to the power and status of those who support the self-regulatory scheme.

For example, in the United States, the *de facto* green building standard is the LEED rating scheme, which was designed and promoted by the USGBC. The USGBC often is misidentified as a US government agency or regulatory body but it is, in fact, a membership-based, not-for-profit trade association. The original LEED v.1.0 certification was designed in the late 1990s by a committee of building industry representatives. The standards draw inspiration from the BREEAM[7] standards launched in the United Kingdom in 1990, but they have evolved with significant differences (Parker 2009). For example, BREEAM standards are based on legislation and/or best practice and quantitative thresholds, whereas LEED certification is based on optional standards and percentage thresholds. Under BREEAM, credits are awarded for minimising the number of car parking spaces, whereas LEED credits are earned for having enough spaces. Energy credits are linked to CO_2 emissions reductions under BREEAM but to dollar amounts under LEED. The USGBC is credited with raising the profile of sustainable building, and its LEED standards have become a recognised eco-label. But this industry association also has begun to produce and reproduce how green buildings are considered in the United States. The authority of the USGBC, for example, to downplay the importance of meeting absolute best practice guidelines, measure progress against emissions reductions projections, and approve numerous parking spaces around sustainable buildings is rarely questioned; rather, these features are absorbed into how green buildings are defined and understood in the United States. However, there is an opportunity cost associated with limiting the range of green solutions for sustainable buildings to the way that the USGBC defines and awards credits in terms of the alternative, more sustainable solutions that are forgone. This opportunity cost is the misrecognition cost associated with the LEED symbol.

The direct costs of symbolic corporate environmentalism are incurred by firms; to that extent, managers have choices about whether to incur them based on whether they perceive a marginal benefit from doing so. However, the indirect costs, whether they are based on inertia, lock-out or misrecognition, are incurred by society. Estimating the social cost of symbolic corporate environmentalism requires quantifying the highly intangible indirect costs identified in the various empirical contexts examined in this book. Chapter 4 explains how we can think about the social energy penalty as a type of utility loss wherein the social costs of corporate environmentalism outweigh the social benefits (see Figure 4.7). Indirect social cost is a loss of social welfare – an allocative inefficiency that results from the misallocation of resources due to corporate discursive power and information asymmetry. The magnitude of the social loss depends on the extent to which firms exercise their discretionary power over the form and quantity of green solutions supplied to consumers. In the following sections, I

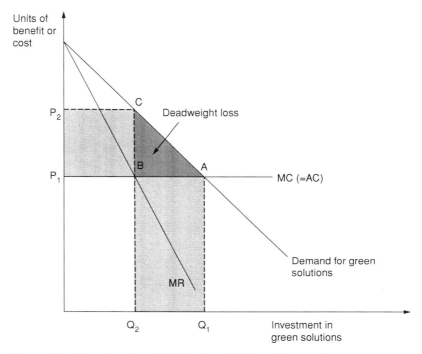

Figure 8.1 Allocational and distributional effects of monopoly power.

introduce two potential methods to estimate the size of this social loss that are based on well-established techniques in microeconomics.

Method 1: Estimation based on deadweight loss triangles

It is a well-known finding in microeconomics that when a firm can affect the overall quantity supplied in a market, it may limit this quantity and push up the price. Figure 8.1 illustrates the basic case of linear demand curves for a good that is produced under constant marginal and average costs by a single supplier – that is, a monopolist.[8] If the market had more competing suppliers, the supply and demand curves would intersect at point A, with equilibrium output Q_1 and price P_1. However, due to the monopolist's power to choose the supply of green solutions in the market, the monopolist would produce where marginal costs (MC) are equal to marginal revenue (MR) at point B.

At this quantity supplied, Q_2, the price of the green solution increases to P_2.

The restriction in output of green solutions from Q_1 to Q_2 represents a misallocation resulting from the monopolist's power. We recall the role of status as a virtual controller described in Chapter 4: maintaining status shapes managers' decisions but does not directly motivate them unless the usual order comes under threat. Under normal conditions, firms cannot risk being perceived as deliberately limiting the supply of green solutions. However, if a firm detects that its discretion on environmental issues is being questioned, it might exert its status as a powerful social actor to control the green solutions available. In these circumstances, a single or small group of suppliers may have the power to limit the supply of green solutions using its non-market power. For example, the group could form an industry association to determine the criteria for a new green building credential. They might develop a performance metric based on symbolic comparability rather than substantive accuracy – which has happened in the carbon accounting context. The group might enthusiastically position an incremental technology such as CCS as the primary solution to climate change. Powerful actors have sufficient status to dominate the terms of the debate on particular issues, regardless of the legitimacy of their actions. This has the effects of limiting the supply of green solutions (i.e., from Q_1 to Q_2); eliminating marginal green solutions that might have been implemented otherwise (i.e., Q_1–Q_2); and pushing up the price paid by consumers for environmental performance in terms of a higher premium on products with green attributes, firm reputation, or other returns that otherwise might have been earned (i.e., from P_1 to P_2).

What are the consequences of this resource misallocation? Limiting the supply of green solutions implies a total loss in consumer surplus in the area P_1P_2CA. The area P_1P_2CB is transferred to the monopolist as additional profits, compared with what it would have earned under perfect competition for green solutions. The area Q_1Q_2BA represents the value of inputs that would have produced green solutions had the quantity not been restricted by the powerful supplier. These resources are available for use elsewhere, but any alternative goods are over-produced relative to the allocatively efficient level. Thus, corporate power to reduce the supply of green solutions leads to (1) firms getting more credit – in the form of a higher price premium or enhanced reputation – than they otherwise would have gained; and (2) resources that otherwise would have been committed to corporate environmentalism being allocated elsewhere. In addition, there is a 'deadweight loss' represented by the triangle ABC that is a loss in consumer surplus that is not transferred to either the producer or the consumers. This is a social cost that arises from the misallocation of resources due to firms exerting their discursive power.

As in any monopoly situation, the extents to which additional profits (i.e., area P_1P_2CB) actually are transferred fully to firms and to which monopolists can control unallocated inputs (i.e., area Q_1Q_2BA) are a matter of policy and social norms. In some cases, firms can fully capture the increased benefits from addressing green issues. For example, they may be able to gain credit for joining industry self-regulation schemes that have weaker entry requirements than those required in the zone Q_2 to Q_1. At a system level, we may be underinvesting in green solutions, reflecting the limited quantity of corporate environmentalism and social decisions to reallocate the inputs to nonenvironmental initiatives. This analysis shows that producers may gain more reputation benefits, consumers may benefit from reassurance that firms are providing green solutions, and resources may be allocated away from green solutions to other productive activities. However, one resource loss is always present because the resources are not transferred to anyone: a 'deadweight loss', defined as the economic benefit forgone by customers due to a firm's power to ration green solutions. Alternatively, it can come from consumers buying a green solution, even if it costs more than it might have otherwise.

Applied economists have been developing techniques to estimate the ABC deadweight loss triangle associated with various forms of market power since Harberger's (1954) seminal estimates based on US manufacturing. Measuring deadweight loss – or, as Harberger sometimes called it, 'the welfare cost' – involves computing the ABC area based on industry output and estimates of elasticities of demand and substitution. Harberger acknowledged that such estimates are imprecise and that 'the best we can hope for is to get a feeling for the general orders of magnitude that are involved' (Harberger 1954: 77). Welfare cost estimates are sensitive to estimates of key parameters, such as the elasticity of demand and substitution that may be impossible to obtain or can be estimated only with substantial error (Harberger 1964). Despite these drawbacks, Harberger's deadweight loss triangles have been widely used to calculate welfare losses associated with firm market power, various taxation regimes and other market distortions.[9]

To estimate the welfare cost of symbolic corporate environmentalism for a particular industry using Harberger's deadweight loss triangles, we need estimates of the oligopoly output and elasticity of demand for each green solution. Some green solutions are easier to estimate in this way than others. Applied economists and marketing scholars have made inroads into estimating the demand effects of eco-labels, and they provide useful guides about how to estimate elasticity of demand for other green solutions. For example, Galarraga, Del Valle, and Gonzalez-Eguino (2011) used revealed preferences data from electrical retailers in Spain to estimate the own- and cross-price elasticities of eco-labelled refrigerators. Refrigerators with the most energy-efficient rating have an own-price elasticity of demand that is an order of magnitude more inelastic than unlabelled refrigerators (i.e., −0.9 to −2.1 for A+ labelled refrigerators compared to −0.25 to − 0.75 for regular refrigerators). Using estimates based on stated preferences from a consumer survey, Larson (2002) estimated the elasticity of demand of coffee labelled as shade-grown at −4.4, which is considerably more inelastic than for the total demand of coffee (i.e., −0.17 to −0.46) but comparable to coffee-brand elasticities estimated in the literature (i.e., −3 to −4). Field experiments also can be used to reveal consumers' preferences and elasticities of demand (see, e.g., Hainmueller, Hiscox, and Sequeira 2011 for a recent example based on fair trade labelling). The methods of estimating demand elasticity in these studies on one form of symbolic corporate environmentalism – that is, eco-labels – could inspire ways to measure the elasticity of demand for other green solutions needed to estimate the deadweight loss triangle.

Measuring social cost using deadweight loss triangles reflects a firm's attempts to gain monopoly power over what constitutes a legitimate green solution. If a firm can do this, for example, by controlling membership criteria of a green solution or lobbying to ensure that its chosen form of self-regulation is deemed legitimate, then it can force down the quantity supplied and drive up the green solution price. Tullock (1967) famously noted that costs associated with these activities should be included in the social cost of monopoly, but they are not accounted for using Harberger's traditional deadweight loss triangle. The opportunity costs of the resources consumed in attempting to establish and protect a monopoly, as well as the resources used to prevent monopolies, also are social costs. In the extreme case of competition among potential suppliers to establish a monopoly, the entire area P_1P_2CB in Figure 8.1 can be consumed through rent-seeking investments to 'build, break or muscle into a monopoly' (Tullock 1967: 232). Tullock further noted (1967: 232): '[P]robably much of the cost of monopoly is spread through companies that do not have a monopoly, but have gambled resources on the hopes of one'. Thus, we should include not only the direct costs of successful attempts to gain control over green solutions but also all of the costs of unsuccessful attempts as part of the social cost.

Tullock's approach reminds us that the social costs of symbolic green solutions include those associated with all unsuccessful attempts to establish an eco-label; environmental industry associations that collapse; unsuccessful lobbying or political donations; and environmental marketing, advertising, or reporting that consumers do not believe; and so on. Several of the empirical chapters in this book demonstrate that significant social energy is used to compete for establishing control over green solutions. These efforts are more intense when there is more profit potential from controlling the preferred green solution (Buchanan and Tullock 1975). Estimates based on the oligopoly power of US manufacturers suggest that traditional deadweight loss might be an underestimate of total social cost by a factor of approximately 20.[10] To compute these losses, we need an estimate of the self-regulatory price increase – that is, the increased premium that self-regulated providers of green solutions could command compared to the price in the absence of a self-regulatory scheme. Interested readers can find inspiration for these estimates for particular schemes and industries within the extensive literature on whether (and when) it pays to be green (see Chapter 3). For a useful illustration of how to calculate the Tullock losses in a related empirical context – that is, corporate political activities – see Bhuyan (2000).

Method 2: Estimation based on utility analysis

In Chapter 4, I adapt Waldfogel's (1993) deadweight loss of gift-giving analysis to the corporate environmentalism context. I describe a utility analysis from the consumer's perspective, showing how much utility consumers achieve by consuming combinations of symbolic and substantive performance produced by firms (see Figure 4.5). I use the analysis to show that as long as a firm's preferences do not exactly match those of stakeholders as consumers of green solutions, there is a welfare loss associated with a firm controlling the exact form of voluntary green solutions, whether or not they are merely symbolic. This analysis opens up alternative methods to estimate social losses resulting from asymmetric preferences and information based on techniques in applied economics and marketing.

Waldfogel's original estimates were calculated from surveys of university students that asked about holiday gifts they had received and what they would have paid to acquire those gifts themselves. In a series of studies built on the original 1993 paper, Waldfogel developed an impressive dataset of more than 3,400 cash and non-cash gifts. He estimated the deadweight loss based on the amount that a gift cost minus the amount a receiver would have paid. He concluded that the value of non-cash gifts is between 10 and 33 per cent less because recipients did not choose them. He then conducted regression-based analyses of the survey data to test how the deadweight loss varies with the giver's and the recipient's preferences and knowledge of those preferences.

Waldfogel hinted that this framework could be used to estimate the deadweight loss of government grant-in-kind programmes such as public housing and Medicare, but these techniques have not been applied to corporate voluntary initiatives. Estimating deadweight loss in the corporate environmentalism context would involve surveying stakeholders on the in-kind green gifts they receive and what they would have paid to acquire them. For example, we could calculate the efficiency losses arising from a firm that donates staff time to a community-garden project compared with donating the equivalent cash to pay experienced gardeners. More ambitiously, we could compare the cost and effort of building and maintaining a voluntary certification scheme, such as ISO 14001, with the amount that stakeholders would have paid to acquire the equivalent information on a firm's environmental performance.[11]

Contemporary economic analyses of giving at the individual level could provide inspiration about how to estimate the welfare effects of different types of green solutions as firm-level giving. For example, DellaVigna, List, and Malmendier (2012) developed two field experiments based on door-to-door charitable fundraising to assess when gifts are either welfare-enhancing or welfare-reducing for the giver.

Their critical insight was that when charitable giving is motivated by altruism, donations are utility maximising for the giver, which leads to a smaller or no deadweight loss. However, when giving is motivated by social pressure, there is a larger gap between the donation and a giver's preferences: that is, giving may be utility reducing for the giver and lead to a deadweight loss. This analysis is consistent with Brennan and Pettit's (2004) esteem-based approach outlined in Chapter 4. It also echoes my conjecture from the CCS demonstration project context that social costs are more substantial when firms are motivated to implement green solutions by legitimation rather than competitiveness motives (see Chapter 6). But the real innovation in DellaVigna et al.'s study is the empirical methods used. It is 'the first in the behavioural literature to provide structural estimates of welfare implications of a field experiment ... [W]hile the fund-raising set-up is specific, it showcases a general methodology' (2012: 2). Their paper provided a model for designing an experiment to assess the extent to which giving leads to welfare losses for the giver. This model could provide inspiration for future estimates of welfare losses from voluntary corporate environmentalism.[12]

The perils and promise of estimating the social cost curve

For more than a half–century, applied economists have been devising increasingly ingenious and sophisticated ways to measure the welfare effects of various forms of market power. Harberger's (1954) warning that the best we can hope for is a feeling for the general orders of magnitude that are involved still rings true, particularly in the new context of corporate environmentalism. This estimation task may be challenging and imprecise but it is still worth doing. Corporate environmentalism researchers tend to downplay the social welfare implications of self-regulation. When they do include welfare effects, they are more interested in showing the positive effects of self-regulation compared with no action or with a forced regulatory change (see, e.g., Husted and Salazar 2006 and Maxwell et al. 2000).

The techniques described in this section have the potential to more fully account for the direct costs of investing in emblems, credentials and kin for both successful and unsuccessful attempts to gain control over the supply of green solutions. The techniques also indicate ways to compare the welfare effects of self-regulation with a Pareto-optimal scenario based on either estimating deadweight loss triangles or preference mismatches between gift givers and receivers.[13] Creatively applying and refining these techniques eventually could yield estimates on the indirect costs resulting from inertia, lock-out and misrecognition related to green solutions in various empirical contexts. Identifying the orders of magnitude involved in different circumstances could allow future researchers to test some of the conjectures in this book about when the social energy penalty is likely to be highest. Recent developments in applied and behavioural economics promise creative routes into the problem of how to estimate the social cost curve.

Estimating the social benefit curve

The social benefit curve illustrates the relationship between the cumulative investment in a new green solution and the incremental value accrued to the next adopter from improved performance of the green solution. The shape of the curve reflects the extent to which new adopters gain additional performance benefits from the investments of earlier adopters. Unlike the social cost curve, which is primarily a reflection of early adopters' discretionary power, the social benefit curve is shaped by a wide range of factors. As described in Chapter 4, these factors range from learning effects and network externalities to the development of complementary assets to the authority of early adopters to force a harmonised solution. Foster himself warned in 1986, when he introduced S-curves to explain technology development, that 'constructing S-curves is time-consuming and should be done only when there is considerable debate about which course to pursue' (Foster 1986: 276).

In this context, the strongest case to invest in estimating the social benefit curve is when social costs are deemed to be high. If social costs are relatively low, there is less likely to be an aggregate net social energy penalty in any case, regardless of the social benefit. However, in circumstances in which direct and indirect social costs are estimated to be high, it may be worth dedicating resources to evaluating whether there are concomitant social benefits. To this extent, I agree with Foster's (1986: 276) assessment that 'S-curves can help communications, but as a general proposition, it is more important to believe that they exist, and to be able to check that belief if necessary, than it is to construct them for each and every case'.

For cases in which the effort of estimating a social benefit curve is justified, the estimation should be based on a logistic curve. We recall from Chapter 4 that the social benefit curve is actually a hybrid of two S-curves: (1) Foster's (1986) technology improvement curve, which maps improving performance of a technology as more cumulative effort is put into developing it; and (2) Rogers' (1991) technology diffusion curve, which traces the number of adopters over time. I simplified these curves into one that traces performance improvement as the number of cumulative adopters increases. To estimate the social benefit curve, we can adapt the logistic functions underlying either of the two curves to this context. For example, Schilling and Esmundo (2009) provided an illustration of how to estimate technology improvement curves for a range of renewable energy technologies. In contrast, Marimon, Llach, and Bernardo (2011) estimated diffusion curves for a well-established green solution (i.e., ISO 14001). Adapting these contrasting analyses for this context, to estimate benefits at any given level of cumulative adoption, we use the following logistic equation:

$$B = \frac{B_0 L}{(L - B_0)e^{-r_0 N} + B_0}$$

where B represents the benefits for any level of cumulative adoption, B_0 represents the benefits from the standalone technology value at the starting point, L is the limit of the benefits, r_0 is the initial growth rate of benefits, and N is the number of cumulative adopters over time. Thus, to estimate social benefits, we need to know three key pieces of information: (1) the standalone technology value of the green solution, (2) the likely limits of social benefits, and (3) the initial rate at which these benefits are generated.

As discussed in Chapter 4, the standalone technology value of the green solution determines the initial height of the social benefit curve (B_0). It depends on the extent to which producing a particular green solution provides an environmental benefit independent of the number of adopters. Thus, to estimate the standalone technology value of a green solution, we need to estimate its net environmental benefits. Green solutions vary in the extent to which they offer substantive environmental improvements – that is, those that otherwise would not be available to society if firms did not implement the green solution. The level B_0 reflects this variation. There is a strong literature concerning techniques to evaluate the substantive impacts of green solutions, including environmental impact assessment in the planning and policy literatures (see, e.g., Glasson, Therivel, and Chadwick 1999 and Wood 2003). However, estimates of B_0 are scarcer in the management literature (see, e.g., Whiteman et al. 2012). One promising approach is to build on literature that compares the substantive performance of several different green solutions to obtain a sense of the factors that influence B_0 and the orders of magnitude involved (see, e.g., Darnall and Sides 2008).

Estimating the likely limits of social benefit (L) involves the assessment of the eventual importance of increasing returns to adoption: What would be the total social benefit of the green solution when all members who are likely to adopt the solution have done so? One approach is to list the potential sources of increasing returns and to ask experts and stakeholders to estimate their importance for the green solution. Chapter 4 outlines the main drivers of increasing returns as learning effects, network externalities and the authority of early entrants. With respect to learning effects, we should ask about the potential benefits from raising awareness of the environmental problem and solutions, learning from early adopters' experience, and the existence of boundary spanners that might disseminate the learning. All of these factors might lower costs or increase benefits for later adopters. For network externalities, the primary determinant of the limit is likely to be the extent to which members reap scale economies in reputation: To what extent does more cumulative adoption provide more visibility and legitimacy to external stakeholders? In considering the authority of early entrants, we need to ask to what extent the high status of early entrants promise more benefits to later adopters who seek to emulate them? Taking all of these factors together, the limits of social benefit (L) is likely to be higher when the ultimate value of the green solution is uncertain, when the participants' state of knowledge about environmental issues is low, when there are boundary spanners to disseminate the solution, when industry participants share a common reputation, when the solution is highly visible, and when the solution is promoted by early high-status actors. Clearly, some of these factors may work against one another, so assessing their relative importance is a difficult matter best accomplished in a collective discussion process by people with complementary expertise. There is minimal empirical evidence on these effects to date, and our ability to estimate the limits of social benefit can only improve as we continue to gather evidence on the long-term symbolic and substantive performance of green solutions.

The third key piece of information is the initial rate at which benefits are generated (r_0). Chapter 4 describes how social benefit curves may be smooth or abrupt, depending on the pace at which additional benefits accrue with adoption. Little or no empirical research so far has been conducted to directly estimate the pace of benefits; therefore, as a first step, estimates are likely to involve discussions of a range of driving factors. These include factors from the technology management literature, such as the importance of an installed base and the complementary assets of stakeholder interest and regulatory enforcement (see, e.g., Schilling 2010 and Suarez and Lanzolla 2007). They also include more institutional factors driving the pace of adoption, such as the power of early adopters (see, e.g., Lawrence et al. 2001). Thus, similar to the limits of social benefits, initial estimates of the pace of benefits likely will rely on a panel of experts making judgements about the importance of these factors in the specific context of green solutions. Much empirical work remains to be done in this area.

Therefore, developing methods to estimate social benefit curves is likely to be an even longer-term project than estimating social cost. We have sound techniques to provide estimates of the standalone technology benefit, but estimates of the pace and limits of social benefits are likely to be informed guesses at first – which may or may not matter. It is worth investing the time and effort in estimating a social benefit curve only when there is significant potential for high social costs. Even then, obtaining a sense of the overall potential for social benefit by asking a structured set of questions on the factors driving the three key variables may be sufficient. Only in extreme situations would it make sense to fully estimate the social benefit curve – and even then, this would be most useful when comparing the relative social benefits of several green solutions. We are still some distance away from full empirical support for the drivers of the social benefits curve.

Measuring the social energy penalty

In this chapter, I outline directions of enquiry for future researchers seeking to quantify the social costs and benefits of symbolic corporate environmentalism. These methods vary in their complexity and completeness. Estimating the direct cost of emblems, credentials and kin, for example, is likely to be the easiest step, although even this involves the difficult issue of how to separate the costs of symbolic from substantive environmentalism. The indirect costs of symbolic corporate environmentalism are a core concern of this book, and I provide two alternative estimation methods to gain understanding of how substantial these costs are likely to be. Neither method promises an easy route but at least they provide clues as to how to estimate the orders of magnitude involved. In time, developing these methods should be able to identify contexts in which the social costs of symbolic corporate environmentalism are sufficiently high so as to justify further analysis of the concomitant social benefits. When the investment in estimating social benefits is justified, we at least now know which three key variables drive the shape of the S-curve. What this chapter primarily demonstrates is how much empirical work remains to be accomplished to more fully capture the social costs and benefits of symbolic corporate environmentalism. The aim of these preliminary discussions is to provide a sense of the work that might be done to apply and test the framework presented in this book.

9 | *Implications and conclusions*

My core aim in this book is to explore symbolic corporate environmentalism as a broader phenomenon after greenwashing. Symbolic corporate environmentalism is defined as shared meanings and representations surrounding changes made by managers within firms that they describe as primarily for environmental reasons. Companies issue environmental reports, build green buildings, create new job titles, develop green technologies, adopt environmental policies and participate in government green schemes to show that they are addressing environmental issues. Some of this activity provides managers, consumers, investors, regulators and other stakeholders with valuable information about a firm's environmental quality, enabling them to make more efficient decisions. However, much of it is an attempt to control the rhetoric and resources around environmental issues and does not change a firm's impact on the natural environment. This book is the first systematic analysis of the drivers and consequences of symbolic corporate environmentalism after greenwashing. In it, I develop a set of tools to distinguish harmful symbolic corporate environmentalism from that which has the potential to signal and coordinate authentic environmental improvements.

This book reveals the drivers and consequences of symbolic corporate environmentalism using the past literature (see Chapter 3), a combination of conceptual frameworks (see Chapter 4) and related empirical studies (see Chapters 5, 6 and 7). My approach offers theoretical contributions to both the conventional and the critical views. I introduce and elaborate on a new concept – the social energy penalty – and also derive new findings for established theory on industry self-regulation and organisational decoupling. In this chapter, I outline each in turn and conclude with implications for practice.

The social energy penalty

The primary new theoretical concept I introduce here is the social energy penalty – that is, the loss of social welfare for a constant resource output that is misdirected into symbolic activities. Developing this new concept was motivated by the need to distinguish between green solutions that are socially beneficial solutions to the problems of information asymmetry and socially costly attempts to control environmental rhetoric and resources. The social energy penalty arises when social costs outweigh social benefits over time (see Chapter 4, Figure 4.7). It is a theoretically powerful idea for three main reasons. First, it explicitly raises the level of analysis of the consequences of symbolic corporate environmentalism from the firm level to the social-system level. Conventional corporate environmentalism research, along with management theory in general, has been criticised for neglecting the social welfare effects of its recommendations. The social energy framework extends and applies ideas already used to explain firm-level environmental decisions, including learning effects, network externalities, and industry concentration, and uses them to predict social outcomes. I adapted conventional corporate environmentalism tools to account for welfare implications. Conventional corporate environmentalism researchers should no longer ignore the social energy penalty simply because it may be an unintended consequence of profit maximisation.

Second, the social energy penalty framework offers a powerful integration of critical and conventional views on the consequences of symbolic corporate environmentalism. As discussed in Chapter 4, critical views assume that high-status actors in a field have the power to manipulate symbolic meanings of everyday greening practices. Conventional views, in contrast, assume that mismatches between corporate green symbols and substantive actions are more benign reflections of imperfect implementation or a stage on the path towards realised corporate greening. These divergent assumptions have encouraged researchers from the two schools to talk past one another and have limited cross-fertilisation between the two largely unconnected research domains. The social energy framework turns these assumptions into an empirical difference across different contexts. Sometimes the critical view is correct, as in the CCS demonstration project example (see Chapter 6): powerful social actors are limiting the range of solutions to those that are acceptable to them, thereby imposing a social energy penalty on society. Sometimes we do not need to be as concerned about the social costs arising from corporate control because adoption helps firms to learn about their environmental impacts, and diffusion can lead to better information quality and authentic social benefit. Thinking in terms of the social energy penalty turns traditionally intractable assumptions into a matter of degree: To what extent might firms be able to exert symbolic control in different contexts? What might the social benefits of an industry-led scheme be over time? There is a social energy penalty only when the control costs are high and there are inadequate compensating social benefits.

The third theoretical contribution is to model the social energy penalty as the interaction of the social costs and benefits of green solutions over time (see Chapter 4, Figure 4.7). As I argue in Chapter 4, the social benefit curve crosses the y axis at the standalone technology value level and then rises with the cumulative adoption of green solutions in an S-curve as both existing and new adopters gain value from learning and network effects. The slope of the social benefit curve is a function of a number of factors. A technology management perspective emphasises the rate of performance improvement in the green solution, the importance of an installed base, and the availability of complementary assets. More institutional explanations for the shape of the social benefit curve focus on the power of stakeholders to force adoption and the extent to which firms share a common reputation. The social cost curve shows the increase in utility losses from the dominance of particular forms of green solutions as the new solution becomes established over time. It reflects social costs resulting from inertia, lock-out and misrecognition. The social cost curve is primarily a reflection of early adopters' discretionary power. The framework provides a theoretically derived list of contextual contingencies for when the social energy penalty is likely to be higher. This opens up a theoretical space for others to extend and refine drivers of the social energy penalty as well as an empirical space to test them.

I labelled the social energy penalty based on a term from one of my empirical contexts: carbon capture and storage (CCS). However, I expect that the phenomenon of using social energy to provide symbolic support over and above that which is justified by material changes will extend far beyond environmental issues. The social energy penalty is likely to occur in any context in which there is uncertainty about how to meet social demands, flexibility in how firms might meet them – particularly through new language or symbols – and when the precise performance implications are difficult to observe. For example, Ahmed (2012) examined corporate equality policies and described them as 'non-performatives that do not bring into effect that which they name'. Alvesson (2013) examined symbolic inflation in higher education, the professions, and working life and argued that organisations increasingly dedicate resources to rhetoric and image. These perspectives resonate with the early greenwashing literature of Greer and Bruno (1996) and Tokar (1997). Critical analyses that point out the social costs of symbolic corporate activity are not new. What I have added to these analyses is a new analytical layer to be able to identify when these social costs are highest and when they might outweigh potential social benefits. I encourage others to explore, test and expand the social energy penalty concept in other contexts.

Industry self-regulation

The ideas in this book also extend theory on industry self-regulation. Much of the conventional view focuses on when, how and why firms voluntarily control their collective actions on environmental issues. Research on voluntary corporate environmentalism has offered mainstream strategy theory new insights on the foundations of competitive advantage (Berchicci and King 2008). But, as I discuss in Chapter 3, evidence from contexts such as the adoption of environmental management systems, disclosure programmes, industry agreements and the implementation of green solutions shows that firms that commit to proactive green solutions are no more likely – and, in some cases, are even less likely – to improve their substantive environmental performance (King et al. 2012). The frameworks in this book contribute to answering Banerjee's (2012) call to explore the boundary conditions surrounding industry self-regulation, particularly by injecting ideas from the critical view on power, status and dominant discourse. My analysis has implications for industry self-regulation at both the firm and the design levels.

At the firm level, I developed two frameworks to demonstrate how managers decide on the quantity and portfolio of investments in green solutions. First, I extended Husted and Salazar's (2006) theory on the optimal quantity of investments in green solutions. I showed how altering assumptions on the functional equivalence of green solutions and how firms can alter the private costs and benefits of green solutions can open up symbolic gaps. Changing Husted and Salazar's (2006) assumptions reveals the overproduction of symbolic green solutions if a firm has the power to limit scrutiny, decouple symbol from substance, define metrics of social output in symbolic terms, or simply face a lower relative cost and higher relative benefit from symbolic rather than substantive green solutions. Previous theory has been slow to explicitly model symbolic gaps in the conventional coerced egoist case, despite empirical evidence of widespread symbolic investments. This analysis also serves as a reminder that managers' decisions on the quantity of green solutions are not disconnected from whether they are primarily symbolic or substantive. Here, I contribute to an effort advocated by Lyon and Maxwell (2011) to integrate the analysis of corporate environmental action and disclosure decisions.

Second, I adapted Brennan and Pettit's (2004) *Economy of Esteem* to the firm level to develop theory on firms' portfolio choices of green solutions. As far as I am aware, this is the first adaptation of Brennan and Pettit's framework into the corporate strategy context. Corporate environmentalism research emphasises symbolic performance in the form of reputation, legitimacy and status as drivers of environmental decision making. I adapted Brennan and Pettit's (2004) framework to describe how a firm invests in a portfolio of green solutions to maximise its symbolic performance (see the discussion about Figure 4.4). The crucial insight from this analysis is that firms maximise their 'audience-seeking' and 'performance-enhancement' activities in order to achieve the highest possible levels of symbolic performance given their budget for green solutions. The relative costs of audience-seeking and performance-enhancement activities will vary according to the context. I argue that large, visible firms have lower audience-seeking costs, and I show in Chapter 5 that this leads them to be more likely to state proactive environmental intentions but no more likely to improve their substantive environmental impacts. I also argue in Chapter 6 that firms that state competitiveness motivations for implementing a pollution control technology will face a flatter budget line than firms with legitimation motives. Therefore, they are more likely to invest in performance-enhancing rather than audience-seeking activities.

These findings are useful preliminary adaptations of a much broader theoretical framework offered in Brennan and Pettit's (2004) work.

We can significantly strengthen industry self-regulation theory by further unpacking this framework. First, it seems likely that the slope of the budget line would differ depending on the characteristics of firms (e.g., visible or high environmental impact), green solutions (e.g., product compared to process), and audiences (e.g., government, investor or NGO), which explains when self-regulation is more likely to be merely symbolic. Some researchers are beginning to seriously examine how firms decide between different self-regulatory schemes (see, e.g., Delmas, Nairn-Birch, and Balzarova 2013 and Prado 2011). The relative costs of audience-seeking and performance-enhancing activities may be an important driver of this decision that has not yet been examined sufficiently.

Second, the framework might provide an explanation for positive symbolic gaps, or what Delmas and Burbano (2011) termed 'silent green firms' (see Chapter 4, Figure 4.3). These firms often are portrayed as unusual in that they do not seem to capitalise fully on their environmental performance by communicating about it. Perhaps these firms simply face flatter budget lines or esteem curves that place their equilibrium investment portfolios towards the bottom right in Figure 4.4.

Third, future research may ask more fundamental questions about this framework. For example, is the budget line always straight? It may be possible that there is positive feedback between symbolic and substantive investments in self-regulation. As firms begin audience seeking, they may get on a course that leads to substantive improvements later (see, e.g., Christensen et al. 2013 and Haack et al. 2012). Future research might investigate whether particular combinations of audience-seeking and performance-enhancement activities over time lead to more utility, resulting in a nonlinear budget line. Furthermore, when applied at the corporate level, the curves are an accumulation of managers' preferences rather than preferences at the individual level, as in Brennan and Pettit's (2004) original version. How sensitive are firms' investments to where environmental decisions are taken within the firm? Do communications or marketing departments lean towards valuing audience-seeking activities relatively more than operations? Can this explain differences in firms' voluntary self-regulation commitments?

The industry self-regulation literature has explored the importance of reputation and legitimacy in driving corporate green decisions. I build on recent research from broader organisational theory to more clearly delineate how reputation, legitimacy and status differ from one another (see Chapter 3, Table 3.2). I then extended the conventional self-regulation literature by modelling status as a virtual controller (see Chapter 4, Figure 4.5). I assumed that managers' environmental decisions are typically driven by reputation and legitimacy seeking until a firm's control over greening comes under threat. If a firm detects that its discretion on environmental issues is being questioned, it might exert its status as a powerful social actor to control the green solutions available. This phenomenon is most obviously observed in the context of CCS in Chapter 6, although it also was evident in a firm's attempt to dominate the design of voluntary carbon measurement and disclosure schemes in Chapter 7. Thinking of status as a virtual controller provides a useful boundary condition for industry self-regulation. Self-regulation may be socially benign as long as firms do not perceive a serious threat to their core business. Status as a virtual controller allows us to integrate the emphasis of the conventional view on reputation and legitimacy and of the critical view on status. Developing this approach would allow us to understand when self-regulation schemes are more likely to be dominated by the high-status firms and would result in symbolic outcomes designed to maintain and protect symbolic capital rather than improve the natural environment. An important future research question in this line of thinking would be to understand when the virtual controller overrides normal reputation and legitimacy seeking. Conventional researchers must focus more attention on the role of status and symbolic power in legitimacy seeking.

My emphasis on status is part of a broader attempt to bridge the two perspectives by injecting power into conventional analyses of corporate environmentalism. Industry self-regulation often is promoted within the conventional view as a way to enhance a firm's competitive positions and to act as an entry barrier, particularly if a firm can persuade regulators to adopt its version of a green solution. Yet, the material, discursive and positional power of those who write the rules too often is neglected in the current industry self-regulation literature. As with the most obvious greenwashing exposed during the 1990s and 2000s, visible attempts by powerful firms to lobby or advocate for particular green solutions may well be exposed by NGOs and journalists. However, most corporate environmentalism is implemented in a more nuanced context, wherein the powerful exhibit high cultural literacy, social prestige, mutual forbearance and limited rivalry. The leaders of prestigious firms, regulatory agencies and NGOs interact with peers within and across the same high-status group, making them more likely to reinforce one another's strategic positions. This limits the environmental problems that are discussed in the public domain and the range of acceptable solutions. Industry self-regulation research needs to take more seriously the power and relational position of key firms as they advance standards, symbols and solutions to suit themselves. One promising line of research for the conventional view could be to investigate whether symbolic gaps can act intrinsically as an entry barrier, particularly when the solution is proposed and supported by powerful incumbents. In contrast, critical scholars might investigate the power of high-status firms to eliminate or hide their presence as powerful social actors.

At the design level, this book serves as a reminder to ensure tight coupling between the organisational means and environmental ends of self-regulatory schemes. Traditionally, conventional researchers recognise the need to design auditing, monitoring and sanctioning into the membership rules and criteria of self-regulation schemes to ensure more than merely symbolic compliance (see, e.g., Christmann and Taylor 2006, Darnall and Sides 2008, Delmas and Terlaak 2001, and Short and Toffel 2010). My contribution here is to use the drivers of the social energy penalty to develop contingencies related to when net social benefit is maximised in industry self-regulation design. For example, net social benefits will be higher when there is mandatory sharing among participants to enhance the benefits of learning; aggressive promotion of the symbol so as to raise awareness and network externalities for all adopters; and a broad range of actors invited to participate in scheme design to mitigate the discretionary power of core members and the appearance of conflict of interest. Optimal design may even include funding or otherwise encouraging monitoring by others to further drive social benefits: the more actively a green solution is monitored, the higher quality is the information available for all agents to make more efficient decisions. More work is needed in developing and evaluating criteria to design standards with the lowest possible social cost – an issue to which I return in the discussion on practical implications.

Finally, this work pushes forward theory on the welfare effects of self-regulation. Conventional researchers make the case that industry self-regulation can lead to more efficient resource allocation, thereby improving overall social welfare (see, e.g., Husted and Salazar 2006 and Maxwell et al. 2000). However, these analyses neglect the importance of firms exerting control over the range of solutions available. When firms voluntarily adopt corporate environmentalism, they can choose which types of initiatives to support or practices to implement. I used Waldfolgel's (1993) approach to model voluntary green solutions as a gift. When firms decide on the form of the green solution, there is less utility gain than if receivers had chosen the form of the gift themselves. This is the case for all non-cash gifts except for the unlikely situation in which the preferences of givers and receivers are identical. Conventional researchers have encouraged managers to invest 'strategically' in corporate environmentalism by adopting green solutions that meet their corporate objectives. Voluntary initiatives as gifts can be used to credibly communicate information about a donor's type. However, they also meet a firm's needs more closely than their consumers or stakeholders, leading to a utility loss.

Much work remains to be done to better understand the welfare effects of corporate environmentalism. These welfare effects are less positive than previous models generally assume. Resolving this debate will rely on more direct empirical tests of the welfare implications of industry self-regulation schemes. In Chapter 8, I suggest some promising directions, building on Waldfogel's utility analysis and the latest experimental research in behavioural economics. For example, future research could adapt DellaVigna et al.'s (2012) experimental setup to the corporate level to estimate the extent to which different green solutions lead to welfare losses for the giver. Experiments could manipulate the characteristics of the self-regulation schemes and the extent to which they offer competitiveness or legitimation benefits. We now have access to long lists of different voluntary standards and eco-labels. Even ranking these according to their distance from the flexibility of cash gifts – as Waldfogel did by comparing gifts with different characteristics – would be a significant step forward in understanding the welfare implications of industry self-regulation.

Conventional industry self-regulation research has contributed much to bring environmental concerns into high-impact management journals, prestigious academic associations, business school curricula and corporate boardrooms. Unfortunately, the evidence in this book reveals that all too often, industry-led solutions do not lead to positive environmental impacts or fix the problems that they are designed to solve. Despite the efforts of managers and academics to promote corporate engagement with environmental issues through apparently less-threatening industry self-regulation schemes, too many symbols have developed shared meanings that are more proactive than their substantive impact. As with Chevron's *People Do* campaign in the early greenwashing era, much industry self-regulation provides social reassurance that companies are fulfilling their proper social function. However, much of this is false reassurance because consumers, voters, investors and managers turn a blind eye to the worsening environmental impacts of industrial activity. Social expectations around environmental issues influence companies in waves of attention over time. Environmental issues have ebbed in social attention during the recent financial downturn; however, as the economy recovers, we can expect attention to turn again to noneconomic factors such as environmental and social sustainability. It may take only one crisis or accident to expose the weaknesses of self-regulation schemes for protecting society from environmental harm. Industry self-regulation proponents must be prepared for the eventual higher monitoring of the various forms of symbolic corporate environmentalism. Otherwise, the self-regulation field risks losing credibility as corporate environmentalism is exposed as merely symbolic, just like The Yes Men's *We Agree* campaign.

In this book, I develop ways to distinguish useful symbolic corporate environmentalism from socially wasteful symbolic manoeuvres. We can use these frameworks to ensure that the baby is not thrown out with the bathwater in criticising corporate environmentalism. Industry self-regulation research should more seriously examine the outcomes and boundary conditions so that it can withstand the stricter scrutiny that may come in time. To help in this effort, I introduce three new ideas to the self-regulation field: (1) explicitly modelling audience-seeking and performance-enhancement investment portfolios, (2) using status as a virtual controller, and (3) exploring the utility implications of controlling the form of voluntary green solutions. Developing each of these ideas would refine industry self-regulation theory and potentially defend the most socially beneficial solutions in the future.

Organisational decoupling

This book also presents implications for understanding decoupling in the broader organisational theory literature. Bromley and Powell's

(2012) recent review highlighted a shift in contemporary organisations from 'policy-practice' decoupling to 'means-ends' decoupling. We might view the shift from greenwashing to broader symbolic corporate environmentalism as a specific application of this broader shift. Traditionally, decoupling has been thought of as a gap between policy and practice. As with greenwashing, however, this policy-practice decoupling is becoming less prevalent in time due to social trends including transparency, monitoring and auditing. Bromley and Powell (2012: 489) argued that policy-practice decoupling is being replaced by means-ends decoupling, when 'policies are implemented but the link between the formal policies and the intended outcome is opaque'.

Symbolic corporate environmentalism is an excellent illustrative context to examine this shift to means-ends decoupling. Firms increasingly must implement the environmental policies and commitments they make, but the connection between green solutions and their eventual outcomes remains tenuous. Indeed, the environmental context is particularly useful here because of the potential to evaluate organisational actions against a basic social outcome – that is, whether green solutions eventually lead to substantive improvements in environmental impacts. Corporate environmentalism exhibits several trends that Bromley and Powell (2012) suggested are typical of means-ends decoupling: (1) there is widespread diffusion of environmental practices and symbols that are of dubious substantive value; (2) firms not only adopt green solutions symbolically but also implement them symbolically (see Chapter 5); (3) firms face increasing pressures of rationalisation and measurement, but the modes of measurement are socially contested (see Chapter 7); and (4) a firm's environmental commitments and programmes are subject to endemic reform as they are constantly adapted and changed in response to increased monitoring.

Analysing symbolic corporate environmentalism offers at least three insights concerning the emerging literature on means-ends decoupling within organisational theory. First, my application of Brennan and Pettit's (2004) *Economy of Esteem* framework offers the potential to explain the links between the means and ends of green solutions (see Chapter 4, Figure 4.4). The means-ends decoupling approach positions investments in shared meanings around corporate environmentalism as adaptive symbols rather than the more traditional ceremonial adoption. Within this view, the weak link between corporate environmentalism and improving environmental impacts does not result because managers are avoiding or failing to implement stated corporate environmentalism policies. Rather, symbolic gaps arise because managers are caught up in larger structural pressures that require them to implement, measure, monitor and report on green solutions regardless of whether these activities have positive outcomes. Restated in Brennan and Pettit's (2004) language, managers' decisions are not necessarily driven by technical cost-benefit considerations but instead by investing in a portfolio of activities to gain social esteem. The means-ends decoupling approach so far does not consider a firm's portfolio of activities in response to institutional pressures – in particular, the balance between audience-seeking and performance-enhancing activities. Neither does contemporary decoupling research typically differentiate between ends: whether the outcomes are improvements in economic, symbolic or environmental performance. I encourage others to use Figure 4.4 to clarify this nuance and potentially identify and analyse different types of means-ends decoupling.

Second, the corporate environmentalism context is fertile ground to further examine the rise of ratings, measuring and auditing as rationalising processes. Bromley and Powell's (2012: 496) means-ends decoupling approach emphasises how 'organisational activities are integrated not through a direct connection to production but rather through operational systems such as accounting, personnel management, evaluation, or monitoring'. As discussed in Chapter 6, environmental credentials, emblems and kin are important carriers in the process of institutionalising CCS as a green solution. These cultural symbols are produced and maintained as institutionalised conceptions of how firms can meet environmental demands. Chapter 7 describes how corporate translation of stakeholder demands for carbon accounting led to practice that prioritises comparability and consistency in reporting rather than accuracy in improving carbon performance. Both studies served as a reminder that measurement, ranking, rating and accounting systems are institutionalised in parallel with the corporate environmental activities they are designed to evaluate. They are perceived as legitimate or not, and they can create distinctions among organisations even when there is no meaningful difference between them. Organisations may implement green solutions not because there is a clear environmental or economic benefit from doing so but rather because they have been caught in symbolic environmental ratings or rankings system (Chatterji and Toffel 2010; Doshi, Dowell, and Toffel

2013). My analysis is a reminder that when valuing environmental performance, we must consider not only economic but also cultural value. The means-ends decoupling approach is alert to the roles of signals and symbols but focuses too little attention on symbolic capital. I argue in Chapter 6 that organisations can gain symbolic capital by possessing cultural symbols that are associated with high prestige, whether or not the prestige is warranted. Future research could investigate the extent to which possessing symbolic capital makes means-ends decoupling more likely.

Third, Bromley and Powell (2012) identified the diversion of resources as a key consequence of means-ends decoupling. They pointed out that in early institutional theory, decoupling was seen as positive, enabling organisations to function effectively in conflicting and contested institutional environments. Over time, this has been replaced by a more cynical view in policy-practice decoupling research, which tends to emphasise the negative consequences of decoupling as managers consciously decide not to implement socially desirable policies in order to manipulate institutional pressures. We saw that in the corporate environmental context, resources are diverted into producing emblems, credentials and kin to provide cultural support for a firm's activities. These may be general categories that are useful in the broader decoupling literature. I also delved underneath the surface of whether decoupling is positive or negative: When might there be net social benefits to means-ends decoupling? The social energy penalty framework should be valuable to research in the means-ends decoupling tradition because it addresses the normative implications of symbolic implementation that might be applied in a variety of empirical contexts. In this way, my analysis can be seen as a response to calls to investigate the society-wide consequences of the rising phenomenon of means-ends decoupling.

Practical implications

Corporate environmentalism poses significant challenges for public and private policy. In public policy, regulators appreciate the need for corporate involvement in achieving environmental aims, but they also know that firms can be self-interested and control access to resources. In private policy, managers face conflicting environmental demands that vary in unpredictable ways across locations and time. They need to somehow meet these demands in a society that values rationalisation and reassurance but is not willing to dramatically change consumption patterns to mitigate environmental impacts. All corporate environmentalism has a symbolic component; the challenge for public and private policy is to separate when symbolic corporate environmentalism is socially harmful from when it might be an inevitable part of an overall positive industry influence on the natural environment. Dismissing all corporate green solutions as merely symbolic risks a stifling of innovation and raising the overall cost of meeting environmental challenges. At the same time, accepting corporate environmentalism at face value can lead to false reassurance that green aims are being achieved and, ultimately, to worse environmental damage. In this book, I propose a contingent view on symbolic corporate environmentalism to help practitioners identify when it is most damaging and to focus their efforts accordingly.

The social costs of symbolic corporate environmentalism are likely to be higher when firms have the discretionary power to design a specific green solution. Firms may not always exercise this power. If the environmental demand is not particularly expensive or disruptive to a firm's core activities, managers may go along with another firm or stakeholder's green solution to gain positive reputation or to maintain legitimacy. But if the firm's core business is threatened, we can expect managers to find ways to use their firm's social status to design a compromise green solution and build cultural support around it. This is most evident in the case of CCS, wherein carbon-intensive firms sensed that they needed a plausible solution to climate change and provided political, economic and discursive support for the new technology. The problem with CCS is not so much that the technology does not work: the scientific consensus is that it does and it could be a vital way to substantially reduce global carbon emissions in a few decades (IPCC 2005). The problem is more that companies that are supposed to fund the development of this technology have no intention of doing so on the required scale or timeline. For CCS, R&D is not so much 'research and development' but rather 'research and delay'. The significant gap between stated project timelines and actual project commissioning is mirrored in the gap between enthusiastic rhetoric and investment realities. Far more investment has been discussed and committed on paper than has actually been spent on CCS projects. Firms are skilled at generating and protecting cultural symbols surrounding these potential projects – such as awards, patents, papers at scientific conventions and endorsement from politicians – making it difficult to see the gap between the social recognition that firms obtain for participating and the negligible concrete progress. CCS is an extreme example of firms having the power to sell a symbolic green solution to society that they have little intention of fully supporting: social costs are potentially high.

In situations in which social costs may be high, it is worth examining further whether there are social benefits. To estimate these properly, we need three key pieces of information: (1) the standalone technology value of the green solution, (2) the likely limits of the social benefit, and (3) the initial rate at which these benefits might be generated. In Chapter 8, I provide ideas on how to estimate each of these. However, it is important to remember that there may be scope for both regulators and managers to influence each parameter. For example: Are there any complementary changes to regulation or company practices that might improve the standalone environmental cost-benefit of the green solution? Are there ways to drive the green solution up the social benefit curve, such as mandatory information sharing from early adopters to encourage learning; supporting others in society such as NGOs or think tanks to act as monitors; publishing official information to make firms' reputations more transparent; and providing regulatory sanctions for noncompliance to underpin the selected green solution?

Balancing social costs against social benefits will determine whether there is an overall social energy penalty. The frameworks and analysis in this book suggest that the social energy penalty from symbolic corporate environmentalism is likely to be higher when:

- the industry is concentrated and dominated by a few powerful firms
- leading firms sense a threat to their core business
- firms can control the definitions and symbols around a green solution
- the stakeholder environment is less monitored (e.g., weak NGOs, direct regulations or investor interest)
- the most powerful actors around the green solution have complementary rather than conflicting logics (e.g., when industry and regulators perceive the problem in the same way)
- the industry is characterised by collaboration and consortia, including with government partners

- one green initiative is seen as a solution to several different social, policy, economic or environmental problems
- there is little potential for newly adopting firms to learn from earlier firms' experience
- firms adopt the green solution primarily for legitimacy rather than competitiveness reasons
- environmental performance standards are based on having measurement and reporting systems rather than changing underlying environmental impacts

In Chapter 1, I began by describing green solutions implemented by HSBC in recent years. The bank invested in a portfolio of environmental activities, including planting virtual trees as part of a new green bank account, commissioning greener corporate buildings, making and then withdrawing a commitment to the 'carbon neutral' label, and signing up to financial industry initiatives such as the Equator Principles. All are examples of corporate environmentalism and all have material and symbolic components: buildings, certificates, logos, charters, a system of counting trees, or new internal job titles, programmes, and departments to manage them. We want to know which of these supposed green solutions have the highest net benefit to society. Are there any that policy makers should discourage, that NGOs should expose as merely symbolic or, alternatively, that other firms should adopt as well? The frameworks in this book help to answer these questions.

First, consider HSBC's virtual trees. HSBC promised to plant one virtual tree in its virtual forest for every account that was switched to a paperless Green HSBC Plus account in 2007. It committed to planting one real tree for every twenty virtual trees, and the bank was criticised for a backlog of tree planting even at this conversion rate. This is an iconic example of symbolic corporate environmentalism in action. Driven by the need to be perceived as doing something on environmental issues, HSBC invented a new product and an accounting system for virtual trees that was decoupled from the bank's underlying impacts. The firm controlled the rules of the scheme, including the conversion rate and the measurement and reporting system that accounted for the virtual trees. There is likely to be a utility loss associated with this solution because HSBC controlled the form of the voluntary initiative. It would have been more efficient for the bank to give a discount or cash back to customers who switched to its paper-less account (which it subsequently implemented). Alternatively, there would have been better environmental impact if the bank had more directly limited carbon emissions by limiting staff travel or altering its lending criteria to fund only less carbon-intensive projects (which it has since promised). Furthermore, there is little potential for social benefit from virtual trees because there is little for other adopting firms to learn about environmental impacts through such a simple green solution. Perhaps recognising these difficulties, HSBC quietly dropped its virtual tree-planting programme and green bank accounts, replacing them with paperless options on all accounts. HSBC is not the only company that has had problems with symbolic virtual trees. In a 2008 online marketing initiative, Timberland promised to plant a virtual tree for each 'like' it received on its Facebook page. Overwhelmed by responses, it subsequently altered the ratio of virtual to actual trees and eventually placed a limit on the number of real trees the firm would pay to plant. There is great potential for a social energy penalty when companies control commensurability (e.g., how new bank accounts or Facebook likes are converted into precise numbers of trees) and when virtual symbols outpace a company's ability to deliver non-core activities such as tree planting in the real world. HSBC's relatively small virtual-trees initiative is fairly easy to dismiss as having little or no net social benefit.

Second, HSBC has committed to achieving LEED Gold certification for the firm's top fifty energy-consuming buildings.[1] The bank commissioned the first buildings to be LEED Gold certified in Latin America and in China and continues a global rollout of certifying its data centres, regional headquarters and larger offices. The buildings are cultural manifestations of corporate environmentalism and have a symbolic component that promises that the bank is taking seriously its social responsibility. The buildings may even be seen as forms of symbolic capital if the bank successfully attaches high-status credentials (e.g., LEED Gold certification) or prestigious kin (e.g., famous architects) to the social understanding of the buildings. However, the value of these credentials and kin are somewhat arbitrary: stakeholders use them as shortcuts to decode the bank's symbolic performance without examining actual environmental performance. To evaluate net social benefit, we must look inside the details of the green building certification schemes. HSBC actively chooses between green building standards, opting for LEED Gold in most countries but for the more stringent BREEAM 'excellent' standard for its headquarters and data centre in the United Kingdom. Which, if any, has a higher social energy penalty?

In Chapter 8, I am critical of LEED compared with the more rigorous BREEAM green building standard but, applying the previous list of criteria, it is evident that both schemes have the potential for a social energy penalty. Both schemes were introduced to symbolise a way for land developers, architects and builders to respond to a threat to their core business – that is, the ability to develop new buildings. Governments and industry players had a shared interest in encouraging new symbols to show local communities that buildings were being built in an environmentally responsible way, protecting construction jobs and local economic development. Firms commission green buildings primarily to maintain social legitimacy rather than to gain direct competitiveness benefits, making firms more likely to choose credentials based on symbolic capital value rather than environmental or economic benefits.

However, there also are significant differences between the symbols (see Chapter 8). Whereas both certifications add cost to a building, the costs are lower for the less-stringent LEED scheme, making it more attractive for legitimacy seekers. The certification criteria for LEED are controlled by the USGBC, an industry-led, membership-based trade association, whereas BREEAM is managed by a former government executive agency that is now an independent approvals organisation operating at arm's length from both industry and government. LEED criteria are based on voluntary standards, whereas BREEAM criteria are based on technical best practice and legislation. Energy efficiencies are translated through dollar amounts under LEED but linked to direct CO_2 emissions reductions under BREEAM. The institutional environment surrounding building regulations and industry self-regulation is more decentralised in LEED's US regulatory system than it is in Europe. All of these factors point to a higher social energy penalty associated with LEED certification than with BREEAM.[2]

Although there may be a social energy penalty associated with LEED certification, at least LEED certification is tied to the building's environmental performance. The third of HSBC's green investments – the carbon neutrality label – lost symbolic value for HSBC because it became decoupled from material changes in internal firm practices.

HSBC was the first large bank to declare itself carbon neutral in 2005; however, by 2011, it announced that it was withdrawing from the symbol. HSBC was not the only large firm to withdraw from carbon neutrality around that time. Companies such as Dell, Nike, PepsiCo and Yahoo all backed away from carbon neutrality language in 2010–2011. Why? When carbon neutrality was first introduced as a label, it included a wide variety of behaviours directed at a goal of net-zero emissions. Precise definitions varied in terms of the scope of companies' emissions included and, in particular, whether firms were required to reduce direct emissions from their own internal activities or whether they could pay others to do so. For example, the UK DECC issued guidance on carbon neutrality, stating that it should not be achieved only by offsetting but also should include internal reductions (DECC 2009). In contrast, the Carbon Neutral Company, which assisted 350 companies in 35 countries to become *Certified CarbonNeutral®*, does not require internal emissions reductions (Carbon Neutral Company 2013). The symbolic flexibility of many meanings of carbon neutrality weakens the signalling value of the label. It imposes a higher social energy penalty because the benefits of the symbol are less clear, and firms can control the particular form of carbon neutrality credentials that they offer to their stakeholders.

Leading companies have backed away from carbon neutral certification because the weaker label advocated by agencies such as the Carbon Neutral Company has gained prominence. They have replaced the label with more precise commitments about improving the energy efficiency of their internal operations (HSBC 2013), reporting their use of the entire suite of GHGs (Nike 2013), and going 'beyond carbon neutrality' by investing in renewable energy projects and offering products that help supply chain partners reduce emissions (Google 2013). Despite the social energy penalty, however, carbon neutrality certification has not vanished. Several major companies, including UPS, Microsoft, and Bain & Company, sought and achieved *CarbonNeutral®* certification in 2012 and 2013. In the case of Microsoft, the company introduced carbon neutrality as a new commitment because it found that it could not meet its previous 2009 commitment to reduce relative carbon emissions by 30 percent by 2012. Its new cloud-computing business model was driving up gross carbon emissions, so the only option was to opt for carbon neutrality, which allows the use of offsets (Microsoft 2012). Microsoft replaced a commitment based on improving internal material changes with one based on changing measurement and reporting systems, leading to a higher social energy penalty.

Finally, HSBC committed to a variety of financial sector initiatives including the United Nations Environment Programme Finance Initiative (at the Rio Conference in 1993), the UN's Global Compact (in 2001) and the Equator Principles (in 2003). The Equator Principles illustrate a particularly good example of how a green solution might turn out to have a net social benefit. Ten large financial institutions voluntarily adopted the principles in June 2003 to improve their environmental and social risk management practices in infrastructure project financing.[3] In the early years (i.e., 2003–2006), the principles were widely criticised as a symbolic attempt to gain legitimacy and repair reputational damage from earlier NGO campaigns (O'Sullivan and O'Dwyer 2009). The original principles had many of the hallmarks of high potential social cost: adopting banks tended to be larger than non-adopters; projects often were financed by consortia of financial institutions, leading to interdependence among major industry players; environmental and social concerns could attract considerable public scrutiny in large infrastructure projects, possibly threatening the viability of the projects; the banks narrowed the scope of the principles to project only finance activities; and firms avoided building in accountability and sanctioning mechanisms to monitor compliance (Haack et al. 2012; O'Sullivan and O'Dwyer 2009; Scholtens and Dam 2007).

Given the high potential social cost, we should assess the potential for social benefits. Here, the picture is more positive. The Equator Principles diffused rapidly, with an average of seven new institutions adopting them per year, and now cover more than 70 per cent of international project-finance debt in emerging companies.[4] Banks reported learning about social and environmental risks surrounding infrastructure projects (Macve and Chen 2010), and they responded to the complementary asset of shared reputation to gradually revise the principles under NGO pressure to become broader and more stringent over time (Balch 2012). As Haack et al. (2012: 835) stated it, after being criticised for greenwashing in the early years, the 'banks ultimately talk[ed] themselves into a new reality of doing project finance'. The third version of the principles published in May 2013 extend their scope and reach far beyond what the originators of the charter imagined ten years earlier (Equator Principles 2013). The principles provide a good example of a green solution with apparent potential for social cost ultimately yielding social benefit. In time, the low cost of signing up to an industry-dominated scheme has drawn almost the entire international project-finance industry into normalising a much higher engagement with environmental and social issues. As Haack et al. (2012: 837) concluded from their careful analysis of the Equator Principles: '[I]nstead of unconditionally sanctioning organizations for decoupling, it might pay off to tolerate their gradual transformation and encourage experimentation informed by mutual learning and dialogue'.

Thus, the frameworks presented in this book should assist practitioners in at least ranking green solutions according to their potential for a social energy penalty. Of the green solutions in HSBC's portfolio, we can expect the highest social energy penalty to be associated with planting virtual trees and the biggest social premium from the Equator Principles. The three intermediate cases are certification schemes with different designs and criteria. Of these, the BREEAM green building standards are likely to have the lowest social energy penalty, followed by USGBC's LEED and then The Carbon Neutral Company's *CarbonNeutral*® certification. The lesson here is that whereas it may be difficult to determine an exact quantification of a social energy penalty for a given symbol, the frameworks in this book and the previous checklist should be useful in ranking alternative industry-led green solutions. They should also be useful in assessing whether a particular symbol is generating a smaller or larger social penalty over time.

A broader reminder from this work for regulators is that policy makers also have a role in generating and perpetuating symbolic greening (Matten 2003; Newig 2007). Symbolic corporate environmentalism is not strictly a corporate phenomenon in the sense that others in society – regulators, politicians, consumers, voters and researchers – must be complicit in not calling firms to account for the social energy penalty to persist. There is a natural political temptation to focus attention on specific lobbying groups in response to deliberate corporate political strategies. In this book, however, I emphasise the parallel cultural temptation in adopting the business language of voluntariness, controllability and green solutions. When designing policy instruments, regulators should (as far as possible) question deference and arbitrary distinctions generated by ratings and rankings. Naïve enthusiasm for business-led solutions should be examined carefully, particularly if the regulatory instrument supports an industry-led green solution that meets some of the checklist conditions stated previously. One promising direction is 'co-regulation', in which self-regulatory solutions are backed up by some regulatory oversight or ratification (Gunningham and Rees 1997).

Managers can now access an increasing range of contemporary advice on how to choose an eco-label (see, e.g., Delmas et al. 2013), how to communicate environmental credentials to a cynical public (see, e.g., Illia et al. 2013), and how to reduce greenwashing (see, e.g., Delmas and Burbano 2011). What my analysis adds is how to be aware of the social costs and benefits of corporate environmentalism. All corporate environmentalism has a symbolic dimension, whether or not it is merely symbolic. My goal has been to increase our sensitivity to when symbolic corporate environmentalism is socially harmful. Managers might use the frameworks to evaluate the social energy penalty associated with particular green solutions to avoid cases in which green solutions are of dubious social or environmental value. Doing so in advance might avoid problems later when the green solution is eventually criticised by others. They might also use these ideas to prioritise solutions that offer the most social benefit for a similar firm-level cost, such as those that are based on substantive performance standards or that encourage learning and sharing.

Limitations

Throughout the book, I build the case that symbolic corporate environmentalism has social costs and benefits, depending on a variety of field-, firm- and solution-level characteristics. However, as I point out in Chapter 8, I did not directly test the overall framework. This important task is left to future researchers, and I hope that Chapter 8 provides guidance on how to do so. As well as testing the frameworks more directly, I encourage further work resulting from two key limitations of my approach: (1) exploring different types of symbolic corporate environmentalism, and (2) expanding the framework to different empirical contexts.

The conceptual frameworks in this book expand our theories from deliberate, disclosure-based greenwashing to include the entire range of symbolic aspects of everyday firm practices. I present empirical studies based on environmental strategies and policies (see Chapter 5), an environmental technology (see Chapter 6) and a carbon measurement system (see Chapter 7). In passing, I discuss examples based on symbols in the built environment and discourses surrounding collaboration with stakeholders. Taken together, these examples cover five of the eight cultural manifestations of corporate environmentalism listed by Forbes and Jermier (2012). I leave it to other researchers to assess whether these ideas can be appropriately applied to the other symbolic domains Forbes and Jermier (2012) identified: organisational structure, human resources processes and incentives, and stories and rituals. There are parallel literatures in organisational behaviour that might evaluate the social implications of green job titles, specialised environmental departments, and environmental training and incentives more thoroughly than I do here. Future research might also link my frameworks with emerging findings on the narrative dimensions of diffusing corporate environmentalism through stories (see, e.g., Haack et al. 2012 and Christensen et al. 2013).

Building on this, there may be potential to develop more nuanced arguments based on different types of symbolic corporate environmentalism. For example, symbolic corporate environmentalism may vary according to its embeddedness in the organisation, its visibility to outsiders, by net cost to the adopter, or whether it is attached to the core organisation rather than a particular event or activity. Furthermore, I focus on increases in symbolic corporate environmentalism by adopting or implementing new green solutions. Future research could gain deeper insights from other changes in symbolic corporate environmentalism, such as corporate withdrawal from symbols they helped design, controversies around changes in criteria, and stopping a particular green solution altogether. Recent examples of companies withdrawing from a standard that they helped to design include Apple's withdrawal from the Electronic Product Environmental Assessment Tool green electronics registry and the UK retailer Tesco dropping its plan to include a carbon footprint label on all of its own brand products. For a controversy about changes in criteria, interested readers should see the negotiation surrounding the USGBC's decision to exclude SFI-certified wood in its rating system. An illustration of the withdrawal of a symbolic green solution is the EPA's phase-out of the voluntary Climate Leaders Program that operated in the United States from 2002 to 2011.

Finally, I focus on the symbolic components of environmental activities in companies. This is a compelling example of firms adopting new organizational practices in response to institutional demands. I encourage other researchers to test the robustness of the findings in other empirical contexts. Any context in which there is scope for gaps between stated intent, the implementation of new practices and actual impact might be profitably explored in this way. Researchers explored the drivers of symbolic gaps in contexts as diverse as corporate governance (Westphal and Zajac 2001), management control systems (Kennedy and Fiss 2009; Oakes et al. 1998), equal opportunity policies (Kelly and Dobbin 1998), ethics codes (Stevens et al. 2005), and public policy (Weber et al. 2009). Although I am unable to generalize beyond symbolic gaps in corporate environmental strategy, future research could investigate to what extent the findings may apply elsewhere.

After greenwashing

Greenwashing seems to be on the decline, at least in the narrow sense of deliberate disclosure by companies of their artificially favourable environmental performance. Activists in a social media era have become better at exposing it, and academics have built models based on twenty years of corporate environmentalism research to understand it. This does not mean that we no longer need to be concerned about the social implications of widespread symbolic corporate greening. The naïve marketing of the 1980s and 1990s – exemplified by Chevron's *People Do* campaign and unrefined online engagement campaigns such as Timberland's Facebook virtual trees programme – is no longer successful in our contemporary social media age. Companies and NGOs are inventing increasingly media-savvy deliberate green communication strategies, such as tweetjacking, astroturfing, astrotweeting and even reverse greenwashing.[5] It remains to be seen which of these deliberate post-greenwash strategies will thrive in the coming years. Some may succeed but it is more likely that these deliberate communications will be caught up in exposure and cynicism over time, just like greenwashing has in recent years.

I focus instead on a more socially embedded and often neglected phenomenon: the shared meanings related to everyday corporate environmentalism. This much broader phenomenon is an inevitable consequence of firm engagement with green issues because all firm activities have a symbolic component. Unlike transitory greenwashing and its new-age successors, symbolic corporate environmentalism is here to stay. My goal was to work out when symbolic corporate environmentalism is more or less socially wasteful. Based on evidence from the frameworks, cases and stories in this book, it is difficult to think of a positive example in which there is an unequivocal social energy premium. The Equator Principles comprise possibly the best example of an industry-led green solution that results in a net social benefit over time. Even in this case, it was necessary to take the long view, looking back over ten years: the symbol was widely criticised in the early stages and had the potential for a high social cost.

This state of affairs might leave advocates of corporate environmentalism pessimistic because so many green solutions have an absolute social energy penalty. Critical theorists may be correct to suspect that organisations within society are defining and constructing solutions for the natural environment in order to control it. But realists accept that corporate involvement in addressing environmental issues is inevitable in the current socioeconomic system. Conventional corporate environmentalism researchers have the tools and a duty to help unpack when the same self-regulation they so often advocate imposes a social energy penalty. Social inefficiency arising from the symbolic component of corporate environmentalism may be an absolute problem, but conventional researchers can design green solutions that are relatively better. This book is a first modest effort in this direction.

Notes

1. Introduction

1 Trees are carbon sinks because as they grow, they absorb more carbon than they release. A forest fire would release the stored CO_2 back into the atmosphere.

2 HSBC's head offices in China, Egypt and Mexico have all been certified to the LEED Gold standard. These were the first buildings to achieve this standard in the Middle East (in 2010) and in Latin America (in 2008).

3 See www.ecolabelindex.com and www.environmentawards.net, respectively, for current lists of eco-labels and awards. For a list and details of all of the voluntary standards recognised by the ITC, see www.standardsmap.org.

4 Further details on each of these Advertising Standards Agency claims are found on the ASA website: Shell Adjudication No. ADJ43476; Lexus Adjudication No. ADJ42574.

2. After greenwashing

1 For an example of this advertising campaign from the 1980s, see www.youtube.com/watch?v=bReBO55XzZc.

2 For more on The Yes Men and their antics, see www.theyesmen.org. Details of the Chevron spoof are found at www.yeslab.org/project/chevron.

3 Other words and phrases identified in the same article that have since entered our common business lexicon include 'coopetition', 'herding cats' and 'presenteeism'.

4 It turned out that these differences in environmental claims between magazine advertisements in the United States and the United Kingdom were persistent because this same difference was noticed fifteen years later by Baum (2012).

5 Strictly speaking, this is probably an overestimate of unique articles because working papers can be listed multiple times on different servers, databases and webpages. That said, it is likely that the Google Scholar

measure provides a realistic sense of increase in literature mentioning 'greenwashing' over time.

6 For more about AirCasting and to see its latest maps, see www.aircasting. org.

7 It is worth noting that current definitions of 'greenwashing' are about selective disclosure of *positive* information rather than information in general. There is emerging literature on selective disclosure of negative information, such as Short and Toffel (2008, 2010). This phenomenon is not actually about greenwashing – where environmental information is assumed to be somehow in excess of performance – but it is a significant phenomenon worthy of more research attention.

8 The United Nations Sustainable Development Knowledge Platform contains a list of these available at sustainabledevelopment.un.org/index. php?menu=1070. As of 24 January 2014, 759 total initiatives were listed.

3. Perspectives on symbolic corporate environmentalism

1 For example, Banerjee (2001: 489) defined corporate environmentalism as 'the *process* by which firms address environmental issues and develop environmental management strategies'; Lee and Rhee (2005: 388) defined it as the 'dominant *attitude or mode of response* to environmental issues'; whereas Hoffman (1999) referred to structural, technical and cultural changes to firms' *practices* around environmental issues (emphases added).

2 For example, critics challenge terms popular in the conventional view such as 'environmental protection' on who is protecting what from whom. Similar difficulties arise with 'environmental investments', wherein critics ask whether fixing environmental damage is an asset or liability, or with 'green practices' that may be talked about more than implemented. Thus, just as green solutions may not solve green problems, environmental protection may not protect, green investments may not generate assets, and green practices may not be practiced.

3 For more detailed reviews of the conventional corporate environmentalism literature, see Etzion (2007), Berchicci and King (2008), and Russo and Minto (2012).

4 As with the conventional view, the critical perspective of corporate environmentalism is really a collection of related perspectives on theorising corporate greening. The two handbook review articles cited here, Jermier et al. (2006) and Banerjee (2012), are excellent introductions into this now quite substantial literature. Readers interested in learning more about the diversity within this critical perspective may enjoy Levy's (1997) Neo-Gramscian critique, Bäckstrand's (2004) eco-feminist view,

and Springett's (2003) critical account of the rise of the sustainable development 'industry'.

5 For a more expanded discussion of the philosophical traditions and subtraditions underpinning corporate environmentalism scholarship and practice, see Rikhardson and Welford (1997).

6 Recall from Chapter 2 that greenwashing is a special case of symbolic corporate environmentalism in which the green solution is merely symbolic and deliberately so.

7 Bitektine (2011), Devers et al. (2009), and Deephouse and Suchman (2008) provided overviews of how these three concepts inter-relate as well as how they compare with other proximate concepts, such as celebrity and stigma.

8 For a comparison of LEED with the earlier UK-based BREEAM building standards, see Parker (2009). For more on corporate influence in the ISO 14001 standards, see Karliner (1997: 185) and Hortensius and Barthel (1997).

9 For more on the origins, definition and operation of symbolic capital, see Chapter 6.

10 A typical and well-cited example is Brunsson's (1989) book on *The Organisation of Hypocrisy*.

11 See, for example, the special issue of *Accounting, Auditing and Accountability* on social and environmental reporting introduced in Deegan (2002).

12 For several examples of this approach, see the special issue of the *Strategic Management Journal* on the 'Psychological Foundations of Strategic Management', edited by Powell, Lovallo, and Fox (2011).

13 Of course, because all organisations operate within institutional fields, there is likely no such outfit as an entirely neutral body. The closest for practical purposes is a government agency that is supposed to reflect the collective will of the people within a jurisdiction. For this reason, the most neutral 'gift' for practical purposes is likely to be in the form of payments to governments, such as to a government-controlled technology fund.

14 This mechanism is explained more fully in Chapter 4.

4. Drivers and consequences of symbolic corporate environmentalism

1 For a recent review of the literature on whether and when it may pay to be green, see Stefan and Paul (2008).

2 Technically speaking, I use the Marshallian demand curve at this stage of the analysis, relying on the assumption that income effects are relatively

unimportant for the market for greening solutions (for more details, see Nicholson 1992).
3 McWilliams and Siegel (2001) admitted that there may be cases in which a firm might produce a CSR activity at the same or even lower cost as its normal operations. They argued that these situations are relatively rare for CSR activities. However, green solutions often offer cost reduction or efficiency improvements; therefore, any analysis of corporate environmentalism needs to take this assumption more seriously. Husted and Salazar's (2006) analysis explicitly modelled the ability of firms to reduce costs as part of their strategic view of investment in green solutions.
4 Husted and Salazar (2006) actually described these curves as social cost and benefit curves rather than private costs and benefits. However, they are clear that their '"social benefit" curve is not the social benefit of welfare economics, but is the private benefit to the firm for its production of social goods . . . [which] might include increased sales, the ability to extract a price premium, or reduced production costs' (2006: 79). Because I use social costs and benefits in the sense of costs and benefits to society later in this chapter, I instead labelled Husted and Salazar's curves 'private costs and benefits' because they represent costs and benefits to the firm.
5 Esteem is related to but distinct from organisational theorists' usual indicators of symbolic performance that I introduce in Chapter 3: reputation, legitimacy and status.
6 This assumption is inspired by Brennan and Pettit's (2004) 'virtual controller', which helps solve the problem of how to demand something without having the appearance of demanding it. See Brennan and Petit (2004: 40–42) for a fuller explanation of the more general case of a virtual controller. In the conditions they outlined (2004: 42), B1 = symbolic green solutions, D1 = maintaining status and power, D2 = reputation or legitimacy, and B2 = substantive green solutions.
7 For a popular and engaging recapitulation of this line of thinking, see Waldfogel (2009).
8 There is an additional complexity in applying Waldfogel's analysis to the preferences of multiple – as opposed to a single – receivers of the gift. I am grateful to the reviewer who pointed this out to me, but I leave this as a challenge for future analysis to resolve.
9 Critical researchers and ENGOs might argue that there is no such thing as 'overproduction of substantive green performance'. They would say that as a society, we need as much environmental impact alleviation as we can get. But here I am using a more conventional criterion of optimising consumer preferences, and it may be possible for firms to over-invest

in environmental impact reduction compared with consumers' desire for environmentally damaging goods. Sadly, ample empirical evidence supports this assumption because consumers and voters consistently tolerate levels of environmental damage higher than our natural systems can cope with, particularly in the short run.

10 There are actually at least two different versions of the S-curve. This S-curve, introduced by Foster (1986), is the technology evolution curve, mapping improving performance of a technology as more cumulative effort is put into developing it. The diffusion S-curve popularised by Rogers (1991) traces the number of adopters of a particular technology over time. These two curves are conceptually distinct but interrelated. In this analysis, I simplify the two curves into one, tracing the improving performance of a technology as the number of cumulative adopters rises. This compound curve will be S-shaped as long as the rate of effort put into the technology stays constant across early and late adopters. In the corporate environmental context, effort put into development is as simple as investing in adopting the standard and it can be decoupled from substantive green improvement. Therefore, this assumption seems reasonable, particularly for symbolic green solutions.

5. Study 1: Symbolic gaps in environmental strategies

1 These three dimensions do not map precisely onto the categories of symbolic or substantive green solutions. However, stated intentions are usually symbolic, at least initially, and actual environmental impact mitigation is, by definition, substantive. Categorising initiative implementation as symbolic or substantive is more contentious: although implementation signals more action than stated intent and therefore has a higher chance of yielding substantive environmental improvements, there is no guarantee that implementation will lead to mitigating environmental harm. For that reason, I use the three separate dimensions of corporate environmentalism in this chapter and resolve empirically whether initiative implementation is more symbolic or substantive.

2 Many thanks to Jessica Dillabough – who was then a PhD student at the University of Calgary – for helping with this coding and analysis process.

3 A full coding table showing how each paper was coded for all moderating variables is available from the author.

4 The most recent decoupling research emphasises separating policy from practices and intended outcomes in this way (Bromley and Powell 2012). My approach is different in that it incorporates realised outcomes for the environment, not intended outcomes for the firm.

6. Study 2: Pollution control technology and the production of symbolic capital

1 Strictly speaking, carbon capture investments can be separated into the two main varieties of pollution abatement: pollution control and pollution prevention. Post-combustion capture is a pollution control technology because it involves separating the CO_2 from the flue gases at the end of an industrial process. In contrast, pre-combustion capture requires the gasification of a fuel source earlier in the process, making pollution prevention easier. Whereas pre-combustion capture technologies may have the potential to become disruptive innovations (Bowen 2011), most current CCS projects listed in Table 5.1 are of the post-combustion, pollution control type. I therefore adopt the simplifying assumption in this chapter that CCS technologies are an example of pollution control.

2 These interviews were carried out informally as part of a related research project. Commitments made during the participant-consent process of that study, including how the interview data might be used, prevent a detailed analysis of the transcripts here. Interviewees' candid off-the-record comments were most useful in shaping and reinforcing the public document discourse analysis. Here, I limit the discussion to general comments on the field structure.

7. Study 3: The evolution of measurement and performance standards

1 This chapter draws heavily from Bowen and Wittneben (2011). With thanks to Bettina Wittneben and Emerald Publishing for their permission to use this material.

2 I want to acknowledge my co-organisers, Chuks Okereke and Bettina Wittneben, for their enthusiastic assistance in organising this workshop. The workshop was funded by the Smith School of Enterprise and the Environment, University of Oxford.

3 According to the IPCC (2007), the major GHGs are carbon dioxide (CO_2), methane (CH_4), nitrous oxide (N_2O), the hydrofluorocarbon (HFCs) and perfluorocarbon (PFCs) families of gases, and sulphur hexafluoride (SF_6).

8. Measurement and methods

1 We recall from Chapter 4 that one of the key assumptions in Husted and Salazar's (2006) model is that firms can indeed move the private cost and benefit curves of green solutions through strategic corporate environmentalism. I argue that investing in green solutions is more likely to move the private cost and benefit curves for symbolic green solutions than for

substantive ones. Thus, firms adopting strategic corporate environmentalism may end up making symbolic investments in green solutions as an unintended consequence of a profit-maximisation strategy.

2 For more detailed definitions and descriptions of emblems, credentials and kin, see Chapter 6.

3 For a current list of The Sustainability Consortium members, see www.sustainabilityconsortium.org/members.

4 This is the cost per square foot estimated for commercial real estate in the cheapest area listed in the United States by CBRE, Inc., in August 2013, in Winston-Salem, NC.

5 Cost estimates are based on the relative cost of hiring an external consultant for a large firm, reporting for the first time and based on data that have already been collected within the firm. Estimates were based on the author's calculations from data provided, available at www.sustainability-reporting.com.au/pricing.php.

6 This change was so controversial with the timber industry lobby that the USGBC was forced to delay the ratification and implementation of the new LEED standards (Fedrizi 2012). SFI-certified wood will not be recognised under the new LEED v. 4 standards. However, to ease the transition, adopters can choose to certify under either the old or the new rules until 2015, when the old version of LEED will be fully phased out.

7 The BREEAM for buildings is 'the world's foremost environmental assessment method and rating system for buildings, with 200,000 buildings with certified assessment ratings and over a million registered for assessment since it was first launched in 1990' (see www.breeam.org/about).

8 For simplicity, I assume that the supply is limited by a single or small coordinated group of suppliers and ignore any competitive interactions among them. The issue of whether it is a single firm, a group of firms or another inner circle of actors that has the ability to limit the supply of greening solutions is an empirical question, depending on the context. But, as described in the CCS demonstration projects study (see Chapter 6), there does not need to be overt collusion among large, powerful firms for them to have a shared interest in limiting the social conversation to a narrow range of potential green solutions.

9 Harberger's original formulation does not consider income effects. The most cited paper in applied economics on deadweight loss is Hausman (1981), who considered income effects and refined Harberger's method based on the observed market demand curve to generate estimates based on an unobserved compensated demand curve. Curious readers are referred to Hausman (1981), which contains formulae for more exact calculations of consumer surplus and deadweight loss.

10 Posner (1975) estimated that with an elasticity of one and a price increase over the competitive level of 10 per cent, Harberger's traditional dead-weight loss is only 5.6 per cent of Tullock's total social cost.

11 The corporate environmental context, in fact, may offer an opportunity to test some extensions and complexities in this debate. For example, there is an ongoing discussion on the welfare implications of giving gift cards as a transitional good between a specific gift and cash (see, e.g., Offenberg 2007). The conceptual equivalent in the corporate environmental context might be giving into an environmental technology fund, in which there is some discretion for stakeholders or consumers on how to spend the gift but with 'strings attached'.

12 For reviews and examples of other similar studies, see Ellingsen and Johannesson (2011) and Kube, Marechal, and Puppe (2012).

13 Clearly, all of these estimation techniques are subject to the usual problems with estimating demand and preferences. Methods based on revealed preferences, such as hedonic pricing, are based on real choices but indirect estimation methods; methods based on stated preferences, such as surveys or comparative choice trials, are based on a hypothetical market in which people know that they do not face real budget constraints. For further details and potential solutions, see an applied economics or marketing research textbook such as Lusk and Shogren (2007).

9. Implications and conclusions

1 HSBC's environmental efficiency commitments are listed at www.hsbc.com/citizenship/sustainability/environmental-efficiency (retrieved 1 August 2013).

2 Similar arguments can be made when comparing several sets of US-based compared with European-based corporate environmentalism symbols. In forestry, for example, the US-based SFI standard is likely to impose a larger social energy penalty than the more stringent FSC (Cashore 2003). In the coffee industry, the more business-friendly US Rainforest Alliance label will generate a higher social energy penalty than more environmentally rigorous labels such as the Soil Association Certified Organic (Raynolds, Murray, and Heller 2007).

3 HSBC was not one of the founding signatories but adopted the Equator Principles in September of that year.

4 For a complete list of members with adoption dates, see www.equator-principles.com.

5 'Tweetjacking' is defined as when an individual or group tweets on one's behalf, usually without their permission, such as when McDonald's

launched a #McDStories tweet that was subsequently hijacked and re-tweeted using unfavourable messages about the company (see Lyon and Montgomery 2013). 'Astroturfing' is a communications strategy that sets up a fake 'grassroots' effort so as to create the impression of a popular movement, which was tried in the corporate political activities of tobacco companies and around climate change (Cho, Martens, Kim, and Rodrigue 2011). 'Astrotweeting' is a combination of these strategies, wherein the false grassroots effort is conducted via social media. 'Reverse greenwashing' is a form of negative marketing in which competitors or other stakeholders make claims of environmental detriment about a focal company (Lane 2013).

References

Abrahamson, E. 1996. 'Management fashion', *Academy of Management Review* 21: 254–285.

Abusow, K. 2012. *LEED Approach to Certification: Slogans or Science?* Washington, DC: Sustainable Forestry Initiative.

Ahmed, N., R. Montagno, and R. Firenze. 1998. 'Organizational performance and environmental consciousness: An empirical study', *Management Decision* 36: 57–62.

Ahmed, S. 2012. *On Being Included: Racism and Diversity in Institutional Life.* Oxford University Press.

Allenby, B. 2012. 'Why Rio+20 was a success (yes, really)', *Environmental Quality Management* 22: 13–18.

Alvesson, M. 2013. *The Triumph of Emptiness: Consumption, Higher Education and Work Organization.* Oxford University Press.

Andrews, K. R. 1971. *The Concept of Corporate Strategy.* Homewood, IL: Irwin.

Aragon-Correa, J. A. 1998. 'Strategic proactivity and firm approach to the natural environment', *Academy of Management Journal* 41: 556–567.

Aragon-Correa, J. A., and E. Rubio-López. 2007. 'Proactive corporate environmental strategies: Myths and misunderstandings', *Long Range Planning* 40: 357–381.

Aragon-Correa, J. A., and S. Sharma. 2003. 'A contingent resource-based view of proactive corporate environmental strategy', *Academy of Management Review* 28: 71–88.

Aravind, D., and P. Christmann. 2010. 'Decoupling of standard implementation from certification', *Business Ethics Quarterly* 21: 73–102.

Arthur, W. B. 1989. 'Competing technologies, increasing returns and lock-in by historical events', *Economic Journal* 99: 116–131.

Ashforth, B., and B. W. Gibbs. 1990. 'The double-edge of organizational legitimation', *Organization Science* 1: 177–194.

Axelrod, R. 1984. *The Evolution of Cooperation.* New York: Basic Books.

Bäckstrand, K. 2004. 'Scientisation vs. civic expertise in environmental governance: Eco-feminist, eco-modern and post-modern responses', *Environmental Politics* 13: 695–714.

Balabanis, G., H. Phillips, and J. Lyall. 1998. 'Corporate social responsibility and economic performance in the top British companies: Are they linked?', *European Business Review* 98: 25–44.

Balch, O. 2013. 'Sustainable finance: How far have the Equator Principles gone?', *The Guardian*, 15 November 2013.

Banerjee, S. B. 1998. 'Corporate environmentalism: Perspectives from organizational learning', *Management Learning* 29: 147–164.

Banerjee, S. B. 2000. 'Whose land is it anyway? National interest, indigenous stakeholders, and colonial discourses: The Case of the Jabiluka uranium mine', *Organization and Environment* 13: 3–38.

Banerjee, S. B. 2001. 'Managerial perceptions of corporate environmentalism: Interpretations from industry and strategic implications for organizations', *Journal of Management Studies* 38: 489–513.

Banerjee, S. B. 2008. 'Corporate social responsibility: The good, the bad and the ugly', *Critical Sociology* 34: 51–79.

Banerjee, S. B. 2012. 'Critical perspectives on business and the natural environment'. In P. Bansal and A. Hoffman (eds.), *The Oxford Handbook of Business and the Natural Environment*, pp. 572–590. Oxford University Press.

Bansal, P. 2005. 'Evolving sustainably: A longitudinal study of corporate sustainable development', *Strategic Management Journal* 26: 197–218.

Bansal, P., and I. Clelland. 2004. 'Talking trash: Legitimacy, impression management and unsystematic risk in the context of the natural environment', *Academy of Management Journal* 47: 93–103.

Bansal, P., and T. Hunter. 2003. 'Strategic explanations for the early adoption of ISO 14001', *Journal of Business Ethics* 46: 289–299.

Bansal, P., and G. Kistruck. 2006. 'Seeing is not believing: Managing the impressions of firms' commitment to the natural environment', *Journal of Business Ethics* 67: 165–180.

Bansal, P., and K. Roth. 2000. 'Why companies go green: A model of ecological responsiveness', *Academy of Management Journal* 43: 717–736.

Barnett, M. L., and A. A. King. 2008. 'Good fences make good neighbors: A longitudinal analysis of an industry self-regulatory institution', *Academy of Management Journal* 51: 1150–1170.

Barney, J. B. 1991. 'Firm resources and sustained competitive advantage', *Journal of Management* 17: 99–120.

Bartley, T. 2003. 'Certifying forests and factories: States, social movements, and the rise of private regulation in the apparel and forest products fields', *Politics and Society* 31: 433–464.

Baum, L. M. 2012. 'It's not easy being green... or is it? A content analysis of environmental claims in magazine advertisements from the United

States and United Kingdom', *Environmental Communication: A Journal of Nature and Culture* 6: 423–440.

Baumol, W. J. 1982. 'Contestable markets: An uprising in the theory of industry structure', *The American Economic Review* 72: 1–15.

Baylis, R., L. Connell, and A. Flynn. 1998. 'Company size, environmental regulation and ecological modernization: Further analysis at the level of the firm', *Business Strategy and the Environment* 7: 285–296.

BBC. 2004. *HSBC Bank to Go Carbon Neutral*. London. 6 December.

Bebbington, J., and C. Larrinaga-Gonzalez. 2008. 'Carbon trading: Accounting and reporting issues', *European Accounting Review* 17: 697–717.

Beder, S. 1997. *Global Spin: The Corporate Assault on Environmentalism*. Totnes, Devon: Green Books Ltd.

Benfield, K. 2008. *What a Joke: Auto-Dependent Corporate HQ in Sprawl Claims to Be "Carbon Neutral"*. Natural Resources Defense Council Staff Blog. New York. 5 July.

Berchicci, L., G. Dowell, and A. King. 2012. 'Environmental capabilities and corporate strategy: Exploring acquisitions among US manufacturing firms', *Strategic Management Journal* 33: 1053–1071.

Berchicci, L., and A. King. 2008. 'Postcards from the edge: A review of the business and environment literature', *Academy of Management Annals* 1: 513–547.

Berrone, P., L. Gelabert, and A. Fosfuri. 2009. *The Impact of Symbolic and Substantive Actions on Environmental Legitimacy*, unpublished Working Paper DI-778-E, IESE Business School, University of Navarra, Spain.

Berrone, P., and L. R. Gomez-Mejia. 2009. 'Environmental performance and executive compensation: An integrated agency-institutional perspective', *Academy of Management Journal* 52(1): 103–126.

Bhuyan, S. 2000. 'Corporate political activities and oligopoly welfare loss', *Review of Industrial Organisation* 17: 411–426.

Biondi, Y., and T. Suzuki. 2007. 'Socio-economic impacts of international accounting standards: An introduction', *Socio-Economic Review* 5: 585–602.

Bitektine, A. 2011. 'Toward a theory of social judgments of organizations: The case of legitimacy, reputation, and status', *Academy of Management Review* 36: 151–179.

Blackman, A., and J. Rivera. 2011. 'Producer-level benefits of sustainability certification', *Conservation Biology* 25: 1176–1185.

Boiral, O. 2007. 'Corporate greening through ISO 14001: A rational myth?', *Organization Science* 18: 127–146.

Boiral, O. 2013. 'Sustainability reports as simulacra: A counter-account of A and A+ GRI reports', *Accounting, Auditing and Accountability Journal* 26(7): 1036–1071.

Boiral, O., and Y. Gendron. 2011. 'Sustainable development and certification practices: Lessons learned and prospects', *Business Strategy and the Environment* 20: 331–347.

Bourdieu, P. 1990. *The Logic of Practice*. Cambridge, UK: Polity Press.

Bourdieu, P. 1991. *Language and Symbolic Power*. Cambridge, UK: Polity Press.

Bourdieu, P. 1995. *Outline of a Theory of Practice*. Cambridge University Press.

Bourdieu, P. 2005. *The Social Structures of the Economy*. Cambridge, UK: Polity Press.

Bourdieu, P., and R. Nice. 1984. *Distinction: A Social Critique of the Judgment of Taste*. Cambridge, MA: Harvard University Press.

Bourdieu, P., and J. C. Passeron. 1977. *Reproduction in Education, Society and Culture*. Beverly Hills, CA: Sage Publications.

Bourdieu, P., and J. B. Thompson. 1991. *Language and Symbolic Power*. Cambridge, MA: Harvard University Press.

Bowen, F. E. 2000a. 'Environmental visibility: A trigger of green organizational response?', *Business, Strategy and the Environment* 9: 92–107.

Bowen, F. E. 2000b. *Does Size Matter? Organisational Slack and Visibility as Alternative Explanations for Environmental Responsiveness*. Unpublished PhD thesis, University of Bath.

Bowen, F. E. 2011. 'Carbon capture and storage as a corporate technology strategy challenge', *Energy Policy* 39: 2256–2264.

Bowen, F. E., and B. Wittneben. 2011. 'Carbon accounting: Negotiating accuracy, consistency and certainty across organisational fields', *Accounting, Auditing and Accountability Journal* 24: 1022–1036.

Boxenbaum, E., and S. Jonsson. 2008. 'Isomorphism, diffusion and decoupling'. In R. Greenwood, C. Oliver, and K. Sahlin-Anderson (eds.), *The Handbook of Organizational Institutionalism*, pp. 78–98. Thousand Oaks, CA: Sage Publications.

Bradford, L., and G. Nagel. 2002. *GEMI Benchmarking Survey on External Memberships and Non-Government Organization Partnerships*. Washington, DC: Global Environmental Management Institute.

Brammer, S., and S. Pavelin. 2006. 'Voluntary environmental disclosures by large UK firms', *Journal of Business Finance and Accounting* 33: 1168–1188.

Brammer, S., and S. Pavelin. 2008. 'Factors influencing the quality of corporate environmental disclosure', *Business Strategy and the Environment* 17: 120–136.

Branzei O., T. J. Ursacki-Bryant, I. Vertinsky, and W. Zhang. 2004. 'The formation of green strategies in Chinese firms: Matching corporate environmental responses and individual principles', *Strategic Management Journal* 25: 1075–1095.

Braun, M. 2009. 'The evolution of emissions trading in the European Union: The role of policy networks, knowledge and policy entrepreneurs', *Accounting, Organizations and Society* 34(3–4): 469–487.

Brennan, G., and P. Pettit. 2004. *The Economy of Esteem*. Oxford University Press.

Bromley, P., and W. W. Powell. 2012. 'From smoke and mirrors to walking the talk: Decoupling in the contemporary world', *Academy of Management Annals* 6: 483–530.

Bruce, J. P., H.-S. Yi, and E. F. Haites. 1996. *Climate Change 1995: Economic and Social Dimensions of Climate Change*. Intergovernmental Panel on Climate Change, Working Group III. Cambridge University Press.

Bruno, K. 1992. *The Greenpeace Book of Greenwash*. Amsterdam: Greenpeace International.

Brunsson, N. 1989. *The Organization of Hypocrisy: Talk, Decisions and Action in Organizations*. New York: Wiley & Sons.

Brunsson, N. 2000. 'Standardization and uniformity'. In N. Brunsson and B. Jacobsson (eds.), *A World of Standards*, pp. 138–150. Oxford University Press.

Buchanan, J., and G. Tullock. 1975. 'Polluters' profits and political response: Direct controls versus taxes', *American Economic Review* 65: 139–147.

Buhr, K., and A. Hansson. 2011. 'Capturing the stories of corporations: A comparison of media debates on carbon capture and storage in Norway and Sweden', *Global Environmental Change* 21: 336–345.

Bumpus, A. G. 2009. *Making Carbon Accounting Count*. International Resource Industries and Sustainability Centre, Executive Briefing #09–01, December. University of Calgary.

Bumpus, A. G., and J. C. Cole. 2009. 'How can the current CDM deliver sustainable development?', *Wiley Interdisciplinary Reviews: Climate Change* 1: 541–547.

Burke, L., and J. M. Logsdon. 1996. 'How corporate social responsibility pays off', *Long Range Planning* 29: 495–502.

Büthe, T., and W. Mattli. 2010. 'International standards and standard-setting bodies'. In D. Coen, W. Grant, and G. Wilson. *The Oxford Handbook of Business and Government*, pp. 440–471. Oxford University Press.

Buysse, K., and A. Verbeke. 2003. 'Proactive environmental strategies: A stakeholder management perspective', *Strategic Management Journal* 24: 453–470.

Callon, M. 2009. 'Civilizing markets: Carbon trading between in vitro and in vivo experiments', *Accounting, Organizations and Society* 34: 535–548.

Camerer, C. 2003. *Behavioral Game Theory: Experiments in Strategic Interaction*. Princeton, NJ: Princeton University Press.

Carbon Neutral Company. 2013. *The CarbonNeutral Protocol: The Global Standard for Carbon Neutral Programmes (Version 8)*. London and New York: The Carbon Neutral Company.

Caruana, R., and A. Crane. 2008. 'Constructing consumer responsibility: Exploring the role of corporate communications', *Organisation Studies* 29: 1495–1519.

Cashore, B. 2003. 'Legitimacy and the privatization of environmental governance: How non-state market-driven NSMD governance systems gain rule-making authority', *Governance* 15: 503–529.

Cashore, B., and I. Vertinsky. 2000. 'Policy networks and firm behaviours: Governance systems and firm responses to external demands for sustainable forest management', *Policy Sciences* 33: 1–30.

Center for Political Accountability 2012. *The 2012 CPA-Zicklin Index of Corporate Political Accountability and Disclosure*. Washington, DC: Center for Political Accountability.

Chan, E. H. W., Q. K. Qian, and P. T. I. Lam. 2009. 'The market for green building in developed Asian cities: The perspectives of building designers', *Energy Policy* 37: 3061–3070.

Chan, R. 2005. 'Does the natural-resource view of the firm apply in emerging economy? A survey of foreign invested enterprises in China', *Journal of Management Studies* 42: 625–672.

Chatterji, A. K., and M. W. Toffel. 2010. 'How firms respond to being rated', *Strategic Management Journal* 31: 917–945.

Chen, Y.-S., and C.-H. Chang. 2013. 'Greenwash and green trust: The mediation effects of green consumer confusion and green perceived risk', *Journal of Business Ethics* 114: 489–500.

Chevron. 2007. 'Chevron announces new global 'Human Energy' advertising campaign.' Available at www.prnewswire.com/news-releases/chevron-announces-new-global-human-energy-advertising-campaign-58337612.html. Accessed 24 January 2014.

Chevron. 2010. 'Chevron launches a new global advertising campaign: "We Agree"'. Available at www.chevron.com/chevron/pressreleases/article/10182010_chevronlaunchesnewglobaladvertisingcampaignweagree.news. Accessed 24 January 2014.

Cho, C. H., M. L. Martens, H. Kim, and M. Rodrigue. 2011. 'Astroturfing global warming: It isn't always greener on the other side of the fence', *Journal of Business Ethics* 104: 571–587.

Christensen, L. T., M. Morsing, and O. Thyssen. 2013. 'CSR as aspirational talk,' *Organization* 20: 372–393.

Christmann, P. 2000. 'Effects of 'best practices' of environmental management on cost advantage: The role of complementary assets', *Academy of Management Journal* 43: 663–680.

Christmann, P. 2004. 'Multinational companies and the natural environment: Determinants of global environmental policy standardization', *Academy of Management Journal* 47: 747–760.

Christmann, P., and G. Taylor. 2001. 'Globalization and the environment: Determinants of firm self-regulation in China', *Journal of International Business Studies* 32: 439–458.

Christmann, P., and G. Taylor. 2006. 'Firm self-regulation through international certifiable standards: Determinants of symbolic versus substantive implementation', *Journal of International Business Studies* 17: 863–878.

Clarkson, P., Y. Li, G. Richardson, and F. Vasvari. 2008. 'Revisiting the relation between environmental performance and environmental disclosure: An empirical analysis', *Accounting, Organizations and Society* 33: 303–327.

Clarkson, P., Y. Li, G. Richardson, and F. Vasvari. 2011. 'Does it really pay to be green? Determinants and consequences of proactive environmental strategies', *Journal of Accounting and Public Policy* 31: 122–144.

Clemens, B. 2006. 'Economic incentives and small firms: Does it pay to be green?', *Journal of Business Research* 59: 492–500.

Conlon, G., P. Patrignani, and A. Litchfield. 2012. 'Assessing the deadweight loss associated with public investment in further education and skills'. BIS Research Paper Number 71. London: The Department for Business Innovation and Skills.

Connelly, B. L., S. T. Certo, R. D. Ireland, and C. R. Reutzel. 2011. 'Signaling theory: A review and assessment', *Journal of Management* 37: 39–67.

Cook, A. 2009. 'Emission rights: From costless activity to market operations', *Accounting, Organizations and Society* 34: 456–468.

Corbett, C., and S. Muthulingam. 2007. *Adoption of Voluntary Environmental Standards: The Role of Signaling and Intrinsic Benefits in the Diffusion of the LEED Green Building Standards*. Los Angeles, CA: Anderson School of Business, UCLA Working Paper.

Cordeiro, J., and J. Sarkis. 2008. 'Does explicit contracting effectively link CEO compensation to environmental performance?', *Business Strategy and the Environment* 17: 304–317.

Cornelissen, J. P., and A. R. Lock. 2000. 'Theoretical concept or management fashion? Examining the significance of IMC', *Journal of Advertising Research* 40: 7–16.

Craig, J., and C. Dibrell. 2006. 'The natural environment, innovation, and firm performance: A comparative study', *Family Business Review* 19: 275–288.

Crane, A. 2000. 'Corporate greening as amoralization', *Organization Studies* 21: 673–696.

Crane, A., D. Matten, and J. Moon. 2008. 'Ecological citizenship and the corporation: Politicizing the new corporate environmentalism', *Organization and Environment* 21: 371–389.

Dacin, T., C. Oliver, and J. Roy. 2007. 'The legitimacy of strategic alliances: An institutional perspective', *Strategic Management Journal* 28: 169–187.

Dapeng, L., and W. Weiwei. 2009. 'Barriers and incentives of CCS deployment in China: Results from semi-structured interviews', *Energy Policy* 37: 2421–2432.

Darnall, N. 2006. 'Why firms mandate ISO 14001 certification', *Business and Society* 45: 354–381.

Darnall, N., and D. Edwards. 2006. 'Predicting the cost of environmental management system adoption: The role of capabilities, resources and ownership structure', *Strategic Management Journal* 27: 301–320.

Darnall, N., I. Henriques, and P. Sadorsky. 2008. 'Do environmental management systems improve business performance in an international setting?', *Journal of International Management* 14: 364–376.

Darnall, N., I. Henriques, and P. Sadorsky. 2010. 'Adopting proactive environmental practices: The influence of stakeholders and firm size', *Journal of Management Studies* 47: 1072–1094.

Darnall, N. and Y. Kim. 2012. 'Which types of environmental management systems are related to greater environmental improvements?', *Public Administration Review* 72: 351–365.

Darnall, N., I. Seol, and J. Sarkis. 2009. 'Perceived stakeholder influences and organizations' use of environmental audits', *Accounting, Organizations and Society* 34: 170–187.

Darnall, N., and S. Sides. 2008. 'Assessing the performance of voluntary environmental programs: Does certification matter?', *Policy Studies Journal* 36: 95–117.

Dasgupta, S., H. Hettige, and D. Wheeler. 2000. 'What improves environmental compliance? Evidence from Mexican industry', *Journal of Environmental Economics and Management* 39: 39–66.

Dastrup, S. R., J. G. Zivin, D. L. Costa, and M. E. Kahn. 2012. 'Understanding the solar home price premium electricity generation and 'green' social status', *European Economic Review* 56: 961–973.

Dauvergne, P., and J. Lister. 2012. 'Big brand sustainability: Governance prospects and environmental limits', *Global Environmental Change* 22: 36–45.

de Coninck, H., J. C. Stephens, and B. Metz. 2009. 'Global learning on carbon capture and storage: A call for strong international cooperation on CCS demonstration', *Energy Policy* 376: 2161–2165.

Deegan, C. 2002. 'Introduction: The legitimising effect of social and environmental disclosures: A theoretical foundation', *Accounting, Auditing & Accountability Journal* 15: 282–311.

Deephouse, D. L., and S. M. Carter. 2005. 'An examination of differences between organizational legitimacy and organizational reputation', *Journal of Management Studies* 42: 329–360.

Deephouse, D., and M. Suchman. 2008. 'Legitimacy in organisational institutionalism'. In R. Greenwood, C. Oliver, R. Suddaby, and K. Sahlin-Andersson (eds.), *The Sage Handbook of Organizational Institutionalism*, pp. 49–77. Thousand Oaks, CA: Sage: Publications.

DellaVigna, S., J. A. List, and U. Malmendier. 2012. 'Testing for altruism and social pressure in charitable giving', *Quarterly Journal of Economics* 127: 1–56.

Delmas, M. A. 2002. 'The diffusion of environmental management standards in Europe and in the United States: An institutional perspective', *Policy Sciences* 35: 91–119.

Delmas, M. A., and V. C. Burbano. 2011. 'The drivers of greenwashing', *California Management Review* 54: 64–87.

Delmas, M., and A. Keller. 2005. 'Free riding in voluntary environmental programs: The case of the U.S. EPA WasteWise program', *Policy Sciences* 38: 91–106.

Delmas, M. A., and M. J. Montes-Sancho. 2010. 'Voluntary agreements to improve environmental quality: Symbolic and substantive cooperation', *Strategic Management Journal* 31: 575–601.

Delmas, M., N. Nairn-Birch, and M. Balzarova. 2013. 'Choosing the right eco-label for your product', *MIT Sloan Management Review* 54: 10–12.

Delmas, M., M. Russo, and M. Montes-Sancho. 2007. 'Deregulation and environmental differentiation in the electric utility industry', *Strategic Management Journal* 28: 189–209.

Delmas, M., and A. Terlaak. 2001. 'A framework for analyzing environmental voluntary agreements', *California Management Review* 43: 44–63.

Delmas, M. A., and M. W. Toffel. 2008. 'Organizational response to environmental demands: Opening the black box', *Strategic Management Journal* 29: 1027–1055.

Department of Energy and Climate Change (DECC). 2009. *Guidance on Carbon Neutrality*. London: DECC.

Devers, C. E., T. Dewett, Y. Mishina, and C. A. Belsito. 2009. 'A general theory of organizational stigma', *Organization Science* 20: 154–171.

Doshi, A. R., G. W. S. Dowell, and M. W. Toffel. 2013. 'How firms respond to mandatory information disclosure', *Strategic Management Journal* 34(10): 1209–1231.

DiCaprio, T. 2012. *Becoming Carbon Neutral: How Microsoft Is Striving to Become Leaner, Greener, and More Accountable*. Redmond, WA: Microsoft.

Douglas, M. 1986. *How Institutions Think*. Syracuse, NY: Routledge/ Syracuse University Press.

Economist, The. 2012. 'Many 'mays' but few 'musts': A limp agreement at the UN's vaunted environmental summit'. London. June 23. Available at www.economist.com/node/21557314. Accessed 24 January 2014.

Edelman, L., and M. Suchman. 1997. 'The legal environments of organizations', *Annual Review of Sociology* 23: 479–515.

Ellingsen, T., and M. Johannesson. 2011. 'Conspicuous generosity', *Journal of Public Economics* 95: 1131–1143.

Emirbayer, M., and V. Johnson. 2008. 'Bourdieu and organizational analysis', *Theory and Society* 37: 1–44.

Endelman, L. B. 1992. 'Legal ambiguity and symbolic structures: Organizational mediation of civil rights law', *American Journal of Sociology* 97: 1531–1576.

Engels, A. 2009. 'The European emissions trading scheme: An exploratory study of how companies learn to account for carbon', *Accounting, Organizations and Society* 34: 488–498.

Equator Principles. 2013. *The Equator Principles III June 2013*. Amsterdam: The Equator Principles.

Eriksson, P., and A. Kovalainen. 2008. 'Qualitative methods in business research'. In Paivi Eriksson and Anne Kovalainen (eds.), *Introducing Qualitative Methods*. London: Sage Publications.

Espeland, W. N., and M. L. Stevens. 1998. 'Commensuration as a social process', *Annual Review of Sociology* 24: 313–343.

Etzion, R. 2007. 'Research on organizations and the natural environment', *Journal of Management* 33: 637–664.

Ezzamel, M., and J. Burns. 2005. 'Professional competition, economic value added and management control strategies', *Organisation Studies* 26: 755–777.

Fairclough, N. 2005. 'Peripheral vision: Discourse analysis in organisation studies: The case for critical realism', *Organisation Studies* 26: 915–939.

Fedrizi, R. 2012. 'Important News about LEED 2012: A Message from Rick Fedrizi'. USGBC, 3 June 2012. Available at www.usgbc.org/articles/important-news-about-leed-2012-message-rick-fedrizzi. Accessed 24 January 2014.

Feldman, M. S., and J. G. March. 1981. 'Information in organizations as signal and symbol', *Administrative Science Quarterly* 26: 171–186.

Field, L., and G. W. Ford. 1995. *Managing Organisational Learning: From Rhetoric to Reality*. Melbourne, Australia: Longman.

Financial Times. 2006. '2006 award winners and special commendations: Sustainable Bank of the Year'. Available at www.ft.com/cms/s/2/c1f6fade-fafa-11da-b4d0-0000779e2340.html#axzz2pETPZq1u. Accessed 24 January 2014.

Fineman, S. 2001. 'Fashioning the environment', *Organization* 8: 17–31.

Fineman, S., and K. Clarke. 1996. 'Green stakeholders: Industry interpretations and response', *Journal of Management Studies* 33: 715–730.

Fiss, P. C., and E. J. Zajac. 2006. 'The symbolic management of strategic change: Sensegiving via framing and decoupling', *Academy of Management Journal* 49: 1173–1193.

Fleming, P., and M. T. Jones. 2013. *The End of Corporate Social Responsibility: Crisis and Critique*. London: Sage Publications.

Fombrum, C., and M. Shanley. 1990. 'What's in a name? Reputation building and corporate strategy', *Academy of Management Journal* 33: 233–258.

Forbes, L. C., and J. Jermier. 2012. 'The new corporate environmentalism'. In P. Bansal and A. Hoffman (eds.), *The Oxford Handbook of Business and the Natural Environment*, pp. 556–571. Oxford Univerisity Press.

Foster, R. N. 1986. *Innovation: The Attacker's Advantage*. New York: Summit Books.

Friedman, M. 1962. *Capitalism and Freedom*. University of Chicago Press.

Fuller, T., and Y. Tian. 2006. 'Social and symbolic capital and responsible entrepreneurship: An empirical investigation of SME narratives', *Journal of Business Ethics* 67: 287–304.

Galarraga, I., D. H. Del Valle, and M. Gonzalez-Eguino. 2011. *Price Premium for High-Efficiency Refrigerators and Calculation of Price-Elasticities for Close-Substitutes: Combining Hedonic Pricing and Demand Systems*, unpublished working paper, Basque Centre for Climate Change Working Paper Series, BC3.

Gass, H. 2011. 'Barclays, HSBC and RBS linked to "dirty financing" for fossil fuels', *The Ecologist*, 14 June.

Gavetti, G., D. A. Levinthal, and J. W. Rivkin. 2005. 'Strategy making in novel and complex worlds: The power of analogy', *Strategic Management Journal* 26: 691–712.

Giddens, A. 2009. *The Politics of Climate Change*. Cambridge, UK: Polity Press.

Gillespie, E. 2008. 'Stemming the tide of greenwash', *Consumer Policy Review* 18: 79–83.

Glass G. V., and B. McGaw. 1981. *Meta-Analysis in Social Research*. London: Sage Press.

Glasson, J., R. Therivel, and A. Chadwick. 1999. *Introduction to Environmental Impact Assessment: Principles and Procedures, Process, Practice, and Prospects*. London: Routledge.

Global CCS Institute. 2011. *The Global Status of CCS 2011*. Canberra, Australia: Global CCS Institute.

Gomez, M. 2010. 'A Bourdesian perspective on strategizing'. In D. Golsorkhi, L. Rouleau, D. Seidl, and E. Vaara (eds.), *Cambridge Handbook of Strategy as Practice*, pp. 141–154. Cambridge University Press.

Google. 2013. *Google Green: The Big Picture*. Available at www.google.co.uk/green/bigpicture. Accessed 1 August 2013.

Gray, W. B., and M. E. Deily. 1996. 'Compliance and enforcement: Air pollution regulation in the U.S. steel industry', *Journal of Environmental Economics and Management* 31: 96–111.

Greenpeace, 2008. *False Hope: Why Carbon Capture and Storage Won't Save the Climate*. London: Greenpeace.

Greenwood, R., C. Oliver, R. Suddaby, and K. Sahlin. 2008. *The Sage Handbook of Organizational Institutionalism*. Thousand Oaks, CA: Sage Publications.

Greer, J., and K. Bruno 1996. *Greenwash: The Reality behind Corporate Environmentalism*. Penang, Malaysia: Third World Network.

Guimond, R. J., and B. Nagle. 2001. *GEMI Benchmarking Survey of EHS Annual Reports*. Portland, OR: Global Environmental Management Initiative.

Gunningham, N., and J. Rees. 1997. 'Industry self-regulation: An institutional perspective', *Law & Policy* 19: 363–414.

Haack, P., D. Schoeneborn, and C. Wickert. 2012. 'Talking the talk, moral entrapment, creeping commitment? Exploring narrative dynamics in corporate responsibility standardization', *Organization Studies* 33: 815–845.

Ha-Duong, M., A. Nadai, and S. Campos. 2009. 'A survey on the public perception of CCS in France', *International Journal of Greenhouse Gas Control* 35: 633–640.

Hainmueller, J., M. J. Hiscox, and S. Sequeira. 2011. *Consumer Demand for the Fair Trade Label: Evidence from a Field Experiment,* unpublished working paper, MIT Political Science Department, Research Paper No. 2011–9B.

Halme, M., and M. Huse. 1997. 'The influence of corporate governance, industry, and country factors on environmental reporting', *Scandinavian Journal of Management* 13: 137–157.

Halme, M., and J. Laurila. 2009. 'Philanthropy, integration or innovation? Exploring the financial and societal outcomes of different types of corporate responsibility', *Journal of Business Ethics* 84: 325–339.

Hansson, A., and M. Bryngelsson, 2009. 'Expert opinions on carbon dioxide capture and storage: A framing of uncertainties and possibilities', *Energy Policy* 37: 2273–2282.

Harberger, A. C. 1954. 'Monopoly and resource allocation', *American Economic Review* 44: 77–87.

Harberger, A. C. 1964. 'Principles of efficiency: The measurement of waste', *American Economic Review* 54: 58–76.

Hargadon, A. 2010. 'Technology policy and global warming: Why new innovation models are needed', *Research Policy* 39: 1024–1026.

Hart, S. L. 1995. 'A natural-resource–based view of the firm', *Academy of Management Review* 20: 986–1014.

Hartman, R., M. Hug, and D. Wheeler. 1997. *Why Paper Mills Clean Up: Determinants of Pollution Abatement in Four Asian Countries.* World Bank Policy Research Department: Working Paper No. 1710.

Hause, M. 2008. *GEMI Benchmarking Survey: Environment, Health and Safety Headcount.* Portland, OR: Global Environmental Management Institute.

Hausman, J. A. 1981. 'Exact consumer's surplus and deadweight loss', *The American Economic Review* 71: 662–676.

Helm, D., and C. Hepburn. 2009. *The Economics and Politics of Climate Change.* Oxford University Press.

Henriques, I., and P. Sadorsky. 1996. 'The determinants of an environmentally responsive firm: An empirical approach', *Journal of Environmental Economics and Management* 30: 381–395.

Henriques, I., and P. Sadorsky. 1999. 'The relationships between environmental commitment and managerial perceptions of stakeholder importance', *Academy of Management Journal* 42: 87–99.

Hepburn, C. 2006. 'Regulation by prices, quantities or both: A review of instrument choice', *Oxford Review of Economic Policy* 22: 226–247.

Hertzog, H., 2009. 'Carbon capture and storage'. In D. Helm and C. Hepburn (eds.), *The Economics and Politics of Climate Change,* pp. 263–283. Oxford University Press.

Hettige, H., M. Huq, S. Pargal, and D. Wheeler. 1996. 'Determinants of pollution abatement in developing countries: Evidence from South and Southeast Asia', *World Development* 24: 1891–1904.

Heugens, P., and M. Lander. 2009. 'Structure! Agency! (and other quarrels): A meta-analysis of institutional theories of organization', *Academy of Management Journal* 52: 61–85.

Hillman, A. J., G. D. Keim, and D. Schuler. 2004. 'Corporate political activity: A review and research agenda', *Journal of Management* 30: 837–857.

Hitchens, D., J. Clausen, M. Trainor, M. Keil, and S. Thankappan. 2003. 'Competitiveness, environmental performance and management of SMEs', *Greener Management International* 44: 45–57.

Hoffman, A. 1999. 'Institutional evolution and change: Environmentalism and the U.S. chemical industry', *Academy of Management Journal* 42: 351–371.

Hoffman, A., and P. Bansal. 2012. 'Retrospective, perspective, and prospective'. In P. Bansal and A. Hoffman (eds.), *The Oxford Handbook of Business and the Natural Environment*, pp. 3–25. Oxford University Press.

Hoffmann, V. H., and T. Busch. 2008. 'Corporate Carbon Performance Indicators', *Journal of Industrial Ecology* 12: 505–520.

Hopwood, A. 2009. 'Accounting and the environment', *Accounting, Organisations and Society* 34: 433–439.

Hortensius, D., and M. Barthel. 1997. 'Beyond 14001: An introduction to the ISO 14000 series'. In C. Sheldon (ed.), *ISO 14001 and Beyond*. pp. 19–44. Sheffield, UK: Greenleaf Publishing.

House, K. Z., C. F. Harvey, M. J. Aziz, and D. P. Schrag. 2009. 'The energy penalty of post-combustion CO_2 capture and storage and its implications for retrofitting the US installed base', *Energy and Environmental Science* 2: 193–205.

HSBC. 2011. *HSBC Carbon Neutrality: Reporting Guidance 2011*. London.

HSBC. 2013. *HSBC Holdings plc Sustainability Report 2012*. London.

Huberman, B. A., C. H. Loch, and A. Önçüler. 2004. 'Status as a valued resource', *Social Psychology Quarterly* 67: 103–114.

Huberty, M., and J. Zysman. 2010. 'An energy system transformation: Framing research choices for the climate challenge', *Research Policy* 39: 1027–1029.

Hunter, J. E., and F. L. Schmidt. 1982. *Meta-Analysis: Cumulating Research Findings across Studies*. London: Sage Publications.

Hunter, J. E., and F. L. Schmidt. 1990. 'Dichotomization of continuous variables: The implications for meta-analysis', *Journal of Applied Psychology* 75: 334–349.

Hunter, J. E., and F. L. Schmidt. 2004. *Methods of Meta-Analysis: Correcting Error and Bias in Research Findings*. Thousand Oaks, CA: Sage Publications.

Husted, B. W., and J. d. J. Salazar. 2006. 'Taking Friedman seriously: Maximising profits and social performance', *Journal of Management Studies* 43: 75–91.

Hwa-Shu, L. 2008. 'Bank takes environmental step into rural town', *New York Times*, 2 July.

Hyman, H. H. 1942. 'The psychology of status', *Archives of Psychology* 269: 1–94.

Illia, L., S. C. Zyglidopoulos, S. Romenti, B. Rodriguez-Canovas, and A. G. Del Valle Brena. 2013. 'Communicating corporate social responsibility to a cynical public', *MIT Sloan Management Review* 54(3): 16–18.

Innovation Norway. 2009. *International Carbon Capture and Storage Technology Survey*. Oslo, Norway.

Intergovernmental Panel on Climate Change. 2001. *Climate Change 2001: The Scientific Basis*. J. T. Houghton, Y. Ding, D. J. Griggs, M. Noguer, P. J. van der Linden, X. Dai, K. Maskell, and C. A. Johnson (eds.). Cambridge University Press.

Intergovernmental Panel on Climate Change. 2005. *IPCC Special Report on Carbon Dioxide Capture and Storage*. Cambridge University Press.

Intergovernmental Panel on Climate Change. 2006. *IPCC Guidelines for National Greenhouse Gas Inventories*. Prepared by the National Greenhouse Gas Inventories Programme. H. S. Eggleston, L. Buendia, K. Miwa, T. Ngara, and K. Tanabe. (eds.). Hayama, Japan: Institute for Global Environmental Strategies.

Intergovernmental Panel on Climate Change. 2007. *Fourth Assessment Report of the Intergovernmental Panel on Climate Change*. In R. K. Pachauri and A. Reisinger (eds.). Cambridge University Press.

International Energy Agency. 2009. *Carbon Capture and Storage: Full-Scale Demonstration Progress Update*. Paris: International Energy Agency.

International Energy Agency. 2010. *Carbon Capture and Storage: Progress and Next Steps*. Paris: International Energy Agency.

Jaffe, A. B., and R. N. Stavins. 1995. 'Dynamic incentives of environmental regulations: The effects of alternative policy instruments on technology diffusion', *Journal of Environmental Economics and Management* 29: S43–S63.

Jahn, G., M. Schramm, and A. Spiller. 2005. 'The reliability of certification: Quality labels as a consumer policy tool', *Journal of Consumer Policy* 28: 53–73.

Jennings, P. D., and W. W. Zandbergen. 1995. 'Ecologically sustainable organizations: An institutional approach', *Academy of Management Review* 20: 1015–1052.

Jermier, J., L. Forbes, S. Benn, and R. Orsato. 2006. 'The new corporate environmentalism and green politics'. In S. R. Clegg, C. Hardy, T. Lawrence, and W. R. Nord (eds.), *The Sage Handbook of Orgranization Studies*, pp. 618–650. Thousand Oaks, CA: Sage Publications.

Jiang, R. J., and P. Bansal. 2003. 'Seeing the need for ISO 14001', *Journal of Management Studies* 40: 1047–1067.

Judge, W. Q., and T. J. Douglas. 1998. 'Performance implications of incorporating natural environmental issues into the strategic planning process: An empirical assessment', *Journal of Management Studies* 35: 241–262.

Judge, W. Q., and D. Elenkov. 2005. 'Organizational capacity for change and environmental performance: An empirical assessment of Bulgarian firms', *Journal of Business Research* 58: 893–901.

Karliner, J. 1997. *The Corporate Planet: Ecology and Politics in an Age of Globalisation*. San Francisco, CA: Sierra Club Books.

Kassinis, G., and N. Vafeas. 2006. 'Stakeholder pressures and environmental performance', *Academy of Management Journal* 49: 145–159.

Kassinis, G., and N. Vafeas. 2009. 'Environmental performance and plant closure', *Journal of Business Research* 62(4): 484–494.

Katz, M. L., and C. Shapiro. 1985. 'Network externalities, competition and compatibility', *American Economic Review* 75: 424–440.

Kelly, E., and F. Dobbin. 1998. 'How affirmative action became diversity management,' *American Behavioral Scientist* 41: 960–984.

Kennedy, M. T., and P. C. Fiss. 2009. 'Institutionalization, framing and diffusion: The logic of TQM adoption and implementation decisions among US hospitals', *Academy of Management Journal* 52: 897–918.

Kerr, C. 2009. 'Carbon capture to save industry', *The Australian*, May 13.

Kim, E. H., and T. P. Lyon. 2011. 'Strategic environmental disclosure: Evidence from the DOE's voluntary greenhouse gas registry', *Journal of Environmental Economics and Management* 61: 311–326.

King, A. A., and M. Lenox. 2000. 'Industry self-regulation without sanctions: The chemical industry's Responsible Care program', *Academy of Management Journal* 43: 698–716.

King, A. A., and M. Lenox. 2001. 'Does it really pay to be green? An empirical study of firm environmental and financial performance', *Journal of Industrial Ecology* 5: 105–116.

King, A. A., and M. Lenox. 2002. 'Exploring the locus of profitable pollution reduction', *Management Science* 48: 289–299.

King, A. A., M. Lenox, and M. L. Barnett. 2002. 'Strategic responses to the reputation commons problem'. In A. Hoffman and M. J. Ventresca (eds.), *Organizations, Policy, and the Natural Environment: Institutional and Strategic Perspectives*, pp. 393–406. Stanford, CA: Stanford University Press.

King, A. A., M. Lenox, and A. Terlaak. 2005. 'The strategic use of decentralized institutions: Exploring certification with the ISO 14001 management standard', *Academy of Management Journal* 48: 1091–1106.

King, A. A., A. Prado, and J. Rivera. 2012. 'Industry self-regulation and environmental protection'. In A. Hoffman and P. Bansal (eds.), *Oxford Handbook of Business and the Environment*, pp. 103–121. Oxford University Press.

Klassen, R. 2000. 'Exploring the linkage between investment in manufacturing and environmental technologies', *International Journal of Operations and Production Management* 20: 127–147.

Klassen, R., and S. Vachon. 2003. 'Collaboration and evaluation in the supply chain: The impact on plant-level environmental investment', *Production and Operations Management* 12: 336–352.

Klassen, R. D., and D. C. Whybark. 1999. 'The impact of environmental technologies on manufacturing performance', *Academy of Management Journal* 42: 599–615.

Kolk, A. 2000. *Economics of Environmental Management*. Harlow, UK: Financial Times/Prentice Hall.

Kolk, A., D. Levy, and J. Pinkse. 2008. 'Corporate responses in an emerging climate regime: The institutionalization and commensuration of carbon disclosure', *European Accounting Review* 17: 719–745.

Kolk, A., and J. Pinkse. 2005. 'Business responses to climate change: Identifying emergent strategies', *California Management Review* 47: 6–20.

Kolk, A., and J. Pinkse. 2010. 'Challenges and trade-offs in corporate innovation for climate change', *Business Strategy and the Environment* 19(4): 261–272.

Konar, S., and M. A. Cohen. 1997. 'Information as regulation: The effect of community right-to-know laws on toxic emissions', *Journal of Environmental Economics and Management* 32: 109–124.

Konar, S., and M. A. Cohen. 2001. 'Does the market value environmental performance?', *Review of Economics and Statistics* 83: 281–289.

Kube, S., M. A. Marechal, and C. Puppe. 2012. 'The currency of reciprocity: Gift exchange in the workplace', *American Economic Review* 102: 1644–1662.

Lamertz, K., and P. Heugens. 2009. 'Institutional translation through spectatorship: Collective consumption and editing of symbolic organisational texts by firms and their audiences', *Organisational Studies*, 30: 1249–1279.

Lane, E. L. 2013. 'Green marketing goes negative: The advent of reverse greenwashing', *Intellectual Property and Technology Law Journal* 25: 20–26.

Lange, D., P. M. Lee, and Y. Dai. 2011. 'Organizational reputation: A review', *Journal of Management* 37: 153–184.

Lankoski, L. 2008. 'Corporate responsibility activities and economic performance: A theory of why and how they are connected', *Business Strategy and the Environment* 17: 536–547.

Larson, B. A. 2002. 'Eco-labels for credence attributes: The case of shade-grown coffee', *Environment and Development Economics* 8: 529–547.

Lash, J., and F. Wellington. 2007. 'Competitive advantage on a warming planet', *Harvard Business Review* 85(3): 94–102.

Laufer, W. S. 2003. 'Social accountability and corporate greenwashing', *Journal of Business Ethics* 43: 253–261.

Lawrence, T. B. 1999. 'Institutional strategy', *Journal of Management* 25: 161–187.

Lawrence, T. B. 2008. 'Power, Institutions and Organizations'. In R. Greenwood, C. Oliver, and K. Sahlin-Anderson (eds.), *The Handbook of Organizational Institutionalism*, pp. 170–197. Thousand Oaks, CA: Sage Publications.

Lawrence, T. B., M. I. Winn, and P. D. Jennings. 2001. 'The temporal dynamics of institutionalization', *Academy of Management Review* 26: 624–644.

Lee, S. 2008. 'Drivers for the participation of small and medium-sized suppliers in green supply chain initiatives', *Supply Chain Management* 13: 185–198.

Lee, S., and Rhee, S. K. 2005. 'From end-of-pipe technology towards pollution preventive approach: The evolution of corporate environmentalism in Korea', *Journal of Cleaner Production* 13: 387–395.

Levin, P., and W. Espeland. 2002. 'Pollution futures: Commensuration, commodification, and the market for air'. In A. Hoffman and M. J. Ventresca (eds.), *Organizations, Policy and the Natural Environment: Institutional and Strategic Perspectives*, p. 119. Stanford, CA: Stanford University Press.

Levy, D. L. 1997. 'Environmental management as political sustainability', *Organization & Environment* 10: 126–147.

Levy, D. L., and D. Egan. 2003. 'A neo-Gramscian approach to corporate political strategy: Conflict and accommodation in the climate change negotiations', *Journal of Management Studies* 40: 803–829.

Linardi, S., and M. A. McConnell. 2011. 'No excuses for good behaviour: Volunteering and the social environment', *Journal of Public Economics* 95: 445–454.

Lipsey, M. W., and D. B. Wilson. 2001. *Practical Meta-Analysis: Applied Social Research Methods*. Thousand Oaks, CA: Sage Publications.

Lockett, A., and S. Thompson. 2001. 'The resource-based view and economics', *Journal of Management* 27: 723–754.

Lohmann, L. 2009. 'Toward a different debate in environmental accounting: The cases of carbon and cost-benefit', *Accounting, Organizations and Society* 34: 499–534.

Lohmann, L. 2010. 'Uncertainty markets and carbon markets: Variations on Polanyian themes', *New Political Economy* 15: 225–254.

Lounsbury, M. 2001. 'Institutional sources of practice variation', *Administrative Science Quarterly* 46: 29–56.

Lounsbury, M., and M. A. Glynn. 2001. 'Cultural entrepreneurship: Stories, legitimacy, and the acquisition of resources', *Strategic Management Journal* 22: 545–564.

Lusk, J. L., and J. F. Shogren. 2007. *Experimental Auctions: Methods and Applications in Economic and Marketing Research*. Cambridge University Press.

Lyon, T. P., and J. W. Maxwell. 2004. *Corporate Environmentalism and Public Policy*. Cambridge University Press.

Lyon, T. P., and J. W. Maxwell. 2011. 'Greenwash: Corporate environmental disclosure under threat of audit', *Journal of Economics and Management Strategy* 20: 3–41.

Lyon, T. P., and A. W. Montgomery. 2013. 'Tweetjacked: The impact of social media on corporate greenwash', *Journal of Business Ethics* 118: 747–757.

MacKensie, D. 2009. 'Making things the same: Gases, emission rights and the politics of carbon markets', *Accounting, Organizations and Society* 34: 439–455.

MacLean, M., C. Harvey, and R. Chia. 2010. 'Dominant corporate agents and the power elite in France and Britain', *Organisation Studies* 31: 327–348.

MacLean, T. L., and M. Behman. 2010. 'The dangers of decoupling: The relationship between compliance programs, legitimacy perceptions and institutionalized misconduct', *Academy of Management Journal* 53: 1499–1520.

Macve, R., and X. Chen. 2010. 'The Equator Principles: A success for voluntary codes?', *Accounting, Auditing and Accountability Journal* 23: 890–919.

Marimon, F., J. Llach, and M. Bernardo 2011. 'Comparative analysis of diffusion of the ISO 14001 standard by sector of activity', *Journal of Cleaner Production* 19: 1734–1744.

Marquis, C., and M. W. Toffel. 2012. *When Do Firms Greenwash? Corporate Visibility, Civil Society Scrutiny, and Environmental Disclosure.* Harvard Business School: unpublished working paper.

Martin-Tapia, I., J. Aragon-Correa, and A. Rueda-Manzanares. 2010. 'Environmental strategy and exports in medium, small and micro-enterprises', *Journal of World Business* 45: 266–275.

Mas-Ruiz, F., and F. Ruiz-Moreno. 2011. 'Rivalry within strategic groups and consequences for performance: The firm-size effects', *Strategic Management Journal* 32: 1286–1308.

Matten, D. 2003. 'Symbolic politics in environmental regulation: Corporate strategic responses', *Business Strategy and the Environment* 12: 215–226.

Maxwell, J. W., T. P. Lyon, and S. C. Hackett. 2000. 'Self-regulation and social welfare: The political economy of corporate environmentalism', *Journal of Law and Economics* 43: 583–617.

McWilliams, A., and D. Siegel. 2001. 'Corporate social responsibility: A theory of the firm perspective', *Academy of Management Review* 26: 117–127.

Meadowcroft, J., and O. Langhelle. 2010. *Caching the Carbon: The Politics and Policy of Carbon Capture and Storage.* Aldershot, UK: Edward Elgar Publishing.

Meckling, J. 2011. *Carbon Coalitions: Business, Climate Politics, and the Rise of Emissions Trading.* Cambridge, MA: MIT Press.

Menguc, B., and L. Ozanne. 2005. 'Challenges of the 'green imperative': A natural-resource–based approach to the environmental orientation-business performance relationship', *Journal of Business Research* 58: 430–438.

Merriam-Webster's Collegiate Dictionary. 2011. Springfield, MA: Merriam-Webster Incorporated.

Merton, R. K. 1968. 'The Matthew effect in science', *Science* 159: 56–63.

Meyer, J. W. 2008. 'Reflections on institutional theories of organizations'. In R. Greenwood, C. Oliver, R. Suddaby, and K. Sahlin (eds.), *The Sage Handbook of Organizational Institutionalism*, pp. 790–811. Thousand Oaks, CA: Sage Publications.

Meyer, J. W., and B. Rowan. 1977. 'Institutionalized organizations: Formal structure as myth and ceremony', *American Journal of Sociology* 83: 340–363.

Meznar, M. B., and D. Nigh. 1995. 'Buffer or bridge? Environmental and organizational determinants of public affairs activities in American firms', *Academy of Management Journal* 38: 975–996.

Miles, M. B., and A. M. Huberman. 1994. *Qualitative Data Analysis: An Expanded Sourcebook*. Thousand Oaks, CA: Sage Publications.

Milne, M. J., K. Kearins, and S. Walton. 2006. 'Creating adventures in wonderland: The journey metaphor and environmental sustainability', *Organization* 13: 801–839.

Mintzberg, H., and J. A. Waters. 1985. 'Of strategies, deliberate and emergent', *Strategic Management Journal* 6: 257–272.

MIT Energy Initiative. 2010. 'Carbon dioxide capture and storage projects'. Available at http://sequestration.mit.edu/tools/projects/index.html. Accessed 15 March 2010.

Molina-Azorín, J. F., E. Claver-Cortés, M. D. López-Gamero, and J. J. Tarí. 2009. 'Green management and financial performance: A literature review', *Management Decision* 47: 1080–1100.

Morris, P. 2007. 'What does green really cost?' *PREA Quarterly Summer*: 55–60.

Mowery, D. C., R. R. Nelson, and B. R. Martin. 2010. 'Technology policy and global warming: Why new policy models are needed or why putting new wine in old bottles won't work', *Research Policy* 39: 1011–1023.

Muhr, T. 2009. *ATLAS.ti 6: The New Features*. Berlin: Scientific Software Development.

Muhr, T., and S. Friese. 2004. *User's Manual for ATLAS.ti 5.0, 2nd ed.* Berlin: Scientific Software Development.

Mumby, D., and R. P. Clair. 1997. 'Organizational discourse'. In T. A. Van Dijk (ed.), *Discourse as Social Interaction*, pp. 181–205. London: Sage Publications.

National Environmental Monitoring Conference. 2003. *Analysing the Cost of Obtaining LEED Certification*. Westford, MA: Northbridge Environmental Management Consultants.

Natural Capital Declaration. 2012a. *The Declaration*. Available at www.naturalcapitaldeclaration.org/the-declaration. Accessed 1 May 2013.

Natural Capital Declaration. 2012b. *Benefits of Signing the NCD*. Available at www.naturalcapitaldeclaration.org/benefits-of-signing-the-ncd. Accessed 1 May 2013.

Newell, P. 2005. 'Race, class and the global politics of environmental inequality', *Global Environmental Politics* 5: 70–94.

Newell, P. 2008. 'Civil society, corporate accountability and the politics of climate change', *Global Environmental Politics* 8: 122–153.

Newig, J. 2007. 'Symbolic environmental legislation and societal self-deception', *Environmental Politics* 16: 276–296.

Nicholson, W. 1992. *Microeconomic Theory: Basic Principles and Extensions*. Orlando, FL: The Dryden Press.

Nike. 2013. *Energy and Climate*. Available at www.nikereponsibility.com/report/content/chapter/energy-and-climate. Accessed 1 August 2013.

O'Sullivan, N., and B. O'Dwyer. 2009. 'Stakeholder perspectives on a financial sector legitimation process: The case of NGOs and the Equator Principles', *Accounting, Auditing and Accountability Journal* 22: 553–587.

Oakes, L. S., B. Townley, and D. J. Cooper. 1998. 'Business planning as pedagogy: Language and control in a changing institutional field', *Administrative Science Quarterly* 43: 257–292.

Offenberg, J. P. 2007. 'Markets: Gift cards', *Journal of Economic Perspectives* 21: 227–238.

Okereke, C. 2007. 'An exploration of motivations, drivers and barriers to carbon management: The UK FTSE 100', *European Management Journal* 25: 475–486.

Okereke, C., B. Wittneben, and F. E. Bowen. 2012. 'Climate change: Challenging business, transforming politics', *Business and Society* 51: 7–30.

Oliver, C. 1991. 'Strategic responses to institutional processes', *Academy of Management Review* 16: 145–179.

Orsato, R. J. 2006. 'When does it pay to be 'green'?', *California Management Review* 48: 128–143.

Oxford English Dictionary. 2012. A. Stevenson (ed.). Oxford University Press.

Ozbilgin, M., and A. Tatli. 2005. 'Book review essay: Understanding Bourdieu's contribution to organizations and management studies', *Academy of Management Review* 30: 855–877.

Pacala, S., and R. Socolow. 2004. 'Stabilization wedges: Solving the climate problem for the next 50 years with current technologies', *Science* 305: 968–972.

Parker, J. 2009. *BREEAM or LEED? Strengths and Weaknesses of the Two Main Environmental Assessment Methods*. Bracknell, UK: Building Services Research and Information Association.

Pearce, F. 2009. 'Greenwash: Calling HSBC to account over green banking claims', *The Guardian*. London. 12 February.

Pearse, G. 2012. *Greenwash: Big Brands and Carbon Scams*. Collingwood, Australia: Black, Inc.

Penrose, E. T. 1959. *The Theory of the Growth of the Firm*. New York: M. E. Sharpe, Inc.

Perrow, C. 2010. 'Comment on Mowery, Nelson, and Martin', *Research Policy* 39: 1030–1031.

Pfeffer, J., and G. R. Salancik. 1978. 'A social information processing approach to job attitudes and design', *Administrative Science Quarterly* 23: 224–253.

Philippe, D., and R. Durand. 2011. 'The impact of norm-conforming behaviours on firm reputation', *Strategic Management Journal* 32: 969–993.

Phillips, D., and E. Zuckerman. 2001. 'Middle-status conformity: Theoretical restatement and empirical demonstration in two markets', *American Journal of Sociology* 107: 379–429.

Pierre-Louis, K. 2012. *Greenwashed: Why We Can't Buy Our Way to a Green Planet*. New York: iG Publishing.

Pinkse, J., and A. Kolk. 2009. *International Business and Global Climate Change*. New York: Routledge.

Pinkse, J., and A. Kolk. 2010. 'Challenges and trade-offs in corporate innovation for climate change', *Business Strategy and the Environment* 19(4): 261–272.

Podolny, J. M. 1994. 'Market uncertainty and the social character of economic exchange', *Administrative Science Quarterly* 39: 458–483.

Podolny, J. M. 2001. 'Networks as the pipes and prisms of the market', *American Journal of Sociology* 107(1): 33–60.

Polonsky, M. J., J. Bailey, H. Baker, C. Basche, C. Jepson, and L. Neath. 1998. 'Communicating environmental information: Are marketing claims on packaging misleading?', *Journal of Business Ethics* 17: 281–294.

Polonsky, M. J., L. Carlson, S. Grove, and N. Kangun, N. 1997. 'International environmental marketing claims: Real changes or simple posturing?', *International Marketing Review* 14: 218–232.

Porter, M. E., and C. Van der Linde. 1995. 'Green and competitive: Ending the stalemate', *Harvard Business Review* 73: 120–134.

Posner, E. A. 2002. *Law and Social Norms*. Cambridge, MA: Harvard University Press.

Posner, R. A. 1975. 'The social costs of monopoly and regulation', *Journal of Political Economy* 83: 807–828.

Potoski, M., and A. Prakash. 2005. 'Green clubs and voluntary governance: ISO 14001 and firms' regulatory compliance', *American Journal of Political Science* 49: 235–248.

Powell, T. C., D. Lovallo, and C. R. Fox 2011. 'Behavioral strategy', *Strategic Management Journal* 32: 1369–1386.

Prado, A. 2011. *Choosing among Environmental and Labor Certifications: An Exploratory Analysis of Producer Adoption*. New York University: Unpublished working paper.

Praetorius, B., and K. Schumacher. 2009. 'Greenhouse gas mitigation in a carbon-constrained world: The role of carbon capture and storage', *Energy Policy* 37: 5081–5093.

Prakash, A. 2000. *Greening the Firm: The Politics of Corporate Environmentalism*. Cambridge University Press.

Prakash, A., and M. Potoski. 2006. *The Voluntary Environmentalists: Green Clubs, ISO 14001 and Voluntary Environmental Regulations*. Cambridge University Press.

Ramchander, S., R. G. Schwebach, and K. Staking. 2011. 'The informational relevance of corporate social responsibility: Evidence from DS400 index reconstitutions', *Strategic Management Journal* 33: 303–314.

Ramus, C. A., and I. Montiel, I. 2005. 'When are corporate environmental policies a form of greenwashing?' *Business and Society* 44: 377–414.

Ranganathan, J., L. Corbier, P. Bhatia, S. Schmitz, P. Gage, and K. Oren. 2004. *The Greenhouse Gas Protocol: A Corporate Accounting and Reporting Standard (revised edition)*. Geneva, Switzerland: World Business Council for Sustainable Development and World Resources Institute.

Rao, H. 1994. 'The social construction of reputation: Certification contests, legitimation, and the survival of organizations in the American automobile industry: 1895–1912', *Strategic Management Journal* 15: 29–44.

Raynolds, L., D. Murray, and A. Heller. 2007. 'Regulating sustainability in the coffee sector: A comparative analysis of third-party environmental and social certification initiatives', *Agriculture and Human Values* 24: 147–163.

Reid, E. M., and M. W. Toffel. 2009. 'Responding to public and private politics: Corporate disclosure of climate change strategies', *Strategic Management Journal* 30: 1157–1178.

Reinhardt, F. 1998. 'Environmental product differentiation: Implications for corporate strategy', *California Management Review* 40: 43–73.

Renard, M.-C. 2005. 'Quality certification, regulation and power in fair trade', *Journal of Rural Studies* 21: 419–431.

Rhee, S. K., and S. Y. Lee. 2003. 'Dynamic change of corporate environmental strategy: Rhetoric and reality', *Business, Strategy and the Environment* 12: 175–191.

Rikhardson, P., and R. Welford. 1997. 'Clouding the crisis: The construction of corporate environmental management'. In R. Welford (ed.), *Hijacking Environmentalism: Corporate Responses to Sustainable Development*, pp. 40–62. London: Earthscan.

Rivera, J. 2010. *Business and Public Policy: Responses to Environmental and Social Protection Processes*. Cambridge University Press.

Rivera, J., and P. de Leon. 2004. 'Is greener whiter? Voluntary environmental performance of Western ski areas', *Policy Studies Journal* 32: 417–437.

Roberts, P. W., and G. R. Dowling. 2002. 'Corporate reputation and sustained superior financial performance', *Strategic Management Journal* 23: 1077–1093.

Rockström, J., W. Steffen, K. Noone, Å. Persson, F. S. Chapin, E. F. Lambin, et al. 2009. 'A safe operating space for humanity', *Nature* 461: 472–475.

Rogers, E. M. 1991. *Diffusion of Innovations*. New York: The Free Press.

Roome, N. 1992. 'Developing environmental management strategies', *Business Strategy and the Environment* 1: 11–24.

Russo, M., and N. Harrison. 2005. 'Organizational design and environmental performance: Clues from the electronics industry', *Academy of Management Journal* 48: 582–593.

Russo, M. V., and P. A. Fouts. 1997. 'A resource-based perspective on corporate environmental performance and profitability', *Academy of Management Journal* 40: 534–559.

Russo, M. V., and A. Minto. 2012. 'Competitive strategy and the environment: A field of inquiry emerges'. In P. Bansal and A. Hoffman (eds.), *The Oxford Handbook of Business and the Natural Environment*, pp. 29–49. Oxford University Press.

Rypdal, K., and W. Winiwarter. 2001. 'Uncertainties in greenhouse gas emission inventories: Evaluation, comparability and implications', *Environmental Science & Policy* 4: 107–116.

Sagie, A., and M. Koslowsky. 1993. 'Detecting moderators with meta-analysis: An evaluation and comparison of techniques', *Personnel Psychology* 46: 629–640.

Schilling, M. A. 1998. 'Technological lockout: An integrative model of the economic and strategic factors driving technology success and failure', *Academy of Management Review* 23: 267–284.

Schilling, M. A. 2010. *Strategic Management of Technological Innovation*. New York: McGraw-Hill Irwin.

Schilling, M. A., and M. Esmundo. 2009. 'Technology S-curves in renewable energy alternatives: Analysis and implications for industry and government', *Energy Policy* 37: 1767–1781.

Scholtens, B., and L. Dam. 2007. 'Banking on the equator: Are banks that adopted the Equator Principles different from non-adopters?', *World Development* 35: 1307–1328.

Schuler, D. 1996. 'Corporate political strategy and foreign competition: The case of the steel industry', *Academy of Management Journal* 39: 720–737.

Schuler, D. A., and K. Rehbein. 1997. 'The filtering role of the firm in corporate political involvement', *Business & Society* 36: 116–139.

Scott, W. R. 1995. *Institutions and Organizations: Ideas and Interests.* Thousand Oaks, CA: Sage Publications.

Scott, W. R., and J. W. Meyer. 1994. *Institutional Environments and Organizations: Structural Complexity and Individualism.* London: Sage Publications.

Scrase, I., and J. Watson. 2009. 'CCS in the UK: Squaring coal use with climate change'. In J. Meadowcroft and O. Langhelle (eds.), *Caching the Carbon: The Politics and Policies of Carbon Capture and Storage*, pp. 187–201. Cheltenham, UK: Edward Elgar.

Sellers, M., A. Verbeke, and F. Bowen 2006. *Corporate Environmental Strategy: An Integrative Resource-Based Framework.* Academy of Management Best Paper Proceedings, K. M. Weaver (ed.), pp. A1–A6.

Shackley, S., and C. Gough. 2006. *Carbon Capture and its Storage: An Integrated Assessment.* Farnham, UK: Ashgate Publishing.

Shafik, N. 1994. 'Economic development and environmental quality: An econometric analysis', *Oxford Economic Papers* 46: 757–773.

Shah, K., and J. Rivera. 2013. 'Industry associations and corporate environmentalism in emerging economies: Evidence from the oil, gas and chemical sectors of Trinidad and Tobago', *Policy Sciences* 46: 39–62.

Sharfman, M., and C. Fernando. 2008. 'Environmental risk management and the cost of capital', *Strategic Management Journal* 29: 569–592.

Sharma, S. 2000. 'Managerial interpretations and organizational context as predictors of corporate choice of environmental strategy', *Academy of Management Journal* 43: 681–697.

Sharma, S., J. Aragon-Correa, and A. Rueda-Manzanares. 2007. 'The contingent influence of organizational capabilities on proactive environmental strategy in the service sector: An analysis of North American and European ski resorts', *Canadian Journal of Administrative Science* 24: 268–283.

Sharma, S., and I. Henriques. 2005. 'Stakeholder influences on sustainability practices in the Canadian forest products industry', *Strategic Management Journal* 26: 159–180.

Sharma, S., and O. Nguan. 1999. 'The biotechnology industry and strategies of biodiversity conservation: The influence of managerial interpretations and risk propensity', *Business Strategy and the Environment* 8: 46–61.

Sharma, S., and H. Vredenburg. 1998. 'Proactive corporate environmental strategy and the development of competitively valuable organizational capabilities', *Strategic Management Journal* 19: 729–753.

Shine, K. P., J. S. Fuglestvedt, K. Hailemariam, and N. Stuber. 2005. 'Alternatives to the global warming potential for comparing climate impacts of emissions of greenhouse gases', *Climatic Change* 68: 281–302.

Shiva, V. 2000. *Stolen Harvest: The Hijacking of the Global Food Supply*. London: Zed Books.

Short, J. L., and M. W. Toffel. 2008. 'Coerced confessions: Self-policing in the shadow of the regulator', *Journal of Law, Economics, and Organization* 24: 45–71.

Short, J. L., and M. W. Toffel. 2010. 'Making self-regulation more than merely symbolic: The critical role of the legal environment', *Administrative Science Quarterly* 55: 361–396.

Siegel, D. S. 2009. 'Green management matters only if it yields more green: An economic/strategic perspective', *Academy of Management Perspectives* 23: 5–16.

Simjee, A. 2013. 'World Water Day: IBM launches WaterWatchers mobile app in South Africa'. Available at www.ibm.com. Accessed 25 July 2013.

Simpson, J. 2000. 'Millennial angst leads a host of buzzwords', *Journal of Commerce* 2(2): 12.

Smith, S. J., and M. L. Wigley. 2004. 'Global warming potentials: 1. Climatic implications of emissions reductions', *Climatic Change*. 44: 445–457.

Springett, D. 2003. 'Business conceptions of sustainable development: A perspective from critical theory', *Business Strategy and the Environment* 12: 71–86.

Steel, P. D., and J. D. Kammeyer-Mueller. 2002. 'Comparing meta-analytic moderator estimation techniques under realistic conditions', *Journal of Applied Psychology* 87: 96–111.

Steelman, T., and J. Rivera. 2006. 'Voluntary environmental programs in the United States: Whose interests are served?', *Organization & Environment* 19: 505–526.

Stefan, A., and L. Paul. 2008. 'Does it pay to be green? A systematic overview', *Academy of Management Perspectives* 22: 45–62.

Stephens, J. C., A. Hansson, Y. Liu, H. de Coninck, and S. Vajjhala. 2011. 'Characterising the international carbon capture and storage community', *Global Environmental Change* 21: 379–390.

Stephens, J. C., and S. Jiusto. 2010. 'Assessing innovation in emerging energy technologies: Socio-technical dynamics of carbon capture and storage CCS and enhanced geothermal systems EGS in the USA', *Energy Policy* 38: 2020–2031.

Stephenson, E., A. Doukas, and K. Shaw. 2012. 'Greenwashing gas: Might a 'transition fuel' label legitimize carbon-intensive natural gas development?', *Energy Policy* 46: 452–459.

Stern, N. H. 2007. *The Economics of Climate Change: The Stern Review.* Cambridge University Press.

Stevens, J. M., H. K. Steensma, D. A. Harrison, and P. L. Cochran. 2005. 'Symbolic or substantive document? The influence of ethics codes on financial executives' decisions', *Strategic Management Journal* 26: 181–195.

Suarez, F. F., and G. Lanzolla. 2007. 'The role of environmental dynamics in building a first mover advantage theory', *Academy of Management Review* 32: 377–392.

Suchman, M. C. 1995. 'Managing legitimacy: Strategic and institutional approaches', *Academy of Management Review* 20: 571–610.

Suddaby, R., D. J. Cooper, and R. Greenwood. 2007. 'Transnational regulation of professional services: Governance dynamics of field level organizational change', *Accounting, Organizations and Society* 32: 333–362.

Suzuki, T. 2003. 'The accounting figuration of business statistics as a foundation for the spread of economic ideas', *Accounting, Organizations and Society* 28: 65–95.

Swartz, D. 2008. 'Bringing Bourdieu's master concepts into organisational analysis', *Theory and Society* 37: 45–52.

Tatli, A. 2011. 'A multi-layered exploration of the diversity management field: Diversity discourses, practices and practitioners in the UK', *British Journal of Management* 22: 238–253.

Telle, K., and J. Larsson. 2007. 'Do environmental regulations hamper productivity growth? How accounting for improvements of plants' environmental performance can change the conclusion', *Ecological Economics* 61: 438–445.

Terlaak, A. 2007. 'Order without law: The role of certified management standards in shaping socially desired firm behaviours', *Academy of Management Review* 32: 968–985.

TerraChoice 2007. *The 'Six Sins of Greenwashing': A Study of Environmental Claims in North American Consumer Markets.* Northbrook, IL: Underwriters Laboratories.

Theyel, G. 2000. 'Management practices for environmental innovation and performance', *International Journal of Operations and Production Management* 20: 249–267.

Thomas, S., R. Repetto, and D. Dias. 2007. 'Integrated environmental and financial performance metrics for investment analysis and portfolio management', *Corporate Governance: An International Review* 15: 421–426.

Tilcsik, A. 2010. 'From ritual to reality: Demography, ideology and decoupling in a post-communist government agency', *Academy of Management Journal* 53: 1474–1498.

Tokar, B. 1997. *Earth for Sale: Reclaiming Ecology in the Age of Corporate Greenwash*. Cambridge, MA: South End Press.

Tolbert, P. S., and L. G. Zucker. 1983. 'Institutional sources of change in the formal structure of organizations: The diffusion of civil service reform', *Administrative Science Quarterly* 28: 22–39.

Tullock, G. 1967. 'The welfare costs of tariffs, monopolies and theft', *Western Economic Journal* 5: 224–232.

Tyler, T. R. 2006. 'Psychological perspectives on legitimacy and legitimation', *Annual Review of Psychology* 57: 375–400.

US Green Building Council. 2012. *LEED Projects and Case Studies Directory*. Washington, DC: US Green Building Council.

Unruh, G. C. 2000. 'Understanding carbon lock-in', *Energy Policy* 28: 817–830.

Vaughan, D. 2008. 'Bourdieu and organisations: The empirical challenge', *Theory and Society* 37: 65–81.

Vergragt, P. J., N. Markusson, and H. Karlsson. 2011. 'Carbon capture and storage, bio-energy with carbon capture and storage, and the escape from the fossil-fuel lock-in', *Global Environmental Change* 21: 282–292.

Vidovic, M., and N. Khanna. 2012. 'Is voluntary pollution abatement in the absence of a carrot or stick effective? Evidence from facility participation in the EPA's 33/50 Program', *Environmental and Resource Economics* 52: 369–393.

Vine, E., G. Katsb, J. Sathayec, and H. Joshid. 2003. 'International greenhouse gas trading programs: A discussion of measurement and accounting issues', *Energy Policy* 31: 211–224.

Vos, J. 2009. 'Actions speak louder than words: Greenwashing in corporate America', *Notre Dame Journal of Ethics and Public Policy* 23: 673–691.

Walck, S. 2006. *Carbon Neutrality: The HSBC Story*. New York: United Nations Environment Programme.

Waldfogel, J. 1993. 'The deadweight loss of Christmas', *American Economic Review* 83: 1328–1336.

Waldfogel, J. 2009. *Scroogenomics: Why You Shouldn't Buy Presents for the Holidays*. Princeton, NJ: Princeton University Press.

Walker, K., and F. Wan. 2012. 'The harm of symbolic actions and greenwashing: Corporate actions and communications on environmental performance and their financial implications', *Journal of Business Ethics* 109: 227–242.

Walley, N., and B. Whitehead. 1994. 'It's not easy being green', *Harvard Business Review* 72: 46–51.

Walmart. 2013. *Walmart Announces New Commitments to Dramatically Increase Energy Efficiency and Renewables*. Bentonville, AR: Walmart, Inc.

Washington, M., and E. J. Zajac. 2005. 'Status evolution and competition: Theory and evidence', *Academy of Management Journal* 48: 282–296.

Weber, K., G. F. Davids, and M. Lounsbury. 2009. 'Policy as myth and ceremony? The global spread of stock exchanges, 1980–2005', *Academy of Management Journal* 52: 1319–1347.

Weigelt, K., and C. Camerer. 1998. 'Reputation and corporate strategy: A review of recent theory and applications', *Strategic Management Journal* 9: 443–454.

Welford, R. 1997. *Hijacking Environmentalism: Corporate Responses to Sustainable Development*. London: Earthscan.

Werbach, A. 2010. 'The failure of Chevron's new 'We Agree' ad campaign', *The Atlantic*, 21 October. Available at www.theatlantic.com/business/archive/2010/10/the-failure-of-chevrons-new-we-agree-ad-campaign/64951. Accessed 24 January 2014.

Wernerfelt, B. 1984. 'A resource-based view of the firm', *Strategic Management Journal* 5: 171–180.

Westphal, J. D., and E. J. Zajac. 1994. 'Substance and symbolism in CEOs' long-term incentive plans', *Administrative Science Quarterly* 39: 367–390.

Westphal, J. D., and E. J. Zajac. 2001. 'Decoupling policy from practice: The case of stock repurchase programs', *Administrative Science Quarterly* 46: 202–228.

Westphal, J. D., R. Gulati, and S. M. Shortell. 1997. 'Customization or conformity? An institutional and network perspective on the content and consequences of TQM adoption', *Administrative Science Quarterly* 42: 366–394.

Whiteman, G., and W. H. Cooper. 2011. 'Ecological sensemaking', *Academy of Management Journal* 54: 889–911.

Whiteman, G., B. Walker, and P. Perego. 2012. 'Planetary boundaries: Ecological foundations for corporate sustainability', *Journal of Management Studies* 50: 307–336.

Whitener, E. M. 1990. 'Confusion of confidence intervals and credibility intervals in meta-analysis', *Journal of Applied Psychology* 75: 315–321.

Winn, M. L., and L. C. Angell. 2000. 'Towards a process model of corporate greening', *Organization Studies* 21: 1119–1147.

Wittneben, B. 2009. 'Exxon is right: Let's re-examine our choice for cap-and-trade over a carbon tax', *Energy Policy* 37: 2462–2464.

Wood, C. 2003. *Environmental Impact Assessment: A Comparative Review*. Harlow, UK: Pearson Education.

Wooten, M., and A. Hoffman. 2008. 'Organizational fields: Past, present and future'. In R. Greenwood, C. Oliver, and K. Sahlin-Anderson (eds.), *The Handbook of Organizational Institutionalism*, pp. 130–147. Thousand Oaks, CA: Sage Publications.

World Business Council for Sustainable Development and the World Resources Institute. 2001. *The Greenhouse Gas Protocol*. Washington, DC: WBCSD/WRI.

World Wide Fund for Nature. 2012. 'WWF Rio+20 Closing Statement'. Available at www.panda.org/?205343/wwf-rio-closing-statement. Accessed 25 July 2013.

Wright, T. P. 1936. 'Factors affecting the cost of airplanes', *Journal of Aeronautical Sciences* 3: 122–128.

Yelle, L. E. 1979. 'The learning curve: Historical review and comprehensive survey', *Decision Sciences* 10: 302–328.

Yin, H., and P. J. Schmeidler. 2009. 'Why do standardized ISO 14001 management systems lead to heterogeneous environmental outcomes?' *Business, Strategy and the Environment* 18: 469–486.

Zeitlyn, D. 2003. 'Gift economies in the development of open source software: Anthropological reflections', *Research Policy* 32: 1287–1291.

Zhu, Q., J. Sarkis, and K. Lai. 2007. 'Green supply chain management: Pressures, practices and performance within the Chinese automobile industry', *Journal of Cleaner Production* 15: 1041–1052.

Index

Advertising Standards Authority, UK, 6
Apple, 248
Association for Manufacturing Excellence, US, 190
audience-seeking, 88–90, 91, 116, 118, 146, 166, 167, 230–231

Bain & Company, 244–245
BASF, 209
Brennan, G., 88, 230, 236
Building Research Establishment and Environmental Assessment Method (BREEAM) UK, 212–213, 243

Capital One Financial, 209
carbon accounting
  as new measurement standard, 182–185
  three accounting organisational fields, 187–196
Carbon Disclosure Project (CDP), 26, 34–35, 169–170, 209
Carbon Neutral Company, 244–245
Carbon Reduction Commitment (CRC) Energy Efficiency Scheme, UK, 191
Chevron, 15–17, 235, 249
Climate Challenge program, 104
Climate Disclosure Standards Board, 190
Cooperative Research Centre for Coal in Sustainable Development (CCSD), 167
core ideas, contributions, 10–14
corporate environmentalism, 39. See also symbolic corporate environmentalism

conventional view, 7, 9–11, 48–49, 50, 51, 52–53, 55, 71, 74, 91–92, 106
critical view, 7, 9–11, 40, 44–45, 46–47, 48–49, 50, 51, 53–54, 55, 65–66, 91–92, 106
corporate social responsibility (CSR), 78–79, 83–84
Costco, 209
CPA-Zicklin Index of Political Accountability and Disclosure, 209
cultural symbols, 140–141, 145, 156–167, 207–210

deadweight loss, social inefficiency, 70, 93–95, 214–218
decoupling, 28, 54, 63–65, 113–115, 117–118, 132–134, 235–238
Deloitte LLP, 190
Deloitte Technology Green 15 Award, 157
Department of Energy and Climate Change, UK, 244
Dow Jones Sustainability Index, 181

eco-labelling, 4–5, 9–11
Electronic Product Environmental Assessment Tool, 248
EnergyStar, 34–35
Equator Principles, 241, 245–246
Esteem (Brennan, Pettit), 88, 230, 236
European Union Emission Trading System (EU ETS), 190

Forest Stewardship Council (FSC), 65, 73

GE Ecomagination campaign, 6
Global CCS Institute, 176

Global Reporting Initiative (GRI),
    164, 210
green solutions, 40–41
    audience-seeking *vs.*
        performance-enhancing activity
        trade-off, 88, 230–231
    coerced egoist case, 81–82
    consumer utility from voluntary
        green solutions, 93–94
    firm-level analysis, private
        costs/benefits, 80–81
    non-market strategies, 85
    optimal firm investment in,
        82–86
    portfolio design, 86–91
    strategic investment, quantity
        decision, 78–86
    typology of firms, environmental
        performance, communication,
        86–88
Greenpeace, 1, 169
greenwashing, 249–250
    academic conceptions, definitions of,
        20, 26
    academic, popular outlets articles,
        17–19
    as information disclosure decision,
        26–27
    benefit to firms *vs.* cost to society,
        30–31
    company-led activity of, 28–30
    definitions of, 17–23
    deliberate, active dissemination,
        selective disclosure, 27–28
    marketing-oriented studies
        definitions, 20–22
    rise, fall of, 15–25
    social media impact on, 24
    strategy scholars, economists
        definitions, 22–23
    symbolic corporate
        environmentalism *vs.*, 31–34,
        37

HabitatMap's Aircasting, 24–25
Harper, Stephen, 163
HSBC
    carbon neutrality policy of, 1–2, 28,
        241–244
    Greenpeace criticism of, 1

LEED certification, 32–33, 242–244
    Natural Resources Defense Council
        (NRDC) and, 32–33
    symbolic corporate
        environmentalism by, 4, 7

IBM, 6, 25
industry self-regulation
    symbolic gaps and, 109–111,
        116–117
    theoretical implications, future
        directions, 229–235
institutional organisation theory, 69.
    See also symbolic organisation
    theory
Intergovernmental Panel on Climate
    Change's (IPCC), 184–185, 189,
    192–196
International Accounting Standards
    Board (IASB), 190, 196
International Carbon Action
    Partnership (ICAP), 191
International Emission Trading
    Association (IETA), 191
International Organisation for
    Standardisation (ISO), 189
ISO 14001, 26, 34–35, 52–54, 69, 73,
    118, 208

Kyoto Protocol, 199

language, terminology, 2–3
LEED building standards, 9, 73–74,
    212–213
    cost of building and, 208–209
    HSBC and, 32–33, 242–244
    symbolic messages and, 32–33
legal compliance, 39
legitimacy, 49, 53, 56, 58, 59–62,
    113–114, 116–117, 143,
    169–170

measurement and methods, social cost
    curve estimation, 179–180
    Building Research Establishment
        and Environmental Assessment
        Method (BREEAM), 212–213
    CPA-Zicklin Index of Political
        Accountability and Disclosure,
        209